Trusts, Wills and Probate Li...

Williams, Mortimer and Sunnucks

on

Executors, Administrators and

Published in 2015 by Thomson Reuters (Professional) UK Limited
Trading as Sweet & Maxwell, Friars House, 160 Blackfriars Road, London SE1 8EZ
(Registered in England & Wales, Company No 1679046.
Registered Office and address for service: 2nd floor, 1 Mark Square, Leonard Street,
London, EC2A 4EG)

Typeset by YHT Ltd, London

Printed in Great Britain by Ashford Colour Press, Gosport, Hants.

For further information on our products and services, visit *www.sweetandmaxwell.co.uk*

No natural forests were destroyed to make this product; only farmed timber was used and
re-planted.

A CIP catalogue record of this book is available for the British Library.

ISBN: 978 04140 34945

Thomson Reuters and the Thomson Reuters logo are trademarks of Thomson Reuters.

Sweet & Maxwell ® is a registered trademark of Thomson Reuters (Professional) UK
Limited.

Crown copyright material is reproduced with the permission of the Controller of HMSO and
the Queen's Printer for Scotland.

Contributors
(in alphabetical order)

John Eidinow
New Square Chambers

Her Honour Judge Jane Evans-Gordon
Birmingham Civil Justice Centre

Charlotte Ford
New Square Chambers

Charles Holbech
New Square Chambers

Kira King
New Square Chambers

Alexander Learmonth
New Square Chambers

Veronica Matthew
Formerly of Leicester De Montfort Law School

Francesca Perselli
New Square Chambers

Leigh Sagar
(Author of new Chapter 49A on the administration of digital
information, as well as a contributor)
New Square Chambers

Alexander Stewart
Hogarth Chambers

First Edition	1832	by Rt. Hon. Sir E. V. Williams
Second Edition	1838	by Rt. Hon. Sir E. V. Williams
Third Edition	1841	by Rt. Hon. Sir E. V. Williams
Fourth Edition	1849	by Rt. Hon. Sir E. V. Williams
Fifth Edition	1856	by Rt. Hon. Sir E. V. Williams
Sixth Edition	1867	by Rt. Hon. Sir E. V. Williams
Seventh Edition	1873	by Rt. Hon. Sir E. V. Williams and W. V. Vaughan Williams
Eighth Edition	1879	by Hon. Sir Roland L. Vaughan Williams and W. V. Vaughan Williams
Ninth Edition	1893	by Hon. Sir Roland L. Vaughan Williams
Tenth Edition	1905	by Hon. Sir Roland L. Vaughan Williams and A. R. Ingpen KC
Eleventh Edition	1921	by Sydney E. Williams, assisted by H. Clifford Mortimer
Twelfth Edition	1930	by Professor David Hughes Parry and John Cherry
Thirteenth Edition	1953	by Sir David Hughes Parry, assisted by D. C. Potter
Fourteenth Edition	1960	by Professor G. W. Keeton, assisted by E. H. Scamell
Fifteenth Edition	1970	by J. H. G. Sunnucks
Sixteenth Edition	1982	by J. H. G. Sunnucks, John Ross Martyn and Kevin Garnett
Seventeenth Edition	1993	by J. H. G. Sunnucks, John Ross Martyn and Kevin Garnett
Eighteenth Edition	2000	by J. H. G. Sunnucks, assisted by John Ross Martyn and Nicholas Caddick
Nineteenth Edition	2008	by John Ross Martyn and Nicholas Caddick
Twentieth Edition	2013	by John Ross Martyn and Nicholas Caddick Q.C.
First Supplement	2015	by Alexander Learmonth and John Ross Martyn

Mortimer on Probate

First edition	1911	by Clifford Mortimer
Second edition	1927	by Clifford Mortimer and Hamish H. H. Coates
Third edition	1970	by J. H. G. Sunnucks
Fourth edition	1982	by J. H. G. Sunnucks, John Ross Martyn and Kevin Garnett
Fifth edition	1993	by J. H. G. Sunnucks, John Ross Martyn and Kevin Garnett
Sixth edition	2000	by J. H. G. Sunnucks, assisted by John Ross Martyn and Nicholas Caddick
Seventh edition	2008	by John Ross Martyn and Nicholas Caddick
Eighth edition	2013	by John Ross Martyn and Nicholas Caddick Q.C.
First Supplement	2015	by Alexander Learmonth and John Ross Martyn

PREFACE

Introduction

The text of the last edition of this book, *Williams, Mortimer and Sunnucks on Executors, Administrators and Probate*, left the hands of the then editors in December 2012, only two and a half years ago. This supplement to update it is, nevertheless, more than 250 pages long. These simple facts illustrate that the areas of law covered by the book are busy and developing ones. The busyness, and even more the developments, are the result of changes in social life, in economic life, and even in some scientific and technical matters. There are new patterns of family life and relationships. The rise in the value of residential property has made the validity of wills a matter of greater significance to family members, and to others with a possible claim on the estates of deceased persons. The development of information technology has created a new area of activity with which testators, beneficiaries and their advisers have to concern themselves.

The changes have prompted Parliament, and the courts, to develop the law and practice of probate and succession in an effort better to do justice, by better serving the public. For example, new patterns of family life and relationships have led to amendments to the law of intestacy, and to the law of family provision. The rise in the value of residential property has made the validity of wills a matter of greater significance to family members, so as to give judicial decisions on probate and administration much greater importance to them. Parliament has had to legislate for information technology, and the courts have had to decide to what extent, and in what manner, existing principles of property law apply to it.

The result is the length of this supplement. It is convenient to refer briefly to the new legislation, and to some of the recent decisions of the courts. The Draft Probate Rules, which are intended to replace the existing Non-contentious Probate Rules, will then be mentioned at somewhat greater length. This will be done in part because of their status as drafts that will very probably, but not certainly, be enacted in their present form, and in part because they have necessarily had to be mentioned frequently in the text. Lastly, the reader will be directed to the new Chapter 49A on digital information.

Legislation

The most important new Act of Parliament is the Inheritance and Trustees' Powers Act 2014. This changes the rules of distribution on intestacy, and amends the Inheritance (Provision for Family and Dependants) Act 1975. The changes to the intestacy rules are mentioned in Chapter 82. The amendments to the 1975 Act are especially important, and are considered at length in Chapters 58 to 61.

The two other Acts of specific importance for this book are the Trusts (Capital and Income) Act 2013, considered in Chapter 80, and the Presumption of Death Act 2013, considered in Chapter 70.

References to these Acts are made elsewhere, as appropriate. The relevant sections of and schedules to the Acts are printed in Appendix One. Appendix Two contains the addition to Part 57 of the Civil Procedure Rules and the new Practice Direction, PD57B, which set out the procedure to be followed under the Presumption of Death Act.

Decisions of the Courts

The most noteworthy reported case considered in this supplement is *Marley v Rawlings*, the first case on probate and related matters to reach the highest court in the land for many years. A lawyer seeing to the execution of the wills of a husband and wife handed the husband's will to the wife, and the wife's will to the husband. This simple error required the court of first instance, the Court of Appeal, and the Supreme Court to consider both the interpretation of the Wills Act 1837, and the statutory power to rectify wills. Subsequently, the Supreme Court had to consider the principles governing the costs of probate actions. The supplement refers to *Marley v Rawlings* in Chapters 13, 39 and 40.

There have been numerous other decisions on the areas of law covered by *Williams, Mortimer and Sunnucks*, but selecting some rather than others might be misleading. The importance of the various decisions will only appear "as time goes by."

The new Probate Rules

New Probate Rules, to replace the Non-contentious Probate Rules 1987, have been in preparation for a considerable while. At the time of writing, these rules (referred to in this supplement as "the Draft Probate Rules") are in a final draft form, following consultation by the rules committee under the chairmanship of His Honour Judge Philip Waller CBE. They have been submitted to the Ministry of Justice for consideration, prior to being put into the form of a draft statutory instrument. It is hoped that the Draft Probate Rules are likely to be published in that form later in 2015, although the Ministry of Justice has not been able to make any firm commitment to that timeframe.

Nevertheless, no significant changes to the Draft Probate Rules are expected. Although it is not yet possible to publish the Rules in their draft form, this supplement therefore includes references to the Draft Probate Rules as they presently stand throughout, with the intention of assisting practitioners to prepare for the change of rules when they are finally brought into force. Readers should remember however that the Draft Probate Rules are not in force, and may be subject to change before they are brought into force. A further supplement may be issued when the Draft Probate Rules are brought into force, if no new edition of this work is then in preparation.

The Draft Probate Rules make few substantive changes to the procedure for acquiring a grant of representation. The amendments are primarily semantic: updating the terminology used to make the Rules more accessible to the public. Thus, references to "devisees" and "legatees" have been replaced by references to "beneficiaries"; oaths and affidavits have been replaced by witness statements; caveats are to be known as "objections", "warnings" as "responses" and citations as "notifications"; and grants *ad colligenda bona* are now called simply "preservation grants".

The most major procedural changes that practitioners will need to be aware of are to the procedure for objections (formerly caveats). First, objections will remain effective for 12 months rather than six. Secondly, instead of the three-stage process whereby the caveator has to enter an appearance to a warning, the response to an objection is the last step prior to a probate claim. Thirdly, once a response is filed, the objection will cease to have effect after three months unless an application is made or a probate claim commenced, putting the onus on the objector to take proceedings.

Digital Information

Lastly, we like to think that the usefulness of this supplement has been decidedly enhanced by a new Chapter 49A, on digital information, written by Leigh Sagar of New Square Chambers. We are most grateful to him.

Conclusion

Nicholas Caddick QC of Hogarth Chambers was one of the general editors of the last edition, and of the edition before that. As such, he made a major contribution. Some members of Hogarth Chambers also contributed to the last edition, as can be seen from its title page. Nicholas and the other Hogarth contributors, with the exception of Alexander Stewart, have now withdrawn, in part because of other commitments. This Preface gives us an opportunity to record our thanks to them.

We thank Taryn Dullisear and Kristiina Kojamo of Sweet & Maxwell, and all other staff involved there, for their help and encouragement in the production of this supplement.

The work on the Chapters was completed during the first three months of 2015 but we have endeavoured to incorporate recent legislation and cases to most Chapters up until April 30, 2015. Not all Chapters required updating from the Main Work. Those Chapters do not feature in this Supplement.

Alexander Learmonth
John Ross Martyn

TABLE OF CONTENTS

CONTENTS

PART 2
Executors and the Admission of Wills to Probate

CONTENTS

PART 3
Administrators

CONTENTS

PART 4
Non-Contentious Practice

21. GRANTS IN COMMON FORM—GENERAL PRACTICE

22. GRANTS WHERE THE DECEASED DIED DOMICILED ABROAD

23. APPLICATIONS TO ADMIT WILLS TO PROOF

24. LIMITED GRANTS

CONTENTS

PART 5
Contentious Practice

PART 6
Devolution and Liability

CONTENTS

CONTENTS

CONTENTS

Table of Cases

Table of Statutes

TABLE OF STATUTES

Table of Statutory Instruments

Table of Non-Contentious Probate Rules and Draft Probate Rules

CHAPTER 1

HISTORY AND JURISDICTION

B.—JURISDICTION OF THE COURTS

Assignment of business—Family Division or Chancery Division

[Replace penultimate sentence "At the time of writing..." to "... status of that process." with the following]   1–11

There is a consultation process for new rules to replace the 1987 Rules which, at the time of writing, are in a final draft form. This supplement includes references to the Draft Probate Rules and any differences they contain. Readers are advised, however, to check the status of any progress in enacting them, whether in their present or an amended form.

County courts—contentious probate jurisdiction

[In second sentence replace "the net estate does not exceed the county court limit which is currently £30,000" with the following]   1–14

the net estate does not exceed £30,000

[Replace text of fn.48 with the following]

High Court and County Courts Jurisdiction Order 1991 (SI 1991/724) art.2(7B) as amended by the High Court and County Court Jurisdiction (Amendment) Order 2014 (SI 2014/821). This is to the same effect as the previous statutory provisions contained in the County Courts Act 1984 s.32(1) and the County Courts Jurisdiction Order 1981 (SI 1981/1123), repealed from April 22, 2014 pursuant to the Crime and Courts Act 2013 Sch.9(1) para.10(3) and the Crime and Courts Act 2013 (Commencement No. 10 and Transitional Provision) Order 2014/954 art.2, subject to transitional provisions.

CHAPTER 2

JURISDICTION WHERE THERE IS A FOREIGN ELEMENT

A.—INTRODUCTION

Inapplicability of international conventions and European Regulations

2–05   *[In fn.8 replace "August 16, 2015" with the following]*

August 17, 2015.

[Add at end of fn.8]
, per art.84.

B.—JURISDICTION AS TO SUCCESSION

Movable property—exercise of jurisdiction in relation to succession

Movables; where the law of domicile is that of an EU state

2–16   *[Replace the first sentence with following text and retain fn.44]*

With regard to persons dying domiciled in an EU state on or after August 17, 2015, the EU Succession Regulation will have effect.

[In paragraph beginning "Thus, where a person dies domiciled in a Member State of the European Union...", replace "after August 15, 2015" with the following]

on or after August 17, 2015.

Immovable property—exercise of jurisdiction in relation to succession

Immovables and intestacy

2–21   *[In fn.64 replace "Yemoah" with the following]*

Yemoh

Immovables; where situated in an EU Member State

2–23   *[In first sentence, change "From August 16, 2012, when the harmonised rules of the Succession Regulation described in para.2–16 above shall apply" to the following]*

For deaths on or after August 17, 2015, when the harmonised rules of the Succession Regulation described in para.2–16 above shall apply

D.—INTERNATIONAL AGREEMENTS REGARDING THE APPLICABLE LAW

The EU Succession Regulation

[Replace "i.e. from August 16, 2015" with the following]

2–26

i.e. from August 17, 2015, per art.88

[Delete last two sentences of paragraph from "At the time of writing..." to "it will be so from 2015."]

CHAPTER 3

DEFINITIONS AND CAPACITY TO ACT

A.—DEFINITIONS

Executor

3–02 *[After "However, there is power for the court to appoint a person (a "substituted personal representative") to act in place of an existing representative.[10]", insert text and new fn.10a]*

This includes the power to remove or replace a person who has been named an executor but has not yet obtained a grant of probate.[10a]

B.—CAPACITY TO ACT AS REPRESENTATIVE

Corporations

3–09 *[Add at end of fn.43]*

Rule 23 of the Draft Probate Rules is to the same effect, although note that a witness statement is required in place of an oath.

[Add to end of paragraph]

The Draft Probate Rules also provide for representation to be granted to any person lawfully appointed to act on its behalf (not being a trust corporation) pursuant to s.15 of the Local Government Act 2000.[44a]

Infants or minors

3–12 *[Add at end of fn.55]*

Rules 41 and 42 of the Draft Probate Rules are to the same effect.

[Add at end of fn.56]

Rule 19 of the Draft Probate Rules is to the same effect.

[10a] *Goodman v Goodman* [2013] EWHC 758 (Ch); [2014] Ch. 186.
[44a] Draft Probate Rules r.23(4).

[Add at end of fn.57]

Draft Probate Rules r.19(2).

Mental disorder

[In fn.78 after "Heywood & Massey, Court of Protection Practice, Ch.23.", add the following]   **3–16**

Rule 43(1) of the Draft Probate Rules is to similar effect.

[After "a person authorised by that court to apply for a grant is given priority.", add the following]

The notice requirement has been removed in the Draft Probate Rules.

The Public Trustee

[In fn.89 delete "81 Chancery Lane, London, WC1A 1DD and its telephone number is 020 7911 7127" and replace with the following]   **3–18**

Victory House, 30–34 Kingsway, London, WC2B 6EX.

[In fn.89 after "detailed history of the offices", add the following]

and a list of telephone numbers for the various departments.

[In fn.89 replace "http://www.officialsolicitor.gov.uk [Accessed September 17, 2012]" with the following]

http://www.justice.gov.uk/about/ospt [Accessed December 15, 2014].

[In fn.91 replace "18th edn (2011), para.19–08" with the following]

19th edn (2015), para.19–011

Estates of persons domiciled abroad

[In sub-paragraph (a) after "ad colligenda bona", add the following]   **3–25**

(referred to as a "preservation grant" in the Draft Probate Rules)

CHAPTER 4

THE ADMINISTRATION OF ESTATES: THE STRUCTURE OF THIS BOOK

PART 4: NON-CONTENTIOUS PRACTICE

4–05 *[Add at end of fn.2]*

These are referred to throughout this book as the "Draft Probate Rules".

[After "in relation to caveats", insert the following]
(renamed "objections" in the Draft Probate Rules)

[After "and citations", insert the following]
(renamed "notifications" in the Draft Probate Rules)

CHAPTER 5

**SIGNIFICANCE OF GRANT FOR EXECUTORS AND
ADMINISTRATORS: ACTION BEFORE GRANT**

C.—ACTION BEFORE GRANT – TITLE OF PUBLIC TRUSTEE

[Replace the last sentence of the paragraph with the following]   **5–18**

The method of service is by sending the notice to him, at the Public Trust Office,
PO Box 3010, London, WC2A 1AX, telephone number 020 3681 2713. The
notice must be submitted in an original NL(1) form, photocopies will not be
accepted.[112]

---

[112] *Practice Direction (Fam. Div.: Probate: Notice to Quit)* [1995] 1 W.L.R. 1120.

CHAPTER 6

WHEN A GRANT IS NEEDED

E.—WHERE A GRANT IS NOT REQUIRED

Assets in particular funds unrelated to the deceased's employment or special situation

(v) Registered societies — building societies and trade unions

6–13   *[Replace "At the age of 16 years a member of a trade union, an industrial, provident or friendly society may nominate a person to receive moneys payable by these institutions at his death." with the following text and new fn.56a]*

At the age of 16 years a member of a trade union, an industrial or friendly society or a registered society under the Co-operative and Community Benefit Societies Act 2014 may nominate a person to receive moneys payable by these institutions at his death.[56a]

[Add at end of fn.57]

Industrial and Provident Societies Act 1965 ss.23 and 25 have now been replaced by Co-operative and Community Benefit Societies Act 2014 ss.37–38 and 40 which are on similar terms. The provision regarding illegitimate members in s.25(2) of the 1965 Act has not been reproduced in s.40 of the 2014 Act pursuant to the recommendation of the Law Commission that there does not seem to be a reason to differentiate between legitimate and illegitimate persons (Consolidation Bill Report of December 2013 (Cm 8768)).

[56a] Provident societies previously registered or treated as registered under the Industrial and Provident Societies Act 1965 have been renamed "registered societies" pursuant to the Co-operative and Community Benefit Societies Act 2014 ss.1(1)(b) and 150.

CHAPTER 8

EXECUTORS—APPOINTMENT AND TRANSMISSION OF OFFICE

A.—APPOINTMENT OF EXECUTORS

Appointments where testator was sole surviving trustee; special representatives

[Add at end of fn.112]   8–28

Rule 47 of the Draft Probate Rules is to similar effect.

B.—TRANSMISSION OF OFFICE OF EXECUTOR: CHAIN OF REPRESENTATION

Chain of representation—the executor of a sole or last surviving executor

[In fn.133 replace "Lewin on Trusts, 18th edn (2011), para.29–95" with the following]   8–34

Lewin on Trusts, 19th end (2015), para.29–105

Grants other than those obtained in England and Wales

[Add at end of fn.158]   8–42

Rule 44 of the Draft Probate Rules is to similar effect.

CHAPTER 9

EXECUTORS—ACCEPTANCE OF OFFICE, CESSATION OF RIGHT TO OFFICE, RETRACTION OF RENUNCIATION

A.—ACCEPTANCE OF OFFICE OF EXECUTOR

Executors cannot be compelled to accept office

9–02   *[Replace the last sentence of fn.8 with the following]*

The shared offices of the Official Solicitor and the Public Trustee are at Victory House, 30-34 Kingsway, London, WC2B 6EX. A list of phone numbers for the various departments can be found at *http://www.justice.gov.uk/about/ospt* [Accessed December 15, 2014].

B.—CESSATION OF RIGHT TO OFFICE OF EXECUTOR

Citation to prove or renounce

9–16   *[After "The exercise of this power is governed by r.47 of the Non-contentious Probate Rules 1987 which provides that a citation may be issued at the instance of any person who would be entitled to a grant in the event of the person citing renouncing his right thereto.", add new fn.49a]*

49a Rule 53 of the Draft Probate Rules is in similar terms.

[Add at end of paragraph]

Citations have been renamed notifications in the Draft Probate Rules.

Citation where executor has intermeddled

9–18   *[Add at end of fn.53]*

Rules 51(2) and 53(1) of the Draft Probate Rules are to the same effect.

Renunciation on behalf of minors and incapable persons

9–21   *[Add at end of fn.63]*

Rules 19(2) and 41 of the Draft Probate Rules are to the same effect.

Renunciation before the application for a grant

[Add at end of fn.66] 9–22

Rule 30(2) of the Draft Probate Rules is to the same effect.

Form of renunciation

[Add at end of fn.69] 9–24

Rule 18(2) of the Draft Probate Rules is to the same effect. Note that the reference to "firm" includes a partnership pursuant to Sch.1.

Effect of renunciation

[Add at end of fn.70] 9–26

Rule 18(1) of the Draft Probate Rules is to the same effect.

[Add at end of fn.73]

Rule 18(3) of the Draft Probate Rules is to the same effect.

Effect of intermeddling on the right to renounce

[Add at end of fn.78] 9–27

Rule 53(5)(c) is in similar terms although note the change in procedure from summons to application notice.

C.—RETRACTION OF RENUNCIATION

Retraction

[Add at end of fn.85] 9–29

Rule 18(4) of the Draft Probate Rules is to the same effect.

[Add at end of fn.85]

The proviso in Rule 18(4) of the Draft Probate Rules is to the same effect as that in N-CPR 1987 r.37(3).

[In fn.89 after "N-CPR 1987 r.37(2A)." insert the following]

Rule 18(2) of the Draft Probate Rules is to the same effect. Note that the reference to "firm" includes a partnership pursuant to Sch.1.

Practice

9–31   *[Add at end of fn.96]*

Rule 18(4) of the Draft Probate Rules is to the same effect, save that affidavits have been replaced by witness statements.

CHAPTER 10

THE NEED FOR PROBATE AND TYPES OF WILL

C.—WILLS EXERCISING A POWER OF APPOINTMENT

[Add at end of the paragraph]

10–05

The reasoning of the Court of Appeal in *Pitt v Holt*[29a] which stated that under the "so-called rule in *Hastings-Bass*" the court had jurisdiction to intervene where trustees had failed to perform their decision-making function. Their Lordships held that the court had a wide degree of flexibility in the application of the rule and in seeking the most appropriate practical solution in a variety of different factual situations. Where a decision was taken by a trustee in the exercise and within the scope of his powers, it was voidable under the rule only where he was in breach of his duty to take into account all relevant matters. Further, where a trustee (acting within his powers) obtained and acted on apparently competent professional advice on relevant matters, he would not be held to be in breach of duty merely because that advice turned out to be wrong.

The decision of the Supreme Court has since been followed at first instance, in decisions including *Top Brands Limited v Sharma* [2014] EWHC 2753.

D.—DUPLICATE WILLS

Practice

[Add at end of fn.56]

10–14

Rules 31 to 36 of the Draft Probate Rules make provision for the proving of wills in accordance with s.9 of the Wills Act 1837.

[29a] [2013] UKSC 26; [2013] 2 A.C. 108. The second conjoined appeal in that case was allowed on the basis of the application of the equitable jurisdiction of mistake; a detailed explanation of the decision is beyond the scope of this book. Accordingly, the Court of Appeal decision reported at [2012] Ch. 132 is reversed in part.

F.—JOINT AND MUTUAL WILLS

Mutual wills

Practice

10–27   *[Add new fn.117a at end of heading "Practice"]*

[117a] In *Fox v Jewell* [2013] EWCA Civ 1152; [2014] W.T.L.R. 283, the Court of Appeal set aside a case management decision ordering a split trial for (a) a claim in proprietary estoppel and (b) issues concerning the will's validity including an allegation that the testatrix and her husband had agreed to make mutual wills, on the basis that all of the issues really concerned a family dispute regarding the inheritance of a farm.

CHAPTER 11

FORMS OF PROBATE

H.—SPECIAL FORMS OF PROBATE

Settled land grants

[Add at end of the paragraph]

11–13

Rule 46(1) of the Draft Probate Rules is to the same effect.

CHAPTER 12

THE FORMAL VALIDITY OF WILLS

A.—INTRODUCTION

Statutory requirements

12–01 *[Add at end of fn.7]*

Rules 31 to 36 of the Draft Probate Rules make provision for the evidence and procedure applicable to proving wills in accordance with s.9 of the Wills Act 1837.

B.—FORMAL VALIDITY UNDER THE WILLS ACT 1837

A will must be signed by the testator

What is a signature?

12–14 *[Add at end of the paragraph]*

In *Re Ashkettle* [2013] EWHC 2125 (Ch); [2013] W.T.L.R. 1331, the court found that there had been "sufficient indication" by a testator such that (despite some tentative concern) a will had been properly executed by a solicitor at the direction of the testator.

The testator must by his signature intend to give effect to that will

12–18 *[Add at end of fn.113]*

The decision regarding the scope of rectification in *Marley v Rawlings* [2014] UKSC 2; [2015] A.C. 129 has been applied in a number of cases, both within and without the context of wills: see *Bank of Scotland plc v Greville Developments Company (Midlands) Limited* [2014] EWHC 128 (r.130 of the Land Registration Rules 2003); *Re Huntley* [2014] EWHC 547; [2014] W.T.L.R. 745 (will, inclusion of inappropriate Nil Rate Band Trust); *Burnard v Burnard* [2014] EWHC 340 (description of property in a gift in a will); *Re Freud* [2014] EWHC 2577; [2014] W.T.L.R. 1453 (interpretation as a contract). See also para.40–17 onwards below.

[Add at end of the paragraph]

However, on appeal to the Supreme Court, their Lordships disagreed with the decisions of the Court of Appeal and the judge at first instance, and found the wills to be valid. Their Lordships held that the requirement in s.9(b) was satisfied because the testator in each case had signed the document which was sought to be admitted to probate; and he "intended" to give effect to it as his will because at the time of signing he believed it was his will.

It is noteworthy (although beyond the scope of this chapter) that their Lordships held that even if this conclusion was wrong, they could go on to consider whether the wills could be rectified because it was not necessary for a will to satisfy the formal requirements of s.9 or for the testator to have knowledge and approval of its contents before it could be treated as a "will" capable of being rectified under s.20: see para.40–17 onwards below for further discussion of the limits of recti-fication of wills.

Testator's signature must be made or acknowledged in the presence of two or more witnesses present at the same time

[Add at end of the paragraph]   **12–19**

In *Watts v Watts* [2014] EWHC 668, the court found the will to be invalid because one of the witnesses did not witness or attest the signature of the testator: she gave clear evidence that she did not see the testator nor the other witness sign the document.

Both attesting witnesses must be present at the signature or acknowledgment

[Add at end fn.116]   **12–20**

Watts v Watts [2014] EWHC 668.

The witnesses' attestation of the will

[Add at end of fn.143]   **12–22**

Watts v Watts [2014] EWHC 668.

C.—PRESUMPTION OF THE DUE EXECUTION OF A WILL

Practice

[Add at end of fn.248]   **12–41**

Rules 29 and 37 of the Draft Probate Rules are to similar effect.

CHAPTER 13

THE SUBSTANTIAL VALIDITY OF WILLS

A.—INTRODUCTION

13–01 *[Add at end of fn.1]*

In *Fox v Jewell* [2013] EWCA Civ 1152; [2013] All E.R. (D) 292, the Court of Appeal gave guidance as to the approach to be taken to case management where issues as to the validity of the will arise together with other (non-validity related) issues.

[Add at end fn.10]

Rules 31–36 of the Draft Probate Rules are to similar effect.

B.—TESTAMENTARY CAPACITY

Mental capacity needed to make a will; the "golden rule"

13–03 *[Add at end of fn.14]*

In *Hubbard v Scott* [2012] W.T.L.R. 29, the testator gave his solicitor information about his property which was broadly correct but contained some inaccuracies regarding its value, the date on which it was purchased and whether it was mortgaged; despite these errors the will was upheld.

[Add new fn.14a to (iii), after "ties with him by blood"]

[14a] In *Vegetarian Society v Scott* [2013] EWHC 4097, there was no dispute that the testator suffered from a disorder of the mind. However, the effect of this disorder on the testator's ability to make a will was disputed. His last will cut out his "blood" family; it was upheld on the basis of a finding that the testator did not feel the bond of natural love and affection with his blood family which usually exists and so made a conscious decision to leave his estate elsewhere.

[Add at end of fn.15]

The decision in *Burgess v Hawes* was upheld by the Court of Appeal with reservation on this issue, [2013] EWCA Civ 94.

[Add at end of fn.20]

The decision in *Key* was applied in *Re Wilson (deceased)* [2013] EWHC 499.

[Add at end of fn.21]

Parker v Litchfield [2014] EWHC 1799; cf. *MacLeish v Marryshow* 15 I.T.E.L.R. 213, where it was held that a non-compliance with the "golden rule" did not demonstrate a lack of capacity, and that the court was in all the circumstances entitled to have placed little weight on the expert's evidence.

[Add at end of sub-paragraph after "If possible, the doctor should be a specialist in old age psychiatry, at least in doubtful or complex cases."]

However, some recent cases have shown a tendency to erode the "golden rule". The Court of Appeal in *Burgess v Hawes* [2013] EWCA Civ 94 (see also the articles by Frost at T.E.L.&T.J. 2013 (May) 4 and Ford & Learmonth at (2013) 157 S.J. 27) found a will to be invalid by reason of a want of knowledge and approval, but did not express a final view on testamentary capacity. In the course of his judgment, Mummery L.J. said "the courts should not too readily upset, on the grounds of mental capacity, a will that has been drafted by an experienced independent lawyer ... The court should be cautious about acting on the basis of evidence of lack of capacity given by a medical expert after the event, particularly when that expert has neither met nor medically examined the testatrix" (at [60]). Sir Scott Baker made a similar comment. The clear implication is that a solicitor's opinion is prima facie reliable evidence of capacity; whilst this may well be true in many cases, it runs counter to the principle behind the "golden rule" that mental incapacity is not always obvious to someone without medical training.

The comments of the Court of Appeal in *Burgess v Hawes* were strictly obiter, but have been applied at first instance in *Greaves v Stolkin* [2013] EWHC 1140 in which Newey J. apparently dismissed the importance of "a good social front"— i.e. that a testator lacking capacity may on a "good day" appear to a non-medically trained solicitor to be perfectly capable. See also *Simon v Byford* [2014] EWCA Civ 280. Although these cases may well be decided correctly on their particular facts, the editors submit that this is a concerning trend, especially when one considers that there have been at least a dozen cases over the last decade or so where wills have been held to be invalid for a want of testamentary capacity, despite having been prepared by solicitors. The failure of the Court of Appeal to refer to these cases must, it is suggested, reduce the authority of the comments of Mummery L.J. and Sir Scott Baker. Maybe they are best regarded as, and indeed perhaps were intended as no more than, words of caution rather than statements of principle.

A degree of optimism may be taken from the cases of *Bateman v Overy* [2014] EWHC 432 and *Re Ashkettle (deceased)* [2013] EWHC 2125. In the latter, the judge noted that in his view the comments of Mummery L.J. "do not go so far as to suggest that, in every case, the evidence of an experienced and independent solicitor will, without more, be conclusive" and that the view of the solicitor must be based on a proper assessment of all the facts of the case, and in addition fully accurate information.

[Add at end of sub-paragraph following "a failure by the testator to understand the extent of his property may, on appropriate facts, be the basis for a plea of want of knowledge and approval."]

This distinction was considered by Lewison L.J. in *Simon v Byford* [2014] EWCA Civ 280, in which he stated that "capacity depends on the potential to understand. It is not to be equated with a test of memory" (at [40]) and "the classic formulation of testamentary capacity ... requires the testator to understand no more than the extent of his property. They do not require him to understand the significance of his assets to other people" (at [46]).

Analogous situations relating to capacity

13–04 *[Delete final sub-paragraph (beginning with "Although the 2005 Act ...") and replace with the following]*

The 2005 Act does not have any effect whatsoever on cases in which the relevant will was executed prior to the Act coming into force, i.e. April 1, 2007: see *Gorjat v Gorjat* [2010] EWHC 1537 (Ch). The application of the 2005 Act to issues of testamentary capacity arising from wills executed after that date has been the subject of some discussion. It was thought that expert witnesses would find the Act's definition of a lack of capacity more straightforward to use and to apply, such that increasing reliance might be applied on the principles set out in the Act. In *Fischer v Diffley* [2013] EWHC 4567 (Ch), the tests in both *Banks v Goodfellow* and the 2005 Act were applied to produce a two-stage test for testamentary capacity: a) whether there was an impairment/disturbance of the mind and if so b) whether as a consequence the person in question was unable to make a decision regarding the transaction in question (see also the article at T.E.L&T.J. 2014 (July/August) 6 in respect of the *Fischer* decision). *Fischer* was followed at first instance in *Bray v Pearce* (06/03/14).

However, the decision in *Fischer v Diffley* has been doubted in a number of more recent decisions. In *Re Smith* (also known as *Kicks v Leigh*) [2014] EWHC 3926, it was held that the appropriate test for capacity to make lifetime gifts remained that in *Re Beaney*, and not the tests contained in ss.2 and 3 of the 2005 Act. One interesting point which arises from the discussion in and decision of *Kicks v Leigh* is that of the role of an explanation of the terms of the will. The 2005 Act raises expressly the requirement to assist someone to make their own decisions; that statutory requirement does not apply to will-making, of course, but the concept is familiar in the common law. *Re Beaney* itself was a case where it was held that the person lacked capacity because an explanation was not given— in other words there was incapacity precisely because the person was incapable of understanding in the absence of an explanation. In *Hoff v Atherton* [2004] EWHC 177 at first instance, Nicholas Warren QC sitting as a Deputy analyses this and agrees that someone who would only understand with explanation does not have capacity if the explanation was not in fact given (although on the facts of that case the person could understand without explanation). Those comments were approved by the Court of Appeal in that case ([2004] EWCA Civ 1554), but more briefly. In the view of the authors, it is arguable that the judge at first instance in *Kicks v Leigh* misunderstands the point, by finding that a testator has capacity if they could understand if an explanation were to be given, even where such an explanation was not in fact given. It is doubtful whether that is, in fact, what the Court of Appeal in *Hoff v Atherton* intended. *Hoff v Atherton* was not cited in

Kicks v Leigh, and as such it seems that the court misread *Re Beaney* without the benefit of the analysis of the same in *Hoff.*

In relation to testamentary capacity, Nicholas Strauss QC in *Walker v Badmin* [2015] W.T.L.R. 493 Ch D confirmed that the "correct and only" test for testamentary capacity was that in *Banks v Goodfellow*. He held that there were clear differences between the tests, so although they might often produce the same results, this would not always be the case. The purpose of the Act was to define when living persons were able to take decisions, and if they could not, how decisions could be taken on their behalf and in their best interests. On that analysis, the Act was inappropriate to evaluate whether the deceased had had capacity at the time he made his will.

Causes of mental incapacity—the medical background

[Add at end of fn.42] 13–05

Key was applied in *Re Wilson (deceased)* [2013] EWHC 499 and *Re Dharamshi* [2013] EWHC 3917.

[In fn.43 replace "[2012] W.T.L.R. 423" with the following]

[2013] EWCA Civ 94

(2) Impairment of the mind

[Add at end of fn.50] 13–09

Cf. *Re Ashkettle (deceased)* [2013 EWHC 2125; [2013] W.T.L.R. 1331 in which it was held that the testatrix had no testamentary capacity where she had been suffering from dementia for in excess of two years.

[Add new fn.69a to the heading "Major psychoses (affective disorder and schizophrenia")] 13–15

[69a] In *Vegetarian Society v Scott* [2013] EWHC 4097, it was accepted that the testator suffered from schizophrenia but the will was nonetheless upheld.

[Add at end of fn.74] 13–16

Applied in *Re Dharamshi* [2013] EWHC 3917, in which a challenge to testamentary capacity on the basis the testator was suffering from a severe bereavement reaction as a result of his wife's death failed.

Delusions

[Add at end of fn.82] 13–19

See *Re Boyes* [2013] EWHC 4027 in which a lack of capacity due to delusions was raised, but dismissed.

Test of the presence of delusion

13–20   *[In fn.89 replace "[2012] W.T.L.R. 423" with the following]*

[2013] EWCA Civ 94

Burden of proving unsoundness of mind

13–21   *[Add at end of fn.98]*

See also *Re Ashkettle* [2013] EWHC 2125; [2013] W.T.L.R. 1331.

C.—KNOWLEDGE AND APPROVAL

13–23   *[Add at end of fn.114]*

See *King v King* [2014] EWHC 2827 (Ch), applying *Fuller v Strum* [2002] 1 W.L.R. 1097.

[Add at end of fn.116]

Gill v Woodall was applied in *Greaves v Stolkin* [2013] EWHC 1140. Cf *King v King* [2014] EWHC 2827, in which it was said that despite applying *Gill v Woodall*, it sometimes might be convenient to approach issues of knowledge and approval in two stages, rather than as a single question, "all things considered".

13–24   *[Add at end of fn.117]*

The decision in *Burgess v Hawes* was upheld on appeal: [2013] EWCA Civ 94.

[Add at end of paragraph]

Lewison L.J. in *Simon v Byford* [2014] EWCA Civ 280 described the principles applying to knowledge and approval as follows: "it is knowledge and approval of the actual will that count: not knowledge and approval of other potential dispositions. Testamentary capacity includes the ability to make choices, whereas knowledge and approval requires no more than the ability to understand and approve choices that have already been made".

(a) General Principles

Proof of knowledge and approval

13–25   *[Add new fn.122a following "There must be a proper and sufficient reading over of the will."]*

[122a] See *Re Ashkettle* [2013] EWHC 2125; [2013] W.T.L.R. 1331 in which there was held to be no knowledge and approval where the testatrix did not read the will herself, would have found the will difficult to understand if it was read to her, and the terms of the will were inexplicable and irrational. Cf *Paynter v Hinch* [2013]

EWHC 13 in which the will was not read over to the testator and the drafter was not present at the execution of the will; but the will was nonetheless held to be valid on the basis that the terms were not complex and there was nothing to rebut the presumption of due execution.

[Add at end of fn.125]

The decision in *Burgess v Hawes* was upheld on appeal: [2013] EWCA Civ 94.

Instructions while the testator is in health; execution when he is in extremis

[Add at end of fn.129]

An attempt to apply the rule in *Parker v Felgate* failed in *Markou v Goodwin* [2013] EWHC 4570, where the medical evidence did not deal with the point.

13–26

When affirmative proof of knowledge and approval must be given

[Add at end of fn.134]

This paragraph was cited with approval in *King v King* [2014] EWHC 2827.

13–28

[Add at end of fn.135]

Burgess v Hawes was upheld on appeal: [2013] EWCA Civ 94.

[Add at end of fn.142]

King v King [2014] EWHC 2827: citing *Fuller v Strum*, and on the assumption that there are no circumstances arousing suspicion, the Master was entitled to conclude the ordinary test was satisfied; "so long as there is no problem of a lack of testamentary capacity, the testator's knowledge and approval of the contents of his will would be assumed from the fact that he has signed the document and had it attested in proper form".

(b) Circumstances which excite the vigilance and suspicion of the court

Particular matters which arouse suspicion

[Add at end of fn.155]

Burgess v Hawes was upheld on appeal: [2013] EWCA Civ 94.

13–29

[Add at end of fn.158]

Tociapski v Tociapski [2013] EWHC 1770. Cf. *Paynter v Hinch* [2013] EWHC 13 in which a will in 1996 gave the estate in equal shares to all three children of the deceased, whilst the last will of 2004 gave the estate all to one child, with a gift over to the other two children, but was still upheld.

13–30

13–31   *[Add at end of fn.166]*

Re Christou [2014] EWHC 79.

[Add at end of fn.167]

Burgess v Hawes [2013] EWCA Civ 94.

(c) Evidence where knowledge and approval is in question

13–33   *[Add at end of fn.191]*

Burgess v Hawes was upheld on appeal: [2013] EWCA Civ 94.

(d) Mistake

Mistake as to the document signed or destroyed

13–39   *[In fn.204 delete references to "Marley v Rawlings [2012] EWCA Civ 61"]*

[Add at end of sub-paragraph, following "even if some of the provisions therein were intended by the signatory"]

At both first instance and in the Court of Appeal in *Marley v Rawlings*, it was held that rectification of a will pursuant to s.20 of the Administration of Justice Act 1982 applied only to a will which was valid under s.9 of the Wills Act 1837. However, on appeal to the Supreme Court, their Lordships disagreed with the decisions of the Court of Appeal and the judge at first instance, and found the wills to be valid. Their Lordships held that the requirement in s.9(b) was satisfied because the testator in each case had signed the document which was sought to be admitted to probate; and he "intended" to give effect to it as his will because at the time of signing he believed it was his will.

It is noteworthy that their Lordships held that even if this conclusion was wrong, they could go on to consider whether the wills could be rectified because it was not necessary for a will to satisfy the formal requirements of s.9 or for the testator to have knowledge and approval of its contents before it could be treated as a "will" capable of being rectified under s.20: see para.40–17 onwards below for further discussion of the limits of rectification of wills. Older authorities reaching a different conclusion should therefore be treated with caution.

Where the words are selected by the drafter

13–43   *[Add at end of fn.216]*

In *Kell v Jones* [2013] W.T.L.R. 507 it was found that the solicitor drafting the will had chosen the words used, such that there was no "inadvertence"—he was mistaken as to the legal effect of the words used, but this did not constitute a clerical error permitting rectification of the will. Cf. *Re Huntley* [2014] EWHC 547; [2014] W.T.L.R. 745, in which the solicitor copied a precedent for a nil rate band trust without appreciating that the wording was inappropriate and would frustrate the testator's intentions—the will was construed by omitting part of the offending clause (construction, and not rectification).

D.—UNDUE INFLUENCE

Chancery definition of undue influence does not apply in probate

[Add at end of fn.258]

13–51

Evans v Lloyd [2013] EWHC 1725, *Hart v Burbidge* [2014] EWCA Civ 992 in which a claim of presumed undue influence in relation to lifetime gifts was upheld.

Undue influence as understood in probate

[Add at end of fn.266]

13–52

Parker v Litchfield [2014] EWHC 1799.

[Add at end of fn.268]

Schrader v Schrader [2013] EWHC 466, *Schomberg v Taylor* [2013] EWHC 2269.

[Add at end of fn.270]

Re Devillebichot [2013] EWHC 2867; see also the article at T.E.L.&T.J. 2014 (May) 9.

Burden of proof in cases where undue influence is alleged

[Add at end of fn.286]

13–56

Jeffery v Jeffery [2013] EWHC 1942.

E.—FRAUD

Fraudulent calumny

[Add at end of the paragraph]

13–61

In *Re Boyes* [2013] EWHC 4027, it was held that the testator's sons had failed to prove the allegation that his daughter had poisoned their father's mind against them by making false statements. The court held that the essence of undue influence was that the person alleged to have been poisoning the testator's mind had to either know the aspersions were false or not care whether they were true or false; in *Boyes* the daughter believed, wrongly or not, the statements she had made.

F.—FORGERY

13–65   *[Add at end of fn.312]*

In *Haider v Syed* [2013] EWHC 4079, the court reiterated that the burden was on the person alleging forgery, and that cogent evidence was required albeit still only to the civil standard of proof. The evidence of the attesting witnesses was not accepted; and the handwriting evidence concluded that it was as equally possible that the testator's signature had been forged as it was that it could be genuine. The court found "without hesitation" that in the light of all the evidence, the testator did not sign the will and that the signature on the will was a forgery.

CHAPTER 14

THE REVOCATION OF WILLS

A.—INTRODUCTION

[In fn.5 replace reference to Snell's Equity]

Snell's Equity, 33rd edn (2015), Ch.12 (estoppel), para.24-038 onwards (constructive trusts)

14–02

B.—REVOCATION BY MARRIAGE OR CIVIL PARTNERSHIP

[Add at end of fn.11]

The Marriage (Same Sex Couples) Act 2013 extended marriage to same sex couples. Section 18 of the Wills Act 1837 has been amended (as of December 10, 2014) to provide that there shall be no revocation of a will where an existing civil partnership is converted into a marriage pursuant to s.9 of the 2013 Act.

14–03

D.—REVOCATION BY A SUBSEQUENT WILL OR CODICIL

Revocation where there is a revocation clause

[Add at end of fn.38]

Macleish v Marryshow 15 I.T.E.L.R. 213.

14–09

E.—REVOCATION BY DULY EXECUTED WRITING DECLARING AN INTENTION TO REVOKE

[Add at end of fn.89]

Rules 31(2)(f) and 36 of the Draft Probate Rules lay down rules relating to wills where there has been an attempted revocation by burning, tearing or otherwise destroying. Rule 36 provides that the court must be satisfied that the will has not been revoked.

14–16

F.—REVOCATION BY DESTRUCTION

The act of destruction

14–18   *[Add at end of fn.100]*

See also rr.31(2)(f) and 36 of the Draft Probate Rules in relation to an attempted revocation.

Burden of proof of the revocation of a will or codicil

(2) Will in testator's possession missing at his death

14–28   *[Add at end of fn.156]*

Cf. Rule 32 of the Draft Probate Rules as regards the evidence required by the court to admit a will to probate if the original of the will is not available.

[Add at end of fn.163]

See also *NT v FS* [2013] EWHC 684, an application to execute a statutory will; in which little weight was attached to hearsay evidence of the patient destroying another will.

Rebuttal of the presumption of the revocation of a missing will

14–30   *[Add at end of fn.167]*

Rule 32 of the Draft Probate Rules sets out the evidence required where the original of a will is not available.

[Add at end of the paragraph]

In *Evans v Lloyd* [2013] EWHC 1725, the fact that a draft will was found after the deceased's death was held to be insufficient evidence that the deceased had executed a will; accordingly the deceased was held to have died intestate.

H.—REVOCATION BY OBLITERATION, INTERLINEATION AND ALTERATION

14–32   *[Add at end of fn.184]*

Rule 31(2)(e) of the Draft Probate Rules makes provision for rules applying where there appears in a will an obliteration, interlineation or alteration which is not authenticated as required by s.21 of the Wills Act 1837.

Interpolated sheets

14–37   *[Add at end of fn.227]*

Rule 30(2) of the Draft Probate Rules is to the same effect.

Chapter 16

PRIVILEGED WILLS

H.—Practice

Written wills

[Add at end of fn.89]

16–18

Rule 38 of the Draft Probate Rules is to the same effect.

[Add at end of fn.90]

Rules 31 and 33 of the Draft Probate Rules are to similar effect.

Oral or nuncupative wills

[Add at end of fn.93]

16–20

Rule 32(2) of the Draft Probate Rules is to the same effect.

[Add at end of fn.94]

Rules 68–70 of the Draft Probate Rules deal with the procedure to be followed in making applications to the court.

[Add at end of fn.95]

Rule 32(3) of the Draft Probate Rules is to the same effect.

[Add at end of fn.96]

Rule 31(3) of the Draft Probate Rules is to the same effect.

CHAPTER 17

APPOINTMENT OF ADMINISTRATORS

B.—ORDER OF PRIORITY FOR THOSE ENTITLED TO A GRANT

17–03 *[Add at end of paragraph]*

The Non-contentious Probate Rules 1987 are shortly to be replaced by new Probate Rules. In their draft form, rules 10 and 11 are in similar form to the present rules 20 and 22 respectively.

[Replace fn.9 text with the following]

N-CPR 1987 r.27(6). Rule 13(7) of the Draft Probate Rules is to the same effect.

C.—CAPACITY TO ACT AS ADMINISTRATOR

17–04 *[Add at end of fn.19]*

Rule 39 of the Draft Probate Rules is to the same effect.

E.—PREFERENCE FOR LIVING INTEREST AND FOR PERSONS SUI JURIS

17–06 *[Add at end of fn.22]*

Rule 13(6) of the Draft Probate Rules is to the same effect.

G.—GRANTS TO CO-ADMINISTRATORS WITH DIFFERING DEGREES OF PRIORITY

17–08 *[Add at end of fn.28]*

Rule 14(1) of the Draft Probate Rules is to the same effect.

[Add at end of fn.29]

Rule 14(2) of the Draft Probate Rules is to the same effect.

[Add at end of fn.30]

Rule 14(3)(a) of the Draft Probate Rules is to the same effect, and refers to rr.41(3) and 43(3).

[Add at end of fn.31]

Rule 14(3)(b) of the Draft Probate Rules is to the same effect.

[Add at end of fn.32]

(soon to be r.11 of the Draft Probate Rules).

H.—GRANTS WHERE THERE IS A MINORITY OR LIFE INTEREST

General rule—requirement for no fewer than two administrators

[Insert new fn.32a at end of first sentence following "than two individuals."]   **17–09**
[32a] Senior Courts Act 1981 s.114(2).

[Add at end of paragraph following "second (additional) administrator."]

For deaths after October 1, 2014, life interests will no longer arise under intestacy: see para.19–16 below. This will mean the requirement for a second administrator will arise less frequently than in the past.

[Add at end of fn.33]

Rule 27(3)(c) of the Draft Probate Rules is to the same effect, save that a witness statement will replace the oath.

[Insert after first sentence of fn.35]

(soon to be r.40 of the Draft Probate Rules).

Selection of administrators where there is a minority or life interest

[Add at end of last sentence of first paragraph following "with a child"]   **17–12**
(in the case of a death before October 1, 2014—see para.19–19 below).

[Add at end of fn.45]

Rule 14(1) of the Draft Probate Rules is to the same effect.

[Add at end of fn.46]

Rule 14(3)(b) of the Draft Probate Rules is to the same effect.

[Add at end of fn.47]

Rule 14(2) of the Draft Probate Rules is to the same effect, save that a witness statement is required rather than an affidavit.

Where the person entitled to the grant is a minor

17–13 *[Add at end of second sentence following "Probate Rules 1987"]*
(soon to be r.41(1) under the Draft Probate Rules).

[Add at end of fn.51]
Rule 41(3) of the Draft Probate Rules is to the same effect.

[Add at end of fn.52]
(r.10 of the Draft Probate Rules).

Where there is only one personal representative

17–16 *[Add at end of fn.60]*
Rule 40 of the Draft Probate Rules is to the same effect.

[Add at end of fn.61]
Rule 40(1) of the Draft Probate Rules is to the same effect, save that a witness statement should be used.

[Add at end of fn.62]
Rule 40(1) of the Draft Probate Rules is to the same effect.

[Add at end of fn.63]
Rule 40(2) of the Draft Probate Rules is to the same effect.

J.—TRUST CORPORATIONS

17–19 *[Replace fn.70 text with the following]*
For a fuller treatment see *Lewin on Trusts*, 19th edn (2014), paras 19–068 to 19–093.

Grants to trust corporations

17–21 *[Add at end of fn.87]*
Rule 23(2) of the Draft Probate Rules is to the same effect.

[Add at end of fn.88]
Rule 23(3) of the Draft Probate Rules is to the same effect.

[Add at end of fn.89]

Rule 23(1) of the Draft Probate Rules is to the same effect, save that a witness statement will be used in place of the oath.

[Add at end of fn.90]

Rule 23(4) of the Draft Probate Rules is to the same effect.

CHAPTER 18

ADMINISTRATORS—ENTITLEMENT TO A GRANT WITH THE WILL ANNEXED

B.—ORDER OF PRIORITY OF RIGHT TO A GRANT WHERE THE DECEASED HAS LEFT A WILL

18–02   *[Add at end of first paragraph following "Rules 1987 (as amended)."]*
Rule 10 of the Draft Probate Rules will be to the same effect.

C.—CLEARING OFF EXECUTORS AND OTHERS ENTITLED IN PRIORITY TO THE APPLICANT

18–03   *[Add at end of fn.6]*
Rule 27(3)(b) of the Draft Probate Rules will be to similar effect, save that a witness statement is required in place of the oath.

[Add at end of fn.8]
Under the Draft Probate Rules, citations will be known as notifications, and entering an appearance will become acknowledging service.

F.—CLASS (A) – THE EXECUTOR

18–06   *[Add at end of fn.17]*
Rule 10(a) of the Draft Probate Rules.

H.—CLASS (C) – ANY OTHER RESIDUARY LEGATEE OR DEVISEE OR A PERSON ENTITLED TO SHARE IN UNDISPOSED OF ESTATE, ETC.

18–08   *[Add at end of fn.21]*
Rule 10(c)(i) of the Draft Probate Rules.

Where there has been disposition of the whole or substantially the whole estate

18–10   *[Add at end of fn.30]*
Rule 26 of the Draft Probate Rules is to the same effect.

[34]

I.—CLASS (D) – THE PERSONAL REPRESENTATIVE OF ANY RESIDUARY LEGATEE OR DEVISEE, ETC.

[Add at end of fn.31]

Rule 10(d) of the Draft Probate Rules.

18–11

J.—CLASS (E) – SPECIFIC LEGATEE, DEVISEE OR CREDITOR

[Add at end of fn.32]

Rule 10(e) of the Draft Probate Rules.

18–12

K.—CLASS (F) – PERSONAL REPRESENTATIVE OF SPECIFIC LEGATEE, DEVISEE OR CREDITOR

[Add at end of fn.34]

Rule 10(f) of the Draft Probate Rules.

18–13

L.—GRANTS TO PERSONS NOT IN THE SPECIFIED CLASSES

(2) Grant to the nominee or attorney of a non-trust corporation

[Add at end of fn.39]

Rule 23(5) of the Draft Probate Rules.

18–15

(3) Grant to an assignee

[Add at end of fn.44]

Rule 15 of the Draft Probate Rules.

18–17

M.—PRACTICE IN OBTAINING GRANTS OF ADMINISTRATION (WITH THE WILL)

[Add at end of fn.52]

The requirement in r.27(4) of the Draft Probate Rules will be to lodge a witness statement rather than an oath. The necessary contents are similar but not identical.

18–20

CHAPTER 19

ADMINISTRATORS—ENTITLEMENT TO A GRANT ON TOTAL INTESTACY

A.—GRANTS ON INTESTACY – GENERAL

19–01   *[Add at end of fn.2 following "see Ch.82, below."]*

New rules governing the distribution on intestacy under the Inheritance and Trustees' Powers Act 2014 came into force on October 1, 2014 and apply to deaths on or after that date.

[Add at end of fn.5]

The Non-contentious Probate Rules 1987 are shortly to be replaced by new Probate Rules. In their draft form, r.54(2) of the Draft Probate Rules is to the same effect as N-CPR 1987 r.48(2). However, citations are referred to as "notifications". The notified person must acknowledge service of the notification rather than enter an appearance to it.

19–02   *[Add new fn.6a after first sentence following "1987 (as amended)."]*

6a The order of entitlement to a grant on total intestacy is set down in the Draft Probate Rules at r.11. It is identical to the order in the current N-CPR r.22.

19–03   *[Add at end of fn.10]*

Under the Draft Probate Rules, citations are known as "notifications".

Adoption

19–13   *[Add at end of paragraph following "a qualifying interest."]*

Section 4 of the Inheritance and Trustees' Powers Act 2014 amends s.69(4) of the Adoption and Children Act 2002 in relation to adoptions made on or after October 1, 2014 so that adopted children retain any contingent interest they may have in the estate of their natural parent.

Practice

19–15   *[Add at end of fn.48]*

Under the Draft Probate Rules, oaths will be replaced by witness statements.

B.—THE RIGHT OF THE SURVIVING SPOUSE OR CIVIL PARTNER TO A GRANT

Priority of spouse who survives 28 days

[Add at end of paragraph following "of 28 days."]   **19–16**

Polygamous spouses recognised as valid under the customary law of the deceased's domicile are entitled under this provision: *Official Solicitor v Yemoh* [2010] EWHC 3727 (Ch); [2011] 1 W.L.R. 1450.

Sole grant to spouse or joint grant to spouse and another person

[Replace the whole paragraph with the following]   **19–17**

Where the surviving spouse or civil partner is entitled to the whole estate of the intestate, then (unless he or she is a minor) the grant will be made to the surviving spouse of civil partner alone. The rights of the surviving spouse or civil partner on intestacy changed for deaths after October 1, 2014 by virtue of s.1 of the Inheritance and Trustees' Powers Act 2014, which replaced the table under s.46(1)(i) of the Administration of Estates Act 1925. The surviving spouse or civil partner may now be entitled to the whole estate where:

- The intestate died on or after October 1, 2014 and left no issue;
- The intestate died before October 1, 2014 and left no issue and no parent, any brother or sister of the whole blood or any issue of such brother or sister; or
- Whether the intestate died before or after October 1, 2014 and there was a surviving relative of the specified sort, but the personal chattels and fixed net sum payable to the surviving spouse absorb the whole of the estate.

For deaths before October 1, 2014, in most cases where the surviving spouse or civil partner is not the only beneficiary, the grant will be taken jointly with another person, because of the life interest arising. It is therefore necessary to consider whether anyone other than the surviving spouse or civil partner has a beneficial interest in an estate on intestacy.

Revised tables of distribution are in Appendix 3.

The fixed net sum

[Add at end of fn.54]   **19–18**

The definition of "personal chattels" has been amended for deaths on or after October 1, 2014 by s.3 of the Inheritance and Trustees' Powers Act 2014.

[Replace second sentence of paragraph with the following.]

The amount payable is now set under the new Sch.1A to the Administration of Estates Act 1925 (inserted by the Inheritance and Trustees' Powers Act 2014), at same amount as that applying when the new provisions came into force on October 1, 2014, though it may be varied by the Lord Chancellor by statutory instrument. By paras 4 and 5 of Sch.1A, the fixed net sum is now index-linked, so that the Lord Chancellor *must* make such an order each time the Consumer Prices Index rises by 15 per cent, or every five years if sooner.

[Replace second sentence of paragraph after table of fixed net sum with the following]

It bears simple interest from the date of death, up to the date of payment or appropriation.[64] For deaths before October 1, 2014, that rate was 6 per cent,[65] but for deaths after that date the interest is fixed at the Bank of England base rate in force on the date of death.

Spouse's interest in the rest of the residuary estate

19–19   *[Replace bulleted list with the following]*

- Where there are issue, then
  o   for deaths before October 1, 2014, a life interest in half the residuary estate left after deduction of the fixed net sum;
  o   for deaths on or after October 1, 2014, half the residuary estate absolutely;
       (subject to this interest, the residuary estate is held on the statutory trusts for the deceased's issue[67])
- Where there are no issue, then:
  o   for deaths before October 1, 2014, half the residuary estate absolutely (the other half passing to a parent or parents of the deceased or, if the deceased leaves no parent, on the statutory trusts for the deceased's brothers or sisters of the whole blood[68]).
       (For deaths on or after October 1, 2014, without issue, the surviving spouse or civil partner takes the whole estate absolutely.)

Practice where there is a surviving spouse; changes in the value of the estate

19–22   *[Insert the following after first two words of second sentence (i.e. "If, however,")]*

in the case of deaths before October 1, 2014, when the Inheritance and Trustees' Powers Act 2014 abolished life interests under intestacy,

[Add at end of fn.71]

Rule 14 of the Draft Probate Rules contains similar provisions, referring to "co-administrators" rather than "joinder".

---

[64] Administration of Estates Act 1925 s.46(1), as amended.
[65] Intestate Succession (Interest and Capitalisation) Order 1977 (SI 1977/1491), as amended by SI 1983/1374.
[67] See para.19–30 below.
[68] See para.19–38 below.

[Add at end of fn.72]

Rule 40 of the Draft Probate Rules contains similar provisions.

[Add at end of fn.75]

Rule 23 of the Draft Probate Rules contains similar provisions.

19–23

Death of surviving spouse—leading grant

[Add at end of fn.80]

Rule 11 of the Draft Probate Rules contains similar provisions.

19–25

[Add at end of fn.81]

Rule 18(1) of the Draft Probate Rules contains identical provisions.

C.—THE RIGHT OF THE CHILDREN OR ISSUE TO A GRANT

Priority of children or issue to a grant

[Add at end of first sentence of second paragraph following "the residuary estate"]

where the deceased died before October 1, 2014, or an absolute interest in half the rest of the residuary estate where the deceased died after that date.

19–29

[Replace second sentence with the following]

Where, there is a surviving spouse the grant will be made to the spouse and the child or issue (in the case of a deaths prior to October 1, 2014); otherwise it will be made to such children or issue as join in applying.[105]

19–33

D.—THE RIGHT OF OTHER RELATIVES TO A GRANT

Death after 1952—where there is a surviving spouse but not children or issue

[Insert the following at beginning of section]

In the case of deaths on or after October 1, 2014, only the surviving spouse or civil partner of an intestate who dies without leaving issue will be entitled to the estate, and other relatives will have no interest. For deaths before that date, however, the following rules apply.

19–36

---

[105] Subject to a maximum of four, see para.17–07, above.

E.—THE RIGHT OF OTHERS TO A GRANT

The right of a creditor to a grant

19–42 *[Add after first sentence of fn.134]*

Rule 11(3) of the Draft Probate Rules is to similar effect.

CHAPTER 20

ADMINISTRATORS—ACCEPTANCE OF OFFICE, RENUNCIATION, RETRACTION OF RENUNCIATION

A.—ACCEPTANCE OF OFFICE OF ADMINISTRATOR

Citation

[Add at end of section following "in Ch.31, below."]

Under the Draft Probate Rules, citations are replaced by notifications. Rule 51 of the Draft Probate Rules operates in substantially the same way as N-CPR r.47.

20–04

B.—RENUNCIATION

Renunciation

[Add at end of fn.6]

N-CPR rr.32 and 34 are reproduced in the Draft Probate Rules in rr.41 and 19 respectively.

20–05

[Add at end of fn.8]

See Tristram and Coote's *Probate Practice* (30th edn) at para.15.03.

Effect of renunciation

[Add at end of fn.10]

N-CPR r.37(2) is reproduced in r.18(3) of the Draft Probate Rules.

20–06

E.—RETRACTION OF RENUNCIATION

General rule—requirement for no fewer than two administrators

[Add at end of fn.11]

N-CPR r.37(3) is reproduced in r.18(4) of the Draft Probate Rules.

20–07

CHAPTER 21

GRANTS IN COMMON FORM—GENERAL PRACTICE

A.—NON-CONTENTIOUS PRACTICE – DEFINITION AND GOVERNING RULES

The rules governing grants in common form

21–02   *[Add at end of paragraph]*

The non-contentious description has been removed from Draft Probate Rules.

21–03   *[In fn.3 add the following after "N-CPR 1987 r.3."]*

Draft Probate Rules r.3 provides only for the CPR (as amended from time to time) to apply.

[Add at end of fn.3]

Draft Probate Rules r.79 is to similar effect. Note that the costs rules have been renumbered and thus the CPR is stated to apply to Pts 44, 46 and 47 except rr.44.3–44.7, 44.13–44.18 and 46.11–46.13.

[Delete from "This process may well lead to the adoption..." to end of paragraph and insert text and new fn.3a]

Draft Probate Rules, in final draft form are under consideration but have not yet been finalised.[3a]

B.—WHERE GRANTS MAY BE OBTAINED

(1) The Principal Registry

21–04   *[Add at end of fn.5]*

Draft Probate Rules rr.21 and 22 are to similar effect. The definition of "probate practitioner" is contained in r.2.

(2) The district registries and sub-registries

21–05   *[Add at end of fn.7]*

Draft Probate Rules r.2 is to the same effect.

[3a] See also the Preface of this book.

[Add at end of fn.8]

Draft Probate Rules r.50(1) is to the same effect. "Contentions" are instead referred to as "disputes".

[Delete "; Administration of Justice Act 1985 s.51" from fn.6]

C.—MODES OF APPLICATION FOR GRANTS

(1) Applications at the principal registry

(i) Applications made through solicitor or probate practitioner

[Add at end of fn.14]

21–08

Draft Probate Rules rr.2 and 20 are to similar effect. References to solicitors have been removed since they are included in the new definition of "probate practitioner".

[Add at end of fn.15]

Draft Probate Rules r.21 is to the same effect.

(ii) Personal applications

[Add at end of fn.17]

21–09

The procedure is set out in rr.22 and 24(3) of the Draft Probate Rules.

[Replace "http://www.justice.gov.uk/courts/probate [Accessed October 5, 2012]" with the following]

http://www.justice.gov.uk/courts/probate [Accessed January 5, 2015]

[At end of first paragraph, replace "http://www.justice.gov.uk/" with]

http://hmctsformfinder.justice.gov.uk/HMCTS/GetForm.do?court_forms_id=735 [Accessed January 5, 2015]

[Add at end of fn.18]

Draft Probate Rules r.22(1) is to the same effect.

[Add at end of fn.19]

Draft Probate Rules r.45 is to the same effect.

[Add at end of fn.24]

Draft Probate Rules r.22(2)(c) is to the same effect.

[Add at end of fn.25]

Draft Probate Rules r.22(2)(b) is to the same effect.

[Add at end of fn.26]

Draft Probate Rules r.22(4) is to the same effect.

[Insert new section (iia) including paragraph 21–09A and fnn.26a–g before section (iii)]:

(iia) Changes to procedure in the Draft Probate Rules

21–09A The Draft Probate Rules will modify the procedure for both personal applications and applications through a probate practitioner. An application by a probate practitioner must[26a]:

- specify the form of grant being applied for;
- be supported by a witness statement by the person seeking the grant setting out all the facts necessary to be established if such a grant is to be made; and
- be accompanied by such other papers as may be required by any relevant Practice Direction;
- give the address of the probate practitioner's place of business within England and Wales.[26b]

An application by a personal applicant shall be made as follows[26c]:

- the applicant shall complete and deliver to the registry a questionnaire in the form set out in the relevant Practice Direction;
- the applicant shall verify the truth of the answers in the manner required by the form;
- the applicant shall deliver to the registry such other papers as may be required by any relevant Practice Direction.

A personal applicant is no longer required to attend a registry or interview venue to swear an oath before an authorised officer but may be required to attend pursuant to Draft Probate Rules r.25, which also applies to probate practitioners, where appropriate. The requirement to produce a certificate of death pursuant to N-CPR r.5(5) has also been removed.

In both cases:

- the above "relevant Practice Directions" may be made pursuant to Draft Probate Rules r.6, which allows the rules to be supplemented by Practice Directions made in accordance with the Constitutional Reform Act 2005 Pt 1 Sch.2;

[26a] Draft Probate Rules r.24(4).
[26b] Draft Probate Rules r.20.
[26c] Draft Probate Rules r.24(3).

- an application for a grant may be made to any registry[26d];
- applications may be delivered to the registry in any of the ways set out in any relevant Practice Direction[26e];
- any applicant shall if requested by the registry provide any further information or any copy or original document requested or specified by the registry; and attend for interview at the registry.[26f]

The witness statement replaces the oath and must[26g]:

- be verified by a statement of truth;
- unless otherwise directed by the court, state:
  - (a) the full name of the deceased (subject to r.28);
  - (b) the date of birth of the deceased as stated on the death certificate or as applicable to the circumstances;
  - (c) the date of death of the deceased as stated on the death certificate;
  - (d) the address of the principal residence of the deceased; and
  - (e) the state or territory where the deceased died domiciled;
- and state:
  - (a) the basis on which the applicant claims to be entitled to a grant;
  - (b) in what manner any person having a prior right to a grant has been cleared off;
  - (c) where the application is for a grant of administration, whether any minority or life interest arises under the will or intestacy; and
  - (d) the gross and net value of the estate of the deceased.

(iii) Procedure after an application has been lodged

[Add to fn.27 after "N-CPR 1987 rr.44(4) and 57."]

21–10

Provision for an index of caveats is contained in Draft Probate Rules r.55(2), renamed a "record of objections". Similarly, a record of grant applications is provided for by r.63(1) and the records are to be searched pursuant to r.63(2).

(2) Applications at a district registry or sub-registry

[Add at end of fn.28]

21–11

For the procedure under the Draft Probate Rules, see para.21–09A.

[Add at end of fn.29]

Draft Probate Rules r.63 is to the same effect.

[26d] Draft Probate Rules r.24(1).
[26e] Draft Probate Rules r.24(2).
[26f] Draft Probate Rules r.25.
[26g] Draft Probate Rules r.27.

(3) Appeals

21–12 *[Add at end of paragraph new text and fn.31a]*

Draft Probate Rules r.73 will set out an altered procedure in which summonses will be replaced by application notices[31a]:

- an appeal against a decision or requirement of a registrar or district judge shall be made to a judge and shall be made by filing a notice of appeal at the Principal Registry;
- the notice of appeal shall be filed within 21 days after the decision or requirement against which the appeal is brought, unless the court specifies a different time, and the appellant shall at the same time serve a copy of the notice of appeal on every other party to the proceedings;
- any reference in CPR pt.52 to a district judge shall be taken to include a district judge of the Principal Registry;
- CPR r.52.3 (Permission to appeal) does not apply to an appeal under Draft Probate Rules r.73;
- Draft Probate Rules r.73 does not apply to an appeal against a decision in proceedings for the assessment of costs (in proceedings for the assessment of costs, an appeal from the decision of a costs judge or district judge lies to a judge of the High Court under CPR pt.52 and an appeal from the decision of an authorised court officer lies to a costs judge or a district judge under CPR rr.47.21 to 47.24).

D.—GENERAL PRACTICE AS TO GRANTS

Papers to be lodged on application for a grant

21–14 *[Add at end of fn.32]*

See para.21–09A above for the procedural changes contained in the Draft Probate Rules.

[Add at end of fn.33]

Draft Probate Rules r.49 is in similar terms.

[Add at end of fn.34]

Draft Probate Rules r.13(7) is to the same effect. Summonses will be replaced by applications.

Fees payable on issue of an original grant

21–15 *[Replace "a flat fee of £45" in the second sentence with]*

a flat fee of £155

[31a] Consistently with similar changes throughout the Draft Probate Rules.

[Replace fn.37 text with the following]

These are set out in the disposable capital test: see Non-Contentious Probate Fees Order 2004 (SI 2004/3120) art.4 and Sch.1A. If the test is met, the amount of any fee remission is calculated by applying the gross monthly income test, also set out in Sch.1A.

[In third paragraph of 21–15, replace "where, owing to the exceptional circumstances of a particular case, payment of the fee would involve undue financial hardship." with]

where the Lord Chancellor is satisfied that there are exceptional circumstances which justify doing so

[In fn.38 replace "and Sch.1A para.8" with the following]

and Sch.1A para.16

[In third paragraph of 21–15 replace "However, such application must be made within six months of the payment" with the following]

However, such application must be made within three months of the payment

[In fn.39 replace "art.5 and Sch.1A, para.9" with the following]

Sch.1A, para.17

Notice to the Crown of application for a grant

[Add at end of fn.42]

Draft Probate Rules r.26 is to the same effect.

21–17

[Add at end of fn.44]

Under Draft Probate Rules r.49 no grant may be made in all cases (whether a grant of probate, letters of administration with the will annexed or grant of letters of administration) within 14 days without the permission of the court.

21–19

Death of the grantee before the official issue of the grant

[Add at end of fn.49]

Draft Probate Rules r.62 is to the same effect.

21–23

Copy grants

[In fn.51 replace "http://www.theprobateservice.gov.uk [Accessed October 5, 2012]" with the following]

21–24

http://hmctsformfinder.justice.gov.uk/HMCTS/GetForm.do?court_forms_id=735
[Accessed January 5, 2015]

E.—THE OATH

21–25   *[Add at end of paragraph]*

See para.21–09A above for changes to the procedure under the Draft Probate Rules, including the requirement for a witness statement in place of an oath and the matters that must be contained therein.

(1) The name, address and description of the deponent

21–26   *[Add at end of fn.56]*

Draft Probate Rules r.49 is to the same effect.

[Add at end of fn.58]

This is not reproduced in Draft Probate Rules r.3, which provides only for the CPR 1998 (as amended from time to time) to apply to probate matters. In any event, both 32PD para.18.1(2) to the CPR and Draft Probate Rules r.20 are to similar effect as regards witness statements in support of a grant.

(2) The name, address, age and description of the deceased

21–27   *[Add at end of fn.65]*

Draft Probate Rules r.28 is to the same effect.

[Add at end of fn.66]

Draft Probate Rules r.28 is to the same effect as regards the witness statement in support of a grant.

(3) The dates of birth and death of the deceased

21–28   *[Add at end of fn.74]*

This is replicated in Draft Probate Rules r.27(2)(c).

(5) The domicile of the deceased

21–31   *[Add at end of paragraph]*

Draft Probate Rules r.27(2)(e) requires the witness statement in support of a grant to state the state or territory where the deceased died domiciled in all cases.

(6) Settled land: life or minority interest

[Add at end of paragraph]

This requirement has been omitted in the Draft Probate Rules.

21–32

(7.2) Orders made to rectify a will

[Add at end of fn.88]

The procedure is set out in Draft Probate Rules r.78; r.78(1) is to the same effect.

21–34

(9) Description of executors

[Add at end of fn.91]

Draft Probate Rules r.13(1) is to the same effect.

21–36

[Add at end of fn.92]

Draft Probate Rules r.13(2) is to the same effect.

(10) Clearing off persons with a prior right to a grant

[Add at end of fn.95]

Draft Probate Rules r.27(3)(b) is to the same effect as regards the witness statement in support of a grant.

21–37

(11) The amount of the estate

[Add at end of first paragraph after "it is not normally necessary to amend the figure given in the oath."]

Draft Probate Rules r.27(3)(d) requires the witness statement in support of a grant to state the gross and net value of the estate of the deceased.

21–38

(12) Proper description of persons interested on intestacy

[Add new fn.102a at end of paragraph]

[102a] This is expressly required by Draft Probate Rules r.27(3)(a).

21–40

(13) Minority or life interest on intestacy

21–41 *[Add at end of paragraph new text and fn.103a]*

The Draft Probate Rules continue the requirement for a statement regarding minority or life interests but omit the provisions regarding settled land.[103a]

(15) Notice to the Treasury Solicitor

21–43 *[Add at end of fn.104]*

Draft Probate Rules r.26 is to the same effect.

(16) Wills of persons on military service and seamen

21–44 *[Replace text of last sentence "is in the testator's handwriting" with]*

was signed by the testator or, if unsigned, that it is in the testator's handwriting.

[Add at end of fn.105]

Draft Probate Rules r.38 is to the same effect.

F.—GUARANTEES

Discretion to require a guarantee

21–45 *[After "The current N-CPR 1987, unlike their 1954 predecessors, do not make specific provision for requiring such guarantees." add the following]*

Nor is specific provision made in the Draft Probate Rules.

[Add at end of fn.109]

Draft Probate Rules r.77 is to the same effect.

[Add at end of fn.112]

Draft Probate Rules r.11(3) is to the same effect.

[Add at end of fn.113]

Draft Probate Rules r.11(3) is to the same effect. "Accretion to the estate" is renamed "increase in the value of the estate".

[Add at end of fn.115]

Draft Probate Rules r.39 is to the same effect.

[103a] Draft Probate Rules r.27(3)(c).

[Add at end of fn.116]

Draft Probate Rules r.41 is to the same effect.

[Add at end of fn.117]

Draft Probate Rules r.43 is to the same effect. The requirement to give notice to the Court of Protection has been omitted.

Enforcing a guarantee

[Add at end of fn.121]   **21–46**

Draft Probate Rules r.77 is to the same effect. The application is made by application notice rather than by summons.

G.—THE INHERITANCE TAX ACCOUNT

Necessity for the Account

[Replace text of fn.129 with the following]   **21–47**

See, for example, *McCutcheon on Inheritance Tax*, 6th edn and Barlow, King & King's *Wills, Administration and Taxation, a Practical Guide*, 11th edn (2014).

[In fn.130 replace "[Accessed October 5, 2012]" with the following]

[Accessed January 5, 2015]

Time for delivery of the Account

[Add at end of fn.132]   **21–48**

For persons liable as trustee of a settlement for tax on an occasion on which tax is chargeable under Chapter III of Pt III of the 1984 Act, the time limit in relation to chargeable transfers made on or after April 6, 2014 is the expiration of the period of six months from the end of the month in which the occasion concerned occurs.

Form of Account

[In fn.135 replace "[Accessed October 5, 2012]" with the following]   **21–49**

[Accessed January 5, 2015]

Exceptions from the obligation to produce Inheritance Tax Account

[In fn.140 replace "http://www.hmrc.gov.uk/manuals/ihtmanual/ IHTM0 6000.htm [Accessed October 5, 2012]" with the following]   **21–53**

http://www.hmrc.gov.uk/manuals/ihtmanual/ihtm06016.htm [Accessed January 5, 2015]

[Add at end of fn.142]

For deaths occurring on or after March 1, 2011 reg.4(6) is subject to reg.4(7A) which provides for certain exempt transfers to be treated as chargeable transfers.

[Replace fn.144 text with the following]

The IHT threshold up to April 5, 2015 is £325,000.

[Replace fn.147 text with the following]

The IHT threshold up to April 5, 2015 is £325,000.

[In sub-paragraph (f) add new fn.145a after "payment of liabilities"]

145a For deaths occurring on or after April 1, 2014 the meaning of "the total liabilities of the estate" is qualified by reg.4(7B).

[Insert new fn.147a after "The third type of excepted estate is where"]

147a SI 2004/2543 reg.4(5).

CHAPTER 22

GRANTS WHERE THE DECEASED DIED DOMICILED ABROAD

A.—APPLICATION OF R.30, NON-CONTENTIOUS PROBATE RULES

[After "governed by r.30 of the Non-Contentious Probate Rules 1987." add the following]   **22–02**

This provision is set out in r.44 of the Draft Probate Rules which makes no changes to the procedure. The numbering of sub-paragraphs is the same as in N-CPR r.30.

B.—GRANTS TO EXECUTORS

[Add at end of fn.4]   **22–03**

Draft Probate Rules r.44(3)(a)(i) is to the same effect.

[After "The executor's oath in such a case must contain a statement as to the place of domicile of the deceased and the grant will only cover the estate of the deceased in England and Wales." add the following]

The oath has been replaced with a witness statement under Draft Probate Rules r.24 which must contain the matters listed in r.27. For a general summary of the procedural changes in the Draft Probate Rules to applications for grants see para.21–09A above.

C.—GRANTS TO EXECUTORS ACCORDING TO THE TENOR

[Add at end of fn.7]   **22–04**

Draft Probate Rules r.44(3)(a)(ii) is to the same effect.

D.—GRANTS OF ADMINISTRATION

[Add at end of paragraph]   **22–06**

Draft Probate Rules r.44(1) is to the same effect.

(a) Grant to the person entrusted by the court of the domicile

[In fn.11 after "satisfied the requirements of N-CPR 1987 r.30(1)" add the following]   **22–07**

(or similarly Draft Probate Rules r.44(1)).

[53]

[In third paragraph replace "As from 2015" with]

As from August 17, 2015

(b) Grant to a person beneficially entitled to the estate by the law of the place of domicile

22–08   *[Add at end of fn.16]*

Draft Probate Rules r.44(1)(b) is to the same effect.

[Add at end of fn.17]

Draft Probate Rules r.29 is to the same effect.

[Add text and new fn.18a at end of paragraph]

The Draft Probate Rules has replaced the affidavit of law with a witness statement of law, and similarly for oaths in respect of applications for grants.[18a]

(c) Grants made in the discretion of a registrar

22–09   *[Add at end of fn.19]*

Draft Probate Rules r.44(1)(c) is to the same effect.

E.—WHEN THE COURT WILL NOT FOLLOW THE FOREIGN LAW OF THE DOMICILE

22–10   *[Add new fn.20a after "Under r.30, the court has a discretion whether to order the making of a grant. In exercising that discretion, the district judge or registrar will clearly have regard to the law of the deceased's domicile."]*

[20a] Draft Probate Rules r.44 is to the same effect. The numbering of sub-paragraphs is the same as under N-CPR r.30.

F.—ADMISSIBILITY TO PROBATE OF WILLS WHERE DECEASED DOMICILED ABROAD

22–11   *[Add at end of fn.33]*

The Draft Probate Rules require a witness statement in place of an affidavit.

[In fourth paragraph replace "As from 2015" with the following]

As from August 17, 2015

[In fn.34 replace "shall apply as from 2015" with the following]

shall apply from August 17, 2015

[18a] See Ch.21 above.

G.—GRANTS WHERE THERE IS A MINORITY OR LIFE INTEREST; GRANTS TO A SECOND ADMINISTRATOR

[Add at end of fn.35]

22–12

Draft Probate Rules r.44(2) is to the same effect. Note that oaths have been replaced with witness statements.

I.—DEATH BEFORE 1926

[Add at end of fn.37]

22–14

Draft Probate Rules r.12 is to the same effect.

J.—PRACTICE WHERE THE DECEASED DIED DOMICILED ABROAD

(1) Modes of application for an order that a grant be made

[Add at end of paragraph]

22–15

Draft Probate Rules r.44 is to the same effect, and has the same sub-paragraph numbering as N-CPR r.30. Oaths have been replaced with witnesses statements.

(2) Papers to be lodged on application for an order that a grant be made

[Add at end of fn.44]

22–16

Draft Probate Rules r.27(2)(e) provides that unless otherwise directed by the court, the witness statement in support of a grant must the state or territory where the deceased died domiciled.

[In fn.48 insert the following text after "r.30(1)(c) N-CPR 1987."]

Draft Probate Rules r.44(1)(c) is to the same effect.

[Add at end of fn.49]

These affidavits of both fact and law have been replaced with witness statements in the Draft Probate Rules.

[Add at end of fn.50]

Oaths have been replaced with witness statements in the Draft Probate Rules.

(3) Wills and copies of wills

[Add at end of fn.53]

22–17

Draft Probate Rules r.32(1) is to the same effect.

[Add at end of fn.54]

These affidavits have been replaced with witness statements in the Draft Probate Rules.

[Add new fn.54a after "Although there is nothing in the N-CPR 1987" in second paragraph]

[54a] Nor in the Draft Probate Rules.

(5) The oath

22–19 *[Add at end of fn.63]*

Draft Probate Rules r.24 requires a witness statement in place of an oath. This must, unless the court directs otherwise, state the state or territory where the deceased died domiciled pursuant to r.27(2)(e).

(6) Affidavits of foreign law

22–20 *[Add at end of fn.66]*

Draft Probate Rules r.19 is to the same effect but replaces affidavits with witness statements.

[Add at end of fn.67]

Draft Probate Rules r.19 is to the same effect but replaces affidavits with witness statements.

(7) Notice to the Treasury Solicitor

22–21 *[Add at end of fn.69]*

Draft Probate Rules r.26 is to the same effect.

CHAPTER 23

APPLICATIONS TO ADMIT WILLS TO PROOF

B.—Documents to be Lodged

[Add at end of paragraph new text and fnn.0 and 0a]

23–02

The changes to the procedure for applying for a grant proposed in the Draft Probate Rules are discussed at para.21–09A above. In particular, the oath has been replaced by a witness statement pursuant to r.24 which must contain the matters set out in r.27. The Draft Probate Rules do not specify the documents that are to be lodged with the application but make provision for Practice Directions to be made[0] which presumably will so specify, if and when the Draft Probate Rules are enacted.[0a]

C.—Marking of Wills

[Add at end of fn.2]

23–03

Draft Probate Rules r.30(1) is to the same effect. It also requires that the marked will be referred to in the witness statement.

[Add at end of fn.3]

Draft Probate Rules r.30(2) is to the same effect.

D.—Engrossment for the purpose of Record

[Add at end of fn.4]

23–04

This provision has been omitted from the Draft Probate Rules.

[Add at end of fn.5]

Draft Probate Rules r.30(3) is to the same effect.

[Add at end of fn.6]

Draft Probate Rules r.30(4) is to the same effect.

---

[0] Draft Probate Rules r.6, in accordance with Pt 1 of Sch.2 to the Constitutional Reform Act 2005.
[0a] This is implicit in Draft Probate Rules rr.24(3) and (4)(c).

E.—AFFIDAVIT OF DUE EXECUTION

23–05   *[Add at end of fn.8]*

Draft Probate Rules rr.31(2)(b) and 33(1) are to the same effect. "Doubt about the due execution" has been replaced by "for any other reason". Affidavits have been replaced by witness statements, which should contain such evidence as the maker of the statement can give with regard to the manner in which the will was executed pursuant to r.33(2).

[Add at end of fn.9]

Draft Probate Rules r.33(1) is to the same effect.

[Add at end of fn.10]

Draft Probate Rules r.33(3)(a) is to the same effect. The will may also be accepted to proof without such evidence pursuant to r.33(3)(b) if any person who might be adversely affected by accepting the will for proof has consented to its proof without evidence.

[Add to fn.14 after "N-CPR r.10(2)"]

Draft Probate Rules r.30(2) is to the same effect.

[Add at end of fn.14]

This may be addressed by any new Practice Direction made pursuant to Draft Probate Rules r.6: see fn.0a above.

[In fourth paragraph add new fn.14a after "exhibiting the consents of such persons to the admission of the will to proof."]

[14a] This is addressed by Draft Probate Rules r.33(3)(b): see amended fn.10 above.

[Add at end of fn.17]

Affidavits have been replaced by witness statements in the Draft Probate Rules.

[Add at end of fn.18]

Draft Probate Rules r.33(2) is to the same effect.

F.—KNOWLEDGE AND APPROVAL BY THE DECEASED

23–06   *[Add at end of fn.19]*

Draft Probate Rules r.34 is to similar effect and applies where the will appears to have been signed by a blind or illiterate testator or by another person by direction of the testator pursuant to r.31(2)(c).

[Add at end of fn.20]

Draft Probate Rules r.31(3)(b) is to the same effect.

G.—POSSIBLE REVOCATION BY THE TESTATOR

[Add at end of fn.21]

Draft Probate Rules rr.31(2)(f) and 36 are to the same effect.

23–07

I.—OBLITERATIONS, INTERLINEATIONS AND OTHER ALTERATIONS

[Add at end of fn.27]

Draft Probate Rules rr.31(2)(e) and 35 are to the same effect. Note that affidavits have been replaced by witness statements.

23–09

J.—INCORPORATION OF DOCUMENTS

[Add at end of fn.37]

Draft Probate Rules r.35(3) is to the same effect. Draft Probate Rules r.35(4) states that a Practice Direction may be made (pursuant to r.6) providing for circumstances in which a document to which r.35(3) applies and which is in a standard form need not be produced.

23–10

Practice

[Add new fn.37a after first sentence "Evidence may be called for, on affidavit if necessary, to establish that the document produced is that referred to in the will."]

[37a] Draft Probate Rules r.31(3)(b) expressly provides for this.

23–11

L.—DATE OF WILL

[Add at end of fn.47]

Draft Probate Rules rr.31(2)(d) and 31(3)(b) are to the same effect.

23–13

N.—APPLICATION TO HAVE PROBATE REFUSED

[Add at end of fn.51]

Draft Probate Rules rr.33(1) and (4) are to the same effect.

23–15

T.—DESCRIPTION OF WILLS IN THE OATH

[Add new fn.68a after first sentence "All wills and codicils submitted for probate must be described in the oath and the dates thereof given."]

23–21

68a Draft Probate Rules r.30(1)(a) expressly provides for this. Oaths have been replaced with witness statements pursuant to r.24.

[Add new fn.68b to second sentence "Where a lost will is admitted to proof the fact that it is "as contained in a draft thereof" or "as contained in a copy", if such is the case, must be deposed to."]

68b Draft Probate Rules r.32 sets out the procedure where original of a will is not available.

U.—OMISSION OF WORDS FROM PROBATE

Wills not governed by s.9 of the Wills Act

23–26   *[Add at end of fn.82]*

Similar provisions are contained in Draft Probate Rules rr.31–36.

[Add at end of fn.83]

Draft Probate Rules r.37 is to the same effect.

V.—APPLICATION TO SEAL WILL TO PREVENT INSPECTION

23–27   *[Add new text and fnn.92–99 at end of paragraph]*

Draft Probate Rules r.65 contains a comprehensive procedure (albeit intended to be supplemented by Practice Directions pursuant to r.6) for applications to prevent inspection. In particular, if the will is the will of the Consort of a Sovereign or former Sovereign; the child of a Sovereign or former Sovereign; or a member of the Royal Family who, at his or her death is the first or second in line of succession to the throne or the spouse or civil partner or child of such a person, the President of the Family Division shall make an order that the will shall not be open to inspection.[92]

In any other case the President of the Family Division may make an order that the will shall not be open to inspection if he is satisfied that the will was made by a person who was the subject of arrangements made under the Serious Organised Crime and Police Act 2005 s.82 ("protection arrangements") or a beneficiary or other person named in the will is subject to protection arrangements; the rights of a beneficiary or other person named in the will under ECHR art.2 (right to life) may be infringed if the will is open to inspection; the will was made by a person to whom an interim or a final gender recognition certificate has been issued under the Gender Recognition Act 2004; or the will is within any other category prescribed by a Practice Direction.[93]

The above applications shall be made by application notice filed at the Principal Registry and returnable in the first instance before the senior district judge.[94] Only

---

[92] Draft Probate Rules r.65(3).
[93] Draft Probate Rules r.65(4).
[94] Draft Probate Rules r.65(5).

the Attorney General is to be made a respondent unless the senior district judge or the President of the Family Division so directs.[95]

Where an order has been made preventing inspection of a will, an application may be made for its inspection or to vary or set aside any such order and shall be heard by the President of the Family Division.[96] The application is made by application notice filed at the Principal Registry and returnable in the first instance before the senior district judge.[97] The respondents are the Attorney General; if the application is not made on behalf of the estate, the personal representatives of the deceased; and any other person (if living) who was a party to the application which led to the order.[98] No other person shall be made a respondent unless the senior district judge or the President of the Family Division so directs.[99]

---

[95] Draft Probate Rules r.65(6).
[96] Draft Probate Rules r.65(7).
[97] Draft Probate Rules r.65(8).
[98] Draft Probate Rules r.65(9).
[99] Draft Probate Rules r.65(9).

CHAPTER 24

LIMITED GRANTS

TYPES OF LIMITED GRANT

24–01   *[Add at end of fn.14]*

Such grants are called preservation grants in the Draft Probate Rules.

A.—LOST, DAMAGED OR UNOBTAINABLE WILLS

24–02   *[Add at end of fn.16]*

Rule 32(2) of the Draft Probate Rules is to the same effect.

[Add at end of fn.17]

There is no reason to suppose that the practice will be any different should the Draft Probate Rules be introduced although the matter may be dealt with in the anticipated Practice Directions.

Applications to the district judge or registrar

24–04   *[Add at end of fn.18]*

There will be no summonses under the Draft Probate Rules, only applications, but the same power appears in the proposed r.68(2). It remains to be seen whether the existing Registrar's Direction will survive.

[Add at end of fn.19]

Rule 32(2) of the Draft Probate Rules is to the same effect.

[Add at end of fn.20]

Rule 32(3) of the Draft Probate Rules is to the same effect.

[Add at end of fn.22]

As in the N-CPR at r.54, there is no express provision in r.32 of the Draft Probate Rules requiring the identification in the evidence of persons prejudiced by the admission of the subject will to probate although it is clearly best practice to include such information in order to avoid delay. Nor is there a specific reference to notice being given to those adversely affected: this is because a generally applicable provision to the same effect is set out in r.31(3)(a) in the Draft Probate Rules.

Evidence

[Add at end of fn.30]

24–05

Rule 32(2) of the Draft Probate Rules will require such a reconstruction.

Unobtainable wills

[Add at end of fn.33]

24–08

Rule 32(1) of the Draft Probate Rules is to the same effect.

[Add at end of fn.34]

Rule 32(4)(b) of the Draft Probate Rules will cover this situation.

B.—GRANTS TO ATTORNEYS AND CONSULAR OFFICERS

[Add at end of fn.38]

24–09

Rules 39 and 43 of the Draft Probate Rules are to the same effect.

[Add at end of fn.39]

Rule 39(1) of the Draft Probate Rules is to the same effect.

[Add at end of fn.40]

Rule 39(3) of the Draft Probate Rules is to the same effect referring to r.43 of those Rules.

Form and execution of the power of attorney

[Add at end of fn.50]

24–12

Rule 39 of the Draft Probate Rules is of the same effect.

Applying for a grant

[Add at end of fn.52]

24–13

Rule 39(2) of the Draft Probate Rules is to the same effect.

Grants to attorneys

24–15 *[Add at end of fn.62]*

Rule 39(2) of the Draft Probate Rules is to the same effect.

[Add at end of fn.63]

Rule 8 of the Draft Probate Rules deals with service generally, including of notices, and provides that service must be in the manner prescribed by Pt 6 of the Civil Procedure Rules.

Oath

24–17 *[Add new fn.65a to the heading]*

65a Under the Draft Probate Rules it is unlikely that an oath, as such, will be required. Draft r.24(3)(b) refers to the verification of the truth of the answers provided in the prescribed form.

C.—GRANTS FOR THE USE OF MINORS

24–20 *[Add at end of fn.72]*

Draft Rule 41 is headed "Grants on behalf of minors", but the text of the draft Rule uses the words "use and benefit" as under the N-CPR 1987.

Entitlement to the grant

24–21 *[Add new fn.72a at end of the first sentence]*

72a Rule 41(1) of the Draft Probate Rules.

[In fn.73 replace "Sch.4" with the following]

Sch.14

24–22 *[Add at end of fn.80]*

Rule 13(6)(a) of the Draft Probate Rules is to the same effect.

[Add at end of fn.81]

The proviso to r.41(1) of the Draft Probate Rules is to the same effect.

[Add at end of fn.82]

Rule 41(2) of the Draft Probate Rules is to the same effect.

[Add at end of fn.83]

Rule 42(1) of the Draft Probate Rules is to the same effect.

[Add at end of fn.84]

Rule 42(2) of the Draft Probate Rules is to the same effect.

[Add at end of fn.85]

Rule 19(1) of the Draft Probate Rules is to the same effect.

[Add at end of fn.86]

Rule 19(2) of the Draft Probate Rules is to the same effect.

[Add at end of fn.88]

Rule 41(3) of the Draft Probate Rules is to the same effect.

Practice and oath

[Add at end of fn.91]

Under those draft rules the oath will be replaced with a witness statement and/or a form which will contain a statement of truth (r.24(3) & r.27(1)).

D.—GRANTS WHERE A PERSON OTHERWISE ENTITLED IS UNDER A DISABILITY (DISABILITY GRANTS)

[Add at end of fn.95]

Rule 43(1) of the Draft Probate Rules is to the same effect.

[Add at end of fn.97]

Rule 43(2) of the Draft Probate Rules is to the same effect.

Those entitled to a grant where there is no-one entitled to the same degree

[Add new fn.98a at end of the first sentence]

[98a] Rule 43(1) of the Draft Probate Rules is to the same effect.

[Add at end of fn.99]

Rule 43(1)(a) of the Draft Probate Rules is to the same effect. Note that the Court of Protection now appoints deputies, not receivers.

[Add at end of fn.100]

Rule 43(1)(b) of the Draft Probate Rules is to the same effect.

24–23

24–24

24–25

24–26

24–27

24–29

[Add at end of fn.101]

Rule 41(3)(c) of the Draft Probate Rules is to the same effect.

[Add at end of fn.102]

Rule 43(3) of the Draft Probate Rules is to the same effect.

Power of district judge or registrar to order a grant

24–30   *[Add at end of fn.103]*

Rule 41(4) of the Draft Probate Rules is to the same effect.

[Add at end of fn.107]

Rule 44(1)(c) of the Draft Probate Rules is to the same effect.

Notice to the Court of Protection

24–31   *[Add at end of fn.108]*

There is no such requirement in the Draft Probate Rules. This may be addressed in a Practice Direction.

F.—GRANTS LIMITED AS TO PROPERTY

Procedure

24–36   *[Add at end of fn.114]*

Rule 47 of the Draft Probate Rules is to the same effect save that a witness statement replaces an affidavit.

[Add at end of fn.115]

Rule 47 of the Draft Probate Rules is to the same effect save that a witness statement replaces an affidavit.

H.—GRANTS *"CAETERORUM"* (REMAINDER GRANTS)

Procedure

24–41   *[Add at end of fn.131]*

The general rules on obtaining grants clearly apply in such cases. It will, it is submitted, plainly fall within the general rules on probate applications under the Draft Probate Rules (rr.24–27).

N.—GRANTS *AD COLLIGENDA BONA* (PRESERVATION GRANTS)

[Add new fn.144a at the end of the section]

24–47

[144a] Ad colligenda grants will be known formally as "preservation grants" under the Draft Probate Rules (see draft r.2(1)).

Procedure

[Add at end of fn.145]

24–48

Rule 48 of the Draft Probate Rules is to the same effect.

[Add at end of fn.149]

Rules 50(1)(a) and 68(2) of the Draft Probate Rules are to the same effect.

[Add at end of fn.159]

Rule 48 of the Draft Probate Rules is to the same effect.

CHAPTER 25

SPECIAL GRANTS

B.—UNADMINISTERED ASSETS – *"DE BONIS NON"*

Administration (with will) for unadministered assets

25–03   *[Add at end of fn.4]*
Rule 10 of the Draft Probate Rules is to the same effect.

[Add at end of fn.7]
Rule 13(6) of the Draft Probate Rules is to the same effect.

[Add at end of fn.8]
and s.19(3) of the Inheritance (Provision for Family and Dependants) Act 1975.

Administration (without will) for unadministered assets

25–04   *[Add at end of fn.9]*
Rule 11(4) of the Draft Probate Rules is to the same effect.

[Add at end of fn.10]
Rule 13(6) of the Draft Probate Rules is to the same effect.

[Add at end of fn.11]
Rule 11(4) of the Draft Probate Rules is to the same effect.

Death of the grantee

Minors

25–13   *[Add at end of fn.26]*
Rule 40 of the Draft Probate Rules is to the same effect.

Mental incapacity

[Add at end of fn.27]   **25–14**

Sub-rr.43(1) and (4) of the Draft Probate Rules are to the same effect as sub-rr.35(2) and (4) of the N-CPR 1987 respectively.

[Add at end of fn.28]

Rule 40 of the Draft Probate Rules is to the same effect.

D.—GRANT OF DOUBLE PROBATE

Procedure

[In fn.34 replace "below" with the following]   **25–18**
above

E.—SETTLED LAND GRANTS

Introduction

[In fn.36 replace "18th edn (2011)" with the following]   **25–19**
19th edn (2015)

Separate grant required for settled land

[Add at end of fn.38]   **25–21**
Rule 46 of the Draft Probate Rules is to the same effect.

Priority in applications for grants to settled land

[Add new fn.39a following the words "r.29 of the N-CPR 1987"]   **25–22**
[39a] Rule 46 of the Draft Probate Rules is to the same effect.

(3) General personal representatives of the deceased

[Add at end of fn.44]   **25–25**
Rule 46(1) of the Draft Probate Rules is to the same effect.

Is the grant of probate or of administration?

25–26 *[Add new fn.45a at end of the sentence "However, r.29 ... Priority set out above."]*

⁴⁵ᵃ Rule 46 of the Draft Probate Rules reflects the current (amended) version of r.29 of the N-CPR 1987.

The application for a settled land grant

25–27 *[Add new fn.48a at the end of the first sentence of the second paragraph]*

⁴⁸ᵃ Rule 46 of the Draft Probate Rules is to the same effect.

Effect on applications for a general grant

25–28 *[Add at end of fn.52]*

Rule 46(2) of the Draft Probate Rules is to the same effect.

CHAPTER 26

DISCRETIONARY GRANTS

B.—THE STATUTORY DISCRETION

Section 116 Senior Courts Act 1981

[Add new text and fnn.4a–4b at the end of the first paragraph following fn.4]

Further, the power extends to cases governed by r.30 of the N-CPR 1987 (grants where the deceased died domiciled abroad) as well as rr.20 and 22 notwithstanding the similar discretion conferred by r.30((1)(c) in such cases.[4a] Absent any words of limitation in s.116 it is submitted that this must be correct. It appears that a s.116 application is not the only means of excluding executors (although not administrators) from a grant. Newey J. has held that s.50 of the Administration of Justice Act 1985 (court's power to remove a personal representative) may be utilised prior to a grant being issued or even applied for.[4b]

26–03

Requirement for "special circumstances" and for the appointment to be "necessary and expedient"

[Throughout this section the words "necessary and expedient" should be replaced with the following]

necessary *or* expedient (emphasis added)

26–04

Procedure on applications under section 116

[Add at end of fn.86]

Rule 48(a) of the Draft Probate Rules is to the same effect.

[Add at end of fn.88]

Rule 68(2) of the Draft Probate Rules is to the same effect.

[Add at end of second paragraph following fn.90]

It appears from anecdotal evidence that there is a private Practice Note which has been circulated to the judges of the Central Family Court (formerly known as the

26–19

[4a] *Guvadze v Kay* [2012] EWHC 1683 per Sales J.
[4b] *Goodman v Goodman* [2013] EWHC 758 (Ch).

Principal Registry of the Family Division), but not to practitioners, to the effect that contentious applications will not be heard in the Central Family Court but will be stayed for one month during which the applicant must issue a fresh application in the Chancery division. If such an application is not issued the application in the Central Family Court will stand dismissed. If the evidence is reliable, and the writer has had personal experience of it, keeping the Practice Note private is unsatisfactory as it puts applicants to unnecessary expense in incurring a second application fee and causes delay. Practitioners should consider issuing applications which they know or suspect will be contentious in the Chancery division.

C.—EXERCISE OF DISCRETION WHERE APPLICANTS ENTITLED IN SAME DEGREE

Disputes between persons entitled to administration in the same degree

26–23   *[Add at end of fn.99]*

Rule 13(5) of the Draft Probate Rules is to the same effect.

[Add at end of fn.102]

Rule 13(7) of the Draft Probate Rules is to the same effect.

[Add at end of fn.103]

Rule 13(9) of the Draft Probate Rules is to the same effect.

[Add at end of fn.104]

Rule 13(6) of the Draft Probate Rules is to the same effect.

D.—LEAVE TO SWEAR DEATH

26–28   *[Add new para.26–28A and fnn.115a–115b after para.26–28]*

Presumption of Death Act 2013 ("PODA 2013")

26–28A   The Presumption of Death Act 2013 ("PODA 2013") came into effect on October 1, 2014.[115a] It governs applications to court for declarations of death in relation to persons who are missing and are thought to have died or who have not been known to be alive for a period of at least seven years.[115b] A full discussion of this Act may be found in the supplement for Ch.70.

It is questionable as to whether or not such applications of this nature should be dealt with under the N-CPR 1987 in the light of PODA 2013. Although the Draft Probate Rules, at draft r.74, still contain provision for such applications the working party on the new Probate Rules has recognised that the rule will have to be removed or amended in light of the new Act. At the time of writing there is no

[115a] SI 2014/1810.
[115b] PODA 2013 s.1.

indication as to what course will be adopted. It is submitted that it would not be helpful or appropriate to have two different procedures for resolving this issue and the question should be dealt with under PODA 2013 and the CPR Part 57, which governs applications under that Act. Paragraphs 26–29 to 26–35 should be read subject to that caveat. As the court has power to make discretionary and protective grants, all necessary orders can be obtained from the same court. If the evidence is clear then the matter can be dealt with on a summary basis, if necessary, in the applications court. Given the Central Family Court's approach to contentious applications as referred to at para.26–19 above, it is recommended that such applications are made in the Chancery Division.

Persons who have not been heard of for a long period

[In fn.120 replace "17th edn (2009)" with the following]   **26–30**
18th edn (2013)

Practice

[Add new fn.123a following the words "Rule 53 of the N-CPR 1987"]   **26–32**
[123a] Rule 74 of the Draft Probate Rules is to the same broad effect.

[Add new fn.130a following the words "r. 53 of the N-CPR 1987"]   **26–34**
[130a] Rule 74 of the Draft Probate Rules is to the same broad effect.

CHAPTER 27

AMENDMENT, NOTATION, REVOCATION AND IMPOUNDING OF GRANTS

A.—AMENDMENT OF GRANTS

27–01   *[Add at end of paragraph]*

Rule 62 of the Draft Probate Rules is to the same effect and retains the same sub-paragraph numbering.

B.—NOTATION OF GRANTS

Election by a spouse to have a life interest redeemed

27–09   *[Replace text of entire paragraph with following text and fnn.11–14]*

Prior to October 1, 2014, where the deceased left both a surviving spouse and issues, the intestacy rules gave the surviving spouse a life interest in half of the residue of the estate.[11] The deceased was entitled to elect to have his or her life interest redeemed.[11a] If that surviving spouse was the sole representative of the deceased, then such election was not effective unless written notice thereof was given to the senior district judge of the Family Division within 12 months of the grant being taken out. The notice was then noted on the grant and the record and is open to inspection.[12]

From October 1, 2014, the surviving spouse is instead entitled to half of the residue absolutely.[13] Thus the provisions regarding the life interest are obsolete and have been repealed.[14]

---

[11] Administration of Estates Act 1925 s.46(1) Table para.(2)(a), in force from December 5, 2005 to September 30, 2014.

[11a] This is discussed further at para.82–07 below.

[12] Administration of Estates Act 1925 s.47A(7), repealed from October 1, 2014, and N-CPR 1987 r.56. Draft Probate Rules r.67 is to the same effect, although will presumably be omitted from any subsequent enactment to reflect the changes to the 1925 Act s.46 that have taken place since the Draft Probate Rules were drafted.

[13] Administration of Estates Act 1925 s.46(1) Table para.(2)(C)(a), as amended by Inheritance and Trustees' Powers Act 2014 s.1.

[14] Inheritance and Trustees' Powers Act 2014 Sch.4 para.1(3), repealing the Administration of Estates Act 1925 s.47A.

Revocation by a district judge or registrar

[Add at end of fn.28]

Draft Probate Rules r.62(1) is to the same effect.

27–18

[Add at end of fn.29]

Draft Probate Rules r.62(2) is to the same effect.

[Add at end of fn.30]

Draft Probate Rules r.40(2) is to the same effect.

Grounds for revoking a grant

(3) Where the grant is, in effect, a nullity

[Add at end of fn.51]

27–27

Under Draft Probate Rules r.49(2) the minimum time for a grant in all cases without the permission of the court is 14 days of death.

Practice

[Add new fn.58a after text "r.41(1) of the Non-Contentious Probate Rules 1987 (N-CPR 1987)" at end of first sentence]

27–32

58a Draft Probate Rules r.62(1) is to the same effect.

C.—Revocation of Grants

Effect of revocation

Legal proceedings to continue

[Replace fn.86 text with the following]

27–41

CPR r.83.2, replacing RSC Ord.46 r.2 (which was previously applicable pursuant to CPR r.50.1) from April 22, 2014.

CHAPTER 28

RECOGNITION AND RESEALING OF GRANTS

B.—RESEALING OF GRANTS

Commonwealth grants in the United Kingdom

28–04   *[Add at end of fn.27]*

Rule 45 of the Draft Probate Rules is to the same effect.

Practice for resealing in the United Kingdom

28–05   *[Add at end of fn.32]*

Rule 45 of the Draft Probate Rules makes no express ruling as to where the application may be made.

[Add at end of fn.33]

Rule 45(2) of the Draft Probate Rules is to similar effect, and refers to r.44. Rule 44 of the Draft Probate Rules is to the same effect as N-CPR 1987 r.30.

[Add at end of fn.37]

Rule 45(4) of the Draft Probate Rules is to the same effect.

[Add at end of fn.39]

There is no similar provision in r.45 of the Draft Probate Rules.

[Add at end of fn.41]

Rule 45(3) of the Draft Probate Rules is to similar effect, save that the permission of "the court" is required, rather than a registrar.

[Add at end of fn.46]

Rule 45(1) of the Draft Probate Rules is to the same effect.

CHAPTER 29

SEARCHES, COPIES, EXEMPLIFICATIONS, DUPLICATES AND DEPOSIT OF WILLS OF LIVING PERSONS

A.—RECORD OF GRANTS MADE

[Add at end of fn.1]

29–01

Rule 63 of the Draft Probate Rules expressly provides that a record shall be kept of every pending application for a grant made in any registry.

B.—INSPECTION AND COPYING OF PROBATE DOCUMENTS

Standing search

[Add at end of fn.5]

29–03

Rule 64 of the Draft Probate Rules is to the same effect, save that the initial search will extend to all grants issued in the 12 months after the entry of the standing search (rather than the current six-month time period).

Copies of documents

[Add at end of fn.7]

29–05

Rule 66 of the Draft Probate Rules is to the same effect, save that copies may also be issued as unsealed office copies.

E.—COPIES OF DOCUMENT IN LEGAL PROCEEDINGS

[At the end of the first sentence of fn.17 please replace "CPR r.5.4(5)" with the following]

29–09

now CPR r.5.4B

CHAPTER 30

CAVEATS

A.—INTRODUCTION

30–01   *[Add at end of paragraph]*

The Non-contentious Probate Rules 1987 are shortly to be replaced by new Probate Rules. In their draft form, rr.55–60 and the procedure therein for "objections" will replace the present caveat procedure contained in rr.44–46.

[Add new section 30–01A after para.30–01 as follows]

The new "objections" procedure

30–01A   Instead of the three-step process detailed in this chapter as regards caveats, the Draft Probate Rules provide that the filing of a response to an objection is the last step before a probate claim. An objector may enter an objection by filing a notice of objection in the prescribed form: r.55. Any person claiming to have an interest in the estate and who wishes to oppose the objection may file a response (in the prescribed form) setting out the reasons for opposing the objection: r.57.

Once a response has been filed, the objection will cease to have effect after three months, unless an application is made or a probate claim has been commenced: r.57(4). The onus is thus placed firmly on the objector to issue proceedings.

Further, instead of the present process whereby a caveat initially has effect for a period of six months, which may be extended by further periods of six months, an objection will have effect for 12 months, and may be extended by a further period of 12 months: r.56.

By r.60, no further objection may be entered by an objector whose objection has been withdrawn or which has ceased to have effect under the Draft Rules or by order of the court.

B.—EFFECT OF A CAVEAT

30–02   *[Add at end of fn.3]*

Rule 55(3) of the Draft Probate Rules is to the same effect, save that *ad colligenda bona* grants will be known as "preservation grants".

C.—ENTRY OF A CAVEAT

[Add at end of fn.8]

Rule 55 of the Draft Probate Rules sets out the procedure for entry of an objection—see para.30–01A above.

[Add at end of fn.9]

Rule 55 of the Draft Probate Rules sets out the procedure for entry of an objection.

D.—DURATION OF A CAVEAT

[Add at end of fn.11]

Rule 56 of the Draft Probate Rules sets out the rules relating to the duration of an objection—an objection shall remain in force for 12 months.

[Add at end of fn.13]

Rule 56 of the Draft Probate Rules sets out the rules relating to the duration of an objection—see para.30–01A above.

[Add at end of fn.14]

Rule 56 of the Draft Probate Rules sets out the rules relating to the duration of an objection.

[Add at end of fn.15]

Rule 61(3) of the Draft Probate Rules is to the same effect.

[Add at end of fn.16]

Rule 61(4) of the Draft Probate Rules is to the same effect as regards objections.

[Add at end of fn.17]

Rule 58 of the Draft Probate Rules is the same effect as regards objections.

E.—EXTENSION AND RENEWAL OF A CAVEAT

[Add at end of fn.19]

Rule 56(2) of the Draft Probate Rules is of similar effect, save that the objection may be extended for a further 12-month period. Rules 56(2) and (3) set out the procedure to be followed.

[Add at end of fn.20]

Rule 59(1) of the Draft Probate Rules sets out the powers of the court in dealing with an application for an extension of an objection pursuant to r.56.

F.—WARNING OF CAVEATS

30–06   *[Add at end of fn.23]*

See para.30–01A, above, for the new procedure in the Draft Probate Rules relating to responses to objections.

[Add at end of fn.27]

Rule 8 of the Draft Probate Rules makes provision for the service of notices and other documents pursuant to the Draft Rules.

G.—WITHDRAWAL OF CAVEATS

30–07   *[Add at end of fn.28]*

Rule 58 of the Draft Probate Rules is to the same effect regarding objections.

[Add at end of fn.30]

Rule 58(2) of the Draft Probate Rules provides that after a response has been filed to an objection, an application to withdraw may be made by filing a written request if all parties agree, but must otherwise be made by application notice.

H.—NON-APPEARANCE TO WARNING

30–08   *[Add at end of fn.31]*

See para.30–01A, above, for the procedure to be applied under the Draft Probate Rules in respect of objections.

I.—APPEARANCE TO WARNING

30–09   *[Add at end of fn.32]*

See para.30–01A, above, for the procedure to be applied under the Draft Probate Rules in respect of objections.

J.—EFFECT OF APPEARANCE

30–11   *[Add at end of fn.39]*

See para.30–01A, above, for the procedure to be applied under the Draft Probate Rules in respect of objections.

K.—NOTIFICATION OF PROBATE CLAIMS TO CAVEATORS

30–12   *[Add at end of fn.40]*

Rule 61(1) of the Draft Probate Rules is to the same effect as regards objections.

[Add at end of fn.41]

Rule 61(2) of the Draft Probate Rules is to the same effect as regards objections.

M.—DISCONTINUANCE OF CAVEAT

(1) No contrary interest shown

[Add at end of fn.44]

30–14

Rule 57(4) of the Draft Probate Rules makes provision for the circumstances in which an objection shall cease to have effect after the filing of a response.

(2) Consent

[Add at end of fn.45]

30–15

Rule 57(4) of the Draft Probate Rules makes provision for the circumstances in which an objection shall cease to have effect after the filing of a response.

(3) After citation

[Add at end of fn.46]

30–16

Rule 57(4) of the Draft Probate Rules makes provision for the circumstances in which an objection shall cease to have effect after the filing of a response.

CHAPTER 31

CITATION

A.—INTRODUCTION

31–01   *[Add at end of paragraph]*

The Non-contentious Probate Rules 1987 are shortly to be replaced by new Probate Rules. In their draft form, rr.51–54 dealing with notifications are in similar form to the present rr.46–48 regarding citations.

Rule 51(1) of the Draft Probate Rules preserves the three situations applicable to citations, and under the Draft Rules notifications, save that the language used has changed. The three types of notification are to be described as: (1) to accept or refuse to take a grant, (2) to give reasons why a person should not be ordered to take a grant and (3) to prove a will by a probate claim. Rule 51(2) provides that no notification shall be issued (i) while proceedings as to the validity of the will are pending or (ii) before the notifier has entered an objection in accordance with r.55 (see Ch.30, above). However, the procedure to be followed once a notification is given will differ from the present practice: see para.31–07A, below.

B.—TYPES OF CITATION

(1) To accept or refuse a grant of probate or administration

31–02   *[Add at end of fn.3]*

Rule 53 of the Draft Probate Rules is to similar effect.

[Add at end of fn.6]

Rule 53(2) of the Draft Probate Rules is to the same effect.

(2) To take probate

31–03   *[Add at end of fn.11]*

Rule 53(3) of the Draft Probate Rules deals with the issue of a notification to an executor who has intermeddled.

[Add at end of fn.12]

This is now expressly provided in relation to all notifications in r.51(2) of the Draft Probate Rules.

[Add at end of fn.15]

See r.53(3) of the Draft Probate Rules.

(3) To propound a will

[Add at end of fn.19]

Rule 54 of the Draft Probate Rules deals with notifications to have a will proved in solemn form.

31–04

C.—APPLICATION FOR THE ISSUE OF A CITATION

[Add at end of fn.23]

Rule 52 of the Draft Probate Rules sets down rules relating to the procedure and evidence required in respect of notifications.

31–05

[Add at end of fn.25]

Rule 52(1) of the Draft Probate Rules is to the same effect as regards notifications.

[Add at end of fn.26]

Rule 52(3) provides that every notification shall be served personally on the person to be notified. This rule is expressly subject to r.52(4), which provides that a court may direct the use of some other method (i.e. advertisement) of service, if it is satisfied by evidence contained in a witness statement that this would be just and expedient.

[Add at end of fn.27]

Rule 51(2) of the Draft Probate Rules is to the same effect, save that the requirement to enter a caveat is replaced with the need to enter an objection.

[Add at end of the first sentence of fn.28]

This requirement is under the Draft Probate Rules contained in r.52(2).

D.—SERVICE OF CITATION

[Add at end of fn.29]

Rules 52(3) and (4) of the Draft Probate Rules are to the same effect.

31–06

[Add at end of fn.31]

Rule 52(4) of the Draft Probate Rules is to the same effect.

E.—APPEARANCE BY CITEE

31–07 *[Add at end of fn.32]*

See para.31–07A, below, for the procedure which will apply under the Draft Probate Rules.

[Add new section 31–07A at the end of the paragraph]

31–07A The procedure applying after a citation has been served is altered in relation to notifications under the Draft Probate Rules, with differing rules applying depending on the type of notification.

In the case of a notification to accept or refuse a grant, there is a requirement on the person receiving the notification to apply by witness statement for an order for a grant: r.53(4). Rules 53(5)–(8) deal with the procedure to be followed in such a case. If the person receiving the notification has not acknowledged service, r.53(5) provides various options to the notifier to apply for a grant to be made. If the person receiving the notification acknowledges service but does not himself apply for a grant or fails to pursue his application with reasonable diligence, r.53(7) provides various options to the notifier to apply for a grant to be made.

In the case of a notification to have a will proved in solemn form, r.54(2) provides the notifier with options for applying for a grant to be made where no person has acknowledged service, or where a person acknowledging service has failed to proceed with reasonable diligence to propound the will.

F.—PROCEDURE AFTER APPEARANCE OR NON-APPEARANCE

(1) Citation to accept or refuse a grant

31–09 *[Add at end of fn.40]*

See para.31–07A, above, for the procedure which will apply under the Draft Probate Rules.

(2) Citation to take probate

31–10 *[Add at end of fn.51]*

See para.31–07A, above, for the procedure which will apply under the Draft Probate Rules.

(3) Citation to propound a will

31–11 *[Add at end of fn.53]*

See para.31–07A, above, for the procedure which will apply under the Draft Probate Rules.

CHAPTER 32

APPLICATIONS AND SUMMONSES IN NON-CONTENTIOUS
PROCEEDINGS

A.—INTRODUCTION

[Add at end of second sentence of the first paragraph]   **32–01**

Rules 68–78 of the Draft Probate Rules govern the making of applications: they
make no provision for the use of summons, only application notices.

[Add at end of fn.3]

Rule 2 of the Draft Probate Rules is to the same effect.

B.—DECISION OR DIRECTION OF A DISTRICT JUDGE OR REGISTRAR

[Add at end of fn.4]   **32–02**

Rule 50(2) of the Draft Probate Rules is to the same effect.

[Add at end of fn.5]

Rule 68(2) of the Draft Probate Rules is to the same effect, save that there is no
reference to the need for a summons; the rule simply provides that the court may
require that any application be made in that fashion.

Applications without notice (ex parte)—duty to be frank and fair

[Add at end of fn.10]   **32–03**

Rule 68 of the Draft Probate Rules makes provision for the procedure to be
followed in issuing applications. Rule 70 of the Draft Probate Rules governs
applications made without notice. Rule 72(1) of the Draft Probate Rules provides
that the court may direct that an application for the service of which no other
provision is made shall be served in such manner as the court may direct.

[Add at end of fn.12]

Rule 2(1) of the Draft Probate Rules is to the same effect.

Summonses to a district judge or registrar

32–04   *[Add at end of fn.13]*

Rule 76 of the Draft Probate Rules provides that an application for an inventory and account may be made by issuing a notice in the prescribed form.

[Add at end of fn.14]

Rule 68(10) of the Draft Probate Rules provides that the court may at any stage give directions for the conduct of a hearing.

Summonses to a judge

32–06   *[Add at end of fn.17]*

Rule 68(3)(b) of the Draft Probate Rules provides that applications to a judge shall be made by filing an application notice at the Principal Registry.

[Add at end of fn.18]

Rule 68(2) of the Draft Probate Rules is to the same effect, save that the application is made by way of application notice.

[Add at end of fn.19]

Rule 73 of the Draft Probate Rules deals with appeals from a registrar, and is to the same effect, save that a notice of appeal shall be filed (rather than a summons).

C.—PROCEDURE ON SUMMONS

32–08   *[Add at end of fn.23]*

Rule 72 of the Draft Probate Rules makes provision for the service of applications.

[Add at end of fn.24]

Rule 72 of the Draft Probate Rules makes provision for the service of applications.

[Add at end of fn.25]

Rule 72 of the Draft Probate Rules makes provision for the service of applications.

CHAPTER 33

COSTS OF NON-CONTENTIOUS BUSINESS

A.—SOLICITOR'S FEES – WHAT IS FAIR AND REASONABLE

Fees based on time spent

[Add at end of fn.9]   33–02

De Courcy v Secretary of State for the Home Department is now also reported at [2012] 3 Costs L.O. 269.

Fees based on the value of the estate

[Add at end of fn.13]   33–03

The Law Society's booklet *Non-Contentious Costs* was updated in July 2012. However, it is currently unavailable (as at April 2015) on the Law Society website whilst the Society's costs guidance is being extensively updated in the light of the significant changes to legal aid made by the Legal Aid, Sentencing and Punishment of Offenders Act 2012.

Fees based on both time spent and the value of the estate

[Add at end of fn.15]   33–04

The Law Society's booklet *Non-Contentious Costs* was updated in July 2012. However, it is currently unavailable (as at April 2015) on the Law Society website whilst the Society's costs guidance is being extensively updated in the light of the significant changes to legal aid made by the Legal Aid, Sentencing and Punishment of Offenders Act 2012.

E.—ASSESSMENT (TAXATION)

[Replace the last sentence of the paragraph with the following]   33–11

The procedure for such assessments is set out in Pts 44, 46 and 47 of the Civil Procedure Rules 1998 (save that rr.44.3–44.7, 44.13–44.18 and 46.11–46.13 shall not apply).

[Add at end of fn.32]

Rule 79 of the Draft Probate Rules provides for the application of the provisions of the CPR to probate matters, subject to certain specified assessments (as set out in para.33–11 above).

Practice

33–15   *[Insert new footnote 43a at the end of the heading "Practice"]*

[43a] The Draft Probate Rules operate as follows: r.79 provides that the CPR shall apply; r.80 sets out the court's discretion as regards costs; r.81 deals with the basis of assessment; r.82 details the factors to be taken into account in assessing costs; r.83 sets down the procedure for assessing costs; and r.84 makes provision for the time limits applicable for complying with costs orders.

[Replace the first two paragraphs with the following]

As mentioned above, the practice in relation to assessment of costs is governed by Pts 44, 46 and 47 of the Civil Procedure Rules 1998 (save that rr.44.3–44.7, 44.13–44.18 and 46.11–46.13 shall not apply), as modified by rr.60(3)–(7) of the Non-Contentious Probate Rules 1987. Rules 79–84 of the Draft Probate Rules set out similar provisions in relation to costs and the assessment thereof.

Of particular importance are CPR r.46.10 and para.6 of the Practice Direction to Pt 46, which set out the procedure in relation to an order by the court under Pt III of the Solicitors Act 1974 for the assessment of the costs payable to a solicitor by his client.

[Replace fn.45 text with the following]

See CPR 46PD.6.4.

[Replace fn.46 text with the following]

CPR r.46.10(2).

[Delete the reference to the CPR Costs PD in fn.47 and replace with the following]

CPR 46PD.6.15.

[Replace fn.48 text with the following]

See CPR r.46.10(3).

[Replace fn.49 text with the following]

See CPR r.46.10(4).

[Replace fn.50 text with the following]

CPR r.46.10(5) and 46PD.6.10.

[Replace fn.51 text with the following]

CPR 46PD.6.11.

[Replace fn.52 text with the following]

CPR r.46.10(6).

[Replace fn.53 text with the following]

33–16

See CPR r.44.1 and 47.4(2) (as modified by, respectively, N-CPR 1987 r.60(4), (7). Rules 79(c) and 83(2) of the Draft Probate Rules are to the same effect).

[Delete references to the CPR in fn.54 and replace with the following]

CPR rr.47.21–47.24.

[Add at end of fn.54]

Rule 73(5) of the Draft Probate Rules provides that in proceedings for the assessment of costs, an appeal from the decision of a costs judge or district judge lies to a judge of the High Court under CPR Pt 52 and an appeal from the decision of an authorised court officer lies to a costs judge or a district judge under CPR rr.47.21–47.24.

G.—Recovering Unpaid Fees

[Add at end of fn.58]

33–19

Truex v Toll was applied in a non-solicitor context in *Francis v Solomon Taylor & Shaw (a firm)* [2013] EWHC 9 (Ch); [2013] BPIR 314.

CHAPTER 34

PRELIMINARY STEPS AND PARTIES

A.—GENERAL

Limitation

34–03   *[Add at end of fn.10]*

See *Liebel v Liebel* (2014 ONSC 4516 (CanLII), *http://canlii.ca/t/g8lzn* [Last accessed November 11, 2014] for the Canadian position: The Canadian Limitations Act 2002 applied to bar proceedings being brought to challenge the validity of a will after the second anniversary of the death of the testator.

Forms of probate claim

(a) Claims for pronouncing for or against a will

34–06   *[Add at end of paragraph new text and fnn.17a–17e]*

When the Draft Probate Rules come into force, the caveat procedure is substituted by an objection procedure.[17a] Once there has been a response to the objection in accordance with Draft r.7, the objection will cease to have effect on the expiry of the period of three months from the date on which the response was filed unless by then a probate claim has been commenced.[17b] Part 12 of the Draft Rules describes the procedure following the issue of a probate claim. Draft r.61 provides that,[17c] upon being advised of the issue of a probate claim, the senior district judge is to give notice of the claim to every objector other than the claimant in the claim in respect of each objection that is in force, including any objection lodged after the commencement of the probate claim.[17d] Unless the court directs otherwise, the commencement of a probate claim operates to prevent the making of a grant (other than one under s.117 of the Senior Courts Act 1981) by the person shown to be entitled to do so by the decision of the court in the probate claim.[17e]

[17a] See Part 11: Objection to the making of a grant.
[17b] Draft r.57(4)(b).
[17c] See Part 12: Probate claims.
[17d] Draft rr.61(1) and (2).
[17e] Draft r.61(3).

(c) Claim for the revocation of grant

[Add at end of fn.29]

34–12

See also *Paynter v Hinch* [2013] EWHC 13 (Ch); [2013] W.T.L.R. 529 (want of knowledge and approval; claim dismissed).

[Add new fn.29a to "made;" on the fifth line]

[29a] Application failed in *Haider v Syed* [2013] EWHC 4079; [2014] W.T.L.R. 387, where the claim was for revocation of the existing grant of letters of administration on the basis of a will document, which was held to be a forgery.

CHAPTER 35

THE CLAIM FORM, ACKNOWLEDGEMENT AND EVIDENCE OF TESTAMENTARY DOCUMENTS

A.—THE CLAIM FORM

35–01   *[Add new paragraph and fnn.9a–9e at the end of 35–01]*

Under the Draft Probate Rules, the caveat procedure is substituted by an Objection procedure.[9a] Once there has been a response to the objection in accordance with Draft r.57, the objection will cease to have effect on the expiry of the period of three months from the date on which the response was filed unless by then a probate claim has been commenced.[9b] Part 12 of the Draft Rules describes the procedure following the issue of a probate claim. Draft r.61 provides that,[9c] upon being advised of the issue of a probate claim, the senior district judge is to give notice of the claim to every objector other than the claimant in the claim in respect of each objection that is in force, including any objection lodged after the commencement of the probate claim.[9d] Unless the court directs otherwise, the commencement of a probate claim operates to prevent the making of a grant (other than one under s.117 of the Senior Courts Act 1981) by the person shown to be entitled to do so by the decision of the court in the probate claim.[9e]

[9a] See Pt 11: Objection to the making of a grant.
[9b] Draft r.57(4)(b).
[9c] See Pt 12: Probate claims.
[9d] Draft rr.61(1) and (2).
[9e] Draft r.61(3).

CHAPTER 36

STATEMENTS OF CASE

A.—PECULIARITIES

[Add at end of fn.10]

36–01

But see *Jeffery v Jeffery* [2013] EWHC 1942 (Ch); [2013] W.T.L.R. 1509 (testatrix's son involved in preparation of her will, under which his children benefited: no evidence of lack of knowledge and approval); *Paynter v Hinch* [2013] EWHC 13 (Ch); [2013] W.T.L.R. 529 (circumstances not such as to excite the suspicion of the court); *Williams v Wilmot* [2012] EWHC 2211 (Ch); [2013] W.T.L.R. 1291 (circumstances of the preparation of the will excited the vigilance and suspicion of the court, shifting onus on the defendant to establish knowledge and consent); *Re Wilson (deceased)* [2013] EWHC 499 (Ch); [2013] W.T.L.R. 899 (circumstances of the making of the will was an additional factor adding to the need to be vigilant as regards the will); and *Re Catling (deceased)* [2014] EWHC 180 (Ch); [2014] W.T.L.R. 955.

CHAPTER 37

PRE-TRIAL PROCEDURE AND CASE MANAGEMENT

PRIVILEGE

37–03   *[Add at end of fn.6]*

See also *Birdseye v Roythorne & Co.* [2015] EWHC 1003 (Ch).

[Insert the following after "caveat" on 10th line]

or, under the Draft Probate Rules, the lodging of an objection

LARKE V NUGUS LETTERS

37–04   *[Add at end of fn.9]*

Although the guidance was given by the Law Society to solicitors, it is also a general statement of best practice that is not confined to solicitors: *Re Catling (deceased)* [2014] EWHC 180 (Ch); [2014] W.T.L.R. 955 at para.[42].

CHAPTER 38

TRIAL

A.—TRIAL IN THE HIGH COURT

Discontinuance or dismissal

[Add at end of fn.23]   **38–07**

But see *Al-Sadi v Al-Sadi* [2013] EWHC 2379 (Ch), where the claimants discontinued their case (not a probate claim but one brought in relation to distribution) because it was so weak that it would have failed at trial. See also Sara-Kennedy T.E.L. & T.J. 2014 (Nov) 18 and Ch.39 (costs).

B.—TRIAL IN THE COUNTY COURT

Jurisdiction

[Replace fn.58 text with the following]   **38–13**

County Courts Act 1984 s.32; Administration of Justice Act 1985; County Courts Jurisdiction Order 1981. Probate claims must be brought only in a county court where there is also a Chancery district registry, or in the Central London County Court: CPR r.57.2(3); see also Practice Direction 2CPD3(3)(a).

CHAPTER 39

COSTS

A.—COURT'S DISCRETION

39–01   *[In fn.2 replace "CPR r.44.3(2)(a)" with the following]*

CPR r.44.2(2)(a)

[In fn.2, after "Spiers v English [1907] P. 122" add the following]

; *Re McKeen deceased* [2013] EWHC 3639 (Ch); [2014] W.T.L.R. 461; *Marley v Rawlings (Costs)* [2014] UKSC 51 at para.[6] and see also paras [14] to [26] for comments on the effect of conditional fee agreements on costs orders. On discontinuance, see *Al-Sadi v Al-Sadi* [2013] EWHC 2379 (Ch), for a discussion on rebutting the presumption in CPR r.38.6 that the claimant must pay the defendant's costs on a discontinuance (proceedings concerned distribution of the estate).

[Add at end of fn.3]

In *Marley v Rawlings (Costs)* [2014] UKSC 51; [2015] A.C. 157 at para.[6], Lord Neuberger said, "the authorities also reveal that, where there is an unsuccessful challenge to the validity of a will, and the challenge is a reasonable one and is based on an error which occurred in the drafting or execution of the will, the court often orders that all parties' costs come out of the estate." See also A. Learmonth, "Counting the cost" T.E.L. & T.J. 2014, 162 (Dec), 4.

[In fn.4 replace "CPR r.44.13(1)" with the following]

CPR r.44.10(1)

[In fn.7 replace "CPR r.44.3(4) and (5)" with the following]

CPR r.44.2(4) and (5)

[In fn.8 replace "CPR r.44.4(1)" with the following]

CPR r.44.3(1)

[In fn.9 replace "See generally the notes to CPR r.44.4(1)" with the following]

See paragraph 44x.4.3 in the 2015 edition of the White Book.

[Add new fn.9a following "proportionate in amount in favour of the paying party."]

[9a] Costs incurred are proportionate if they bear a reasonable relationship to (a) the sums in issue in the proceedings; (b) the value of any non-monetary relief in issue in the proceedings; (c) the complexity of the litigation; (d) any additional work generated by the conduct of the paying party; and (e) any wider factors involved in the proceedings, such as reputation or public importance. (See CPR 44.3(5)).

[In fn.10 replace "CPR r.44.4(2), (3)" with the following]

CPR r.44.3(2)

[Add new paragraph and fn.11a after the penultimate paragraph ending with "of demonstrating proportionality."]

In deciding the amount of costs the court will also have regard to (a) the conduct of all the parties, including in particular, (i) conduct before, as well as during, the proceedings; and (ii) the efforts made, if any, before and during the proceedings in order to try to resolve the dispute; (b) the amount or value of any money or property involved; (c) the importance of the matter to all the parties; (d) the particular complexity of the matter or the difficulty or novelty of the questions raised; (e) the skill, effort, specialised knowledge and responsibility involved; (f) the time spent on the case; (g) the place where and the circumstances in which work or any part of it was done; and (h) the receiving party's last approved or agreed budget.[11a]

[Add at end of fn.12]

; as there are no costs provisions in Pt 11 of the Draft Probate Rules, the practice is likely to be applied to the costs of and associated with objections.

Exceptions to the general rule

(2) Where the litigation has been caused by the conduct of the testator

[In fn.22, after "[2010] W.T.L.R. 1479" add the following]   **39–04**

; but see *Re McKeen deceased* [2013] EWHC 3639 (Ch); [2014] W.T.L.R. 461, where the defendant had misinstructed her expert, exaggerated evidence at trial, rejected multiple offers, and had conducted litigation in a combative, rather than investigative, fashion (also includes comments on the effect of ATE insurance on costs liability)

[11a] CPR 44.4(3). In a probate claim, the court may order that the costs management provisions of CPR r.3 will apply (CPR 3.12). For the practice involved in costs budgeting, see section II of CPR Pt 3 and Practice Direction 3E.

(4) Where circumstances afford reasonable grounds for investigation

39–06   *[Add at end of fn.46]*

; see also *Re McKeen deceased* [2013] EWHC 3639 (Ch); [2014] W.T.L.R. 461.

B.—COSTS OF PARTICULAR PARTIES

Executors

39–09   *[Add at end of fn.80]*

On discontinuance, see *Al-Sadi v Al-Sadi* [2013] EWHC 2379 (Ch), for a discussion on rebutting the presumption in CPR r.38.6 that the claimant must pay the defendant's costs on a discontinuance (proceedings concerned distribution of the estate).

Additional parties

39–12   *[In fn.108 replace "CPR r.48.4; 48 PD 50.A" with the following]*

CPR r.46.3; 46PD.1

Assessment of costs

39–16   *[In fn.121 replace "As to interim costs orders under CPR r.44.3(8)," with the following]*

There is no longer an express power for the court to order an amount to be paid on account before the costs are assessed but, presumably, this can be done under the general discretion conferred by CPR 44.2(1)(c) as to when costs are to be paid, and

CHAPTER 40

THE EFFECT OF A GRANT AND RECTIFICATION OF WILLS

I.—GRANT CONCLUSIVE BUT TRUST MAY BE IMPOSED WHERE OBTAINED BY FRAUD

[In fn.36 replace "18th edn (2011), para.1–12" with the following]   **40–09**
19th edn (2015), para.1–012

[In fn.37 replace "Snell's Equity, 32nd edn (2010), para.24–23 et seq" with the following]
Snell's Equity, 33rd edn (2015) para.24–023 onwards

[In fn.37 replace "Lewin on Trusts, 18th edn (2011), para.3–76 et seq with the following]
Lewin on Trusts, 19th edn (2015), para.3–076 onwards

O.—RECTIFICATION OF WILLS

The test for rectification

[Delete text and fn.68: "Assuming, therefore, that there is a valid will,[68]..." and   **40–18**
retain the following]
Section 20 requires the court to consider three questions:

[After list, add the following text and new fn.69a]
The word "will" in s.20 is not confined to a will which complies with the
requirements of formal validity imposed by s.9 of the Wills Act 1837 but may
include any document which on its face is bona fide intended to be a will and
which, once rectified, would be a valid will.[69a]

[Replace first sentence, from "As to the third ..." to "... transcription of his will"   **40–21**
and fn.72 with text and fnn.72–72b]
As to the third of these questions, the expression "a clerical error" does not have a
precise, well-established or technical meaning.[72] It is not limited to an error made

---

[69a] *Marley v Rawlings* [2014] UKSC 2; [2015] A.C. 129, reversing the decision of the Court of Appeal
in [2012] EWCA Civ 61.
[72] *Marley v Rawlings* [2014] UKSC 2; [2015] A.C. 129.

in the process of recording the intended words of the testator in the drafting or transcription of his will,[72a] but also extends to a mistake arising out of routine office work such as preparing, filing, or organising the execution of a document.[72b]

[Add new text and fn.77a at end of paragraph]

There is no limit to the amount of text that may be corrected. In appropriate circumstances a wholesale correction of the document may be a permissible exercise of the court's power to rectify, as in *Marley v Rawlings*,[77a] where the solicitor to both the deceased and his wife drafted wills in mirror form and by mistake caused each testator to sign the other's will. The mistake was not noticed until both had died. The Supreme Court held that the deceased's will should be rectified pursuant to s.21 so that it contained the typed parts of the will signed by the deceased's wife in place of the typed parts of the will signed by the deceased.

Practice

40–24 *[Add at end of fn.81]*

Draft Probate Rules r.78 is to the same effect, save that the application must be instead made by application notice and witness statement rather than by affidavit.

40–25 *[In second paragraph replace text and fn.87 "leaving out of account any grants limited to settled land or trust property, and a grant limited to real or personal estate is also left out of account unless a grant limited to the remainder of the estate has previously been made or is made at the same time.[87]" with the following text and fnn.87–87a]*

leaving out of account any grant limited to settled land or to trust property; any grant that does not permit any of the estate to be distributed; a grant limited to real estate or to personal estate, unless a grant limited to the remainder of the estate has previously been made or is made at the same time; and a grant, or its equivalent, made outside the United Kingdom.[87] A grant sealed under Colonial Probates Act 1892 s.2, however, counts as a grant made in the United Kingdom but is to be taken as dated on the date of sealing.[87a]

[72a] As interpreted in *Wordingham v Royal Exchange Trust Co Ltd* [1992] Ch. 412 at 419.
[72b] Per *Marley v Rawlings* [2014] UKSC 2; [2015] A.C. 129.
[77a] [2014] UKSC 2; [2015] A.C. 129.
[87] Administration of Justice Act 1982 s.20(4).
[87a] Administration of Justice Act 1982 s.20(5).

CHAPTER 41

VESTING IN THE PERSONAL REPRESENTATIVE

B.—PERSON IN WHOM ESTATE VESTS

Vesting in the Public Trustee (formerly the Probate Judge)

[Replace text in fn.27 from "www.justice.gov.uk/about/ospt. . ." to the end with the following]   **41–07**

https://www.gov.uk/government/organisations/official-solicitor-and-public-trustee [Last accessed January 5, 2015]. The contract address is Official Solicitor and Public Trustee, Victory House, 30–34 Kingsway, London, WC2B 6EX, enquiries@offsol.gsi.gov.uk.

C.—THE NATURE OF THE REPRESENTATIVE'S INTEREST

Merger with representative's own interest in the same property

[In fn.67 replace "Snell's Equity, 31st edn (2005), para.42–002" with the following]   **41–20**
Snell's Equity, 33rd edn (2015), para.42-002

[In fn.70 replace "Snell's Equity, 31st edn (2005), para.42–003" with the following]
Snell's Equity, 33rd edn (2015), paras 42-002 and 42-004

D.—WHAT VESTS

Property bought in another's name

[In fn.120 replace "Snell's Equity, 32nd edn (2010), para.5–020 et seq" with the following]   **41–31**
Snell's Equity, 33rd edn (2015), para.5-005 onwards

[In fn.124 replace "Snell's Equity, 32nd edn (2010), para.5–25" with the following]
Megarry & Wade: The Law of Real Property, 8th edn (2012), para.13-036 onwards

[In fn.150 replace "Lewin, Trusts (17th edn), Ch.9 with the following]   **41–38**

Lewin on Trusts, 19th edn (2015), Ch.9

[In fn.150 replace "Snell's Equity (31st edn), Ch.25 with the following]
Snell's Equity, 33rd edn (2015), Ch.25

F.—NATURE OF RIGHTS WHERE GRANT IS ADMINISTRATION DE BONIS NON

Rights in respect of judgment obtained by the original representative

41–52   *[Replace text in first sentence "RSC Ord.46 r.2" with]*
CPR r.83.2

[Retain fn.199 and replace text with the following]
This replaced RSC Ord.46 r.2 (which was previously applicable pursuant to CPR r.50.1) from April 22, 2014.

CHAPTER 42

VESTING OF ASSETS IN OTHERS: DONATIONES MORTIS CAUSA

B.—*DONATIONES MORTIS CAUSA – AN ANOMALOUS DOCTRINE*

[Add at end of paragraph new text and fn.9a]   42–02

Sen v Headley was recently applied and approved in *Vallee v Birchwood*.[9a]

D.—REQUIREMENTS FOR A DONATIO MORTIS CAUSA

[Add at end of fn.21]   42–05

See also *Vallee v Birchwood* [2014] Ch. 271.

(1) Contemplation of death

[Add at end of fn.23]   42–06

See also *Vallee v Birchwood* [2014] Ch. 271 at [25].

[Add after "gift was made in contemplation of death.[31]" new text and fn.31a]

Although, in *Vallee v Birchwood* it was held that most people would consider that a person who anticipated the possibility of his death within five months was contemplating his "impending death". It was not necessary for a person to be in extremis.[31a]

(3) Dominion and delivery

[Add at end of fn.42]   42–08

See also *Vallee v Birchwood* [2014] Ch. 271 at [28]–[43].

[Add at end of fn.50]   42–11

See also *Vallee v Birchwood* [2014] Ch. 271. See also *King v Dubrey* [2014] W.T.L.R. 1411 (which is currently subject to an appeal).

[9a] [2014] Ch. 271. See also *King v Dubrey* [2014] W.T.L.R. 1411 (which is currently subject to an appeal) and for further comment Conv. (2014) 525 and T.E.L & T.J. (2014) 18.
[31a] *Vallee v Birchwood* [2014] Ch. 271 at [26].

42–13 *[Add at end of fn.66]*

See also *Vallee v Birchwood* [2014] Ch. 271 at [36–37] and [43].

42–14 *[Add at end of fn.67]*

See also *Vallee v Birchwood* [2014] Ch. 271. See also *King v Dubrey* [2014] W.T.L.R. 1411 (which is currently subject to an appeal).

42–15 *[Add at end of fn.71]*

See also *Vallee v Birchwood* [2014] Ch. 271 at 41–43. See also *King v Dubrey* [2014] W.T.L.R. 1411 (which is currently subject to an appeal).

(4) Property capable of being the subject-matter of a *donatio mortis causa*

42–17 *[Add after second sentence of fn.74]*

Sen v Headley has now been followed in *Vallee v Birchwood* [2014] Ch. 271 on this point.

42–18 *[Add at end of fn.80]*

See also *Vallee v Birchwood* [2014] Ch. 271.

G.—DISTINGUISHING A DONATIO MORTIS CAUSA FROM OTHER GIFTS

Comparison with a legacy

42–31 *[Replace item 2 on the list with the following]*

2. The former requires the donor to part with dominion over the subject-matter of the gift during his lifetime. The latter does not.

CHAPTER 43

SOCIAL SECURITY BENEFITS AND TAX CREDITS

A.—INTRODUCTION

Changes to the social security benefits scheme—introduction of universal credit

[Add at end of paragraph]

43–01

A personal representative who is in receipt of means-tested benefits and receives a benefit under the Will or intestacy may need to notify the Department of Work and Pensions of the change to his circumstances. The need will arise where the benefit received takes the personal representative over the capital limits. In the table of mean-tested benefits in Appendix 4 the capital limits are given for each benefit.

[Add at end of fn.1]

43–02

The benefits that will disappear are known as "legacy benefits".

[Replace the last two sentences of the first paragraph with the following new text and fn.1a]

A House of Commons Select Committee reported on February 25, 2015 that by October 2014 fewer than 18,000 people were claiming Universal Credit, 0.3 per cent of the eligible population. The timetable for the transfer of claimants to this new benefit has been extended to the end of 2019.[1a]

[Add new fn.1b at the end of the second paragraph, after "requirements."]

[1b] Universal Credit Regulations 2013 (SI 2013/376) (UCR) regs 8–16.

[Add at end of the third paragraph the following new text and fn.2a]

A benefit cap of £500 per week for a lone parent or a couple and £350 for a single person was introduced in July 2013. In practice the amount of Housing Benefit is reduced or for claimants in receipt of Universal Credit the amount of that benefit will be reduced. The benefits of claimants who are not in receipt of Housing Benefit or Universal Credit are not capped. Benefit cap exceptions include

---

[1a] *http://www.parliament.uk/business/committees/committees-a-z/commons-select/public-accounts-committee/news/report-universal-credit-progress-update/* [Accessed April 6, 2015].

claimants in receipt of earnings, those in receipt of certain disability benefits and claimants over the qualifying age for state pension credit.[2a]

The public bodies involved

43–03 *[Replace paragraph (1) in the list with the following paragraph]*

The Department of Work and Pensions is responsible for the payment of most social security benefits and pensions. Jobcentre Plus, run by the Department of Work and Pensions, administers most benefits for people of working age and payments from the Social Fund. The Pensions Service covers retirement pensions, state pension credit and the winter fuel payment. Regional Disability Benefits Centres administer disability living allowance, personal independence payment and attendance allowance. The central Carer's Allowance Unit administers all carer's allowance claims.

[Add the following new text and fn.2b at end of paragraph (2) in the list]

On April 1, 2013 council tax benefit was replaced by council tax reduction schemes administered by local authorities.[2b]

[Add at end of fn.4]

All the reported Commissioners' decisions are now on a single website: *www.osscsc.gov.uk/Aspx* [Accessed April 6, 2015].

Legislative abbreviations

43–05 *[In the second row of the table delete references to CTBR and add the regulations listed below. On April 1, 2013 council tax benefit was replaced by council tax reduction schemes administered by local authorities.]*

CTRS(Eng)R Council Tax Reduction Schemes (Prescribed Requirements)(England) Regulations 2012 (SI 2012/2885)
CTRS(Wales)R Council Tax Reduction Schemes (Prescribed Requirements)(Wales) Regulations 2012 (SI 2012/3144)

[Add the following to the table]

SSPIPR Social Security (Personal Independence Payment) Regulations 2013 (SI 2013/377)
UCR Universal Credit Regulations 2013 (SI 2013/376)

[2a] UCR regs 78–81; Housing Benefit Regulations 2006 (SI 2006/213) (HBR) regs 75A, 75B and 75C: main requirements for benefit cap to apply. UCR reg.82, HBR reg.75E earnings exceptions; UCR reg.83, HBR reg.75F disability benefit recipients' exceptions.
[2b] Council Tax Reduction Schemes (Prescribed Requirements)(England) Regulations 2012 (SI 2012/2885) and Council Tax Reduction Schemes (Prescribed Requirements)(Wales) Regulations 2012 (SI 2012/3144).

C.—BENEFITS AND TAX CREDITS PAYABLE TO THE ESTATE

Types of benefit and tax credits

Means-tested benefits

[Add at end of the paragraph the following new text and fnn.35a–35b] **43–14**

A benefit cap of £500 per week for a lone parent or a couple and £350 for a single person was introduced in July 2013. In practice the amount of Housing Benefit is reduced. For claimants in receipt of Universal Credit the amount of that benefit will be reduced. The benefits of claimants who are not in receipt of Housing Benefit or Universal Credit are not capped. Benefit cap exceptions include claimants in receipt of earnings, those in receipt of certain disability benefits and claimants over the qualifying age for state pension credit.[35a]

There will also be a deduction from Housing Benefit if the property is deemed to be too large for the claimant. This deduction is known officially as "the spare room subsidy" but has been christened "the bedroom tax".[35b]

[Replace the whole paragraph (1) in the list with the following paragraph. Delete fn.36 and replace with a new fn.36] **43–15**

The discretionary social fund has been abolished. Since April 2013 local authorities have taken over the administration of grants and loans for situations formerly covered by community care grants and crisis loans. The qualifying conditions, backdating rules, etc. are determined locally. Budgeting loans are currently administered by the Department of Work and Pensions. Applications for budgeting loans should be made to the local Jobcentre Plus office. For Universal Credit claimants budgeting loans have been replaced by payments on account.[36]

[In paragraph (2) in the list delete "regulated"]

[Delete the whole of the last paragraph which starts "Community care grants ...."]

Non-means tested benefits

[Add at end of paragraph (1) in the list] **43–16**
, personal independence payment;

[35a] UCR regs 78–81; Housing Benefit Regulations 2006 (SI 2006/213) (HBR) regs 75A, 75B and 75C: main requirements for benefit cap to apply. UCR reg.82, HBR reg.75E earnings exceptions; UCR reg.83, HBR reg.75F disability benefit recipients' exceptions.
[35b] HB Regs 2006 (SI 2006/213) reg.B13.
[36] WRA s.70.

Tax credits

43–19   *[Replace the second paragraph with the following new text and fnn.62–62a]*

Both Working Tax Credit and Child Tax Credit will be abolished and replaced with Universal Credit.[62] A House of Commons Select Committee reported on February 25, 2015 that by October 2014 fewer than 18,000 people were claiming Universal Credit, 0.3 per cent of the eligible population. The timetable for the transfer of claimants to this new benefit has been extended to the end of 2019.[62a]

Effect of death on claims and appeals

Making claims after death

43–21   *[In the second sentence replace "regulated social fund" with the following]*

social fund

[Add at end of the third paragraph the following new text and fn.70a]

On April 1, 2013 Council Tax Benefit was replaced by council tax reduction schemes administered by local authorities.[70a]

Pursuing existing claims

43–22   *[Add at end of the third paragraph the following new text and fn.80a]*

On April 1, 2013 Council Tax Benefit was replaced by council tax reduction schemes administered by local authorities.[80a]

[Replace fnn.81, 82, and 83 with the following]

[81] HBR reg.97(1).
[82] Defined in HBR reg.97(2).
[83] HBR reg.97(3).

---

[62] WRA s.33.
[62a] *http://www.parliament.uk/business/committees/committees-a-z/commons-select/public-accounts-committee/news/report-universal-credit-progress-update/* [Accessed April 6, 2015].
[70a] Council Tax Reduction Schemes (Prescribed Requirements)(England) Regulations 2012 SI (2012/2885) and Council Tax Reduction Schemes (Prescribed Requirements)(Wales) Regulations 2012 (SI 2012/3144).
[80a] Council Tax Reduction Schemes (Prescribed Requirements)(England) Regulations 2012 SI (2012/2885) and Council Tax Reduction Schemes (Prescribed Requirements)(Wales) Regulations 2012 (SI 2012/3144).

Rights of Challenge to Decisions

[Add at end of the third paragraph the following new text and fn.92a]   **43–23**

On April 1, 2013 council tax benefit was replaced by council tax reduction schemes administered by local authorities.[92a]

D.—BENEFITS PAYABLE TO A DECEASED'S FAMILY

Bereavement benefits

[Add at end of the second paragraph the following new text and fn.103a]   **43–24**

The new benefit support payment will be introduced in April 2016 at the earliest. The conditions of entitlement are in the Pensions Act 2014.[103a]

Retirement pensions

[Add at end of the second paragraph the following new text and fn.122a]   **43–29**

For people who reach state pension age on or after April 6, 2016 the government is planning to introduce a flat rate state pension based on a 35-year national insurance contribution record. This flat rate pension will be reduced proportionally for people with fewer national insurance contributions. The new system will be based solely on an individual's record; the spouse or civil partner's record will not confer any entitlement.[122a]

Funeral expenses payable by the social fund

Right to claim funeral expenses

[Replace the website reference in fn.136 with the following]   **43–33**

https://www.gov.uk/government/publications/the-social-fund-technical-guidance/ the-social-fund-technical-guidance#funeral-payments [Accessed April 6, 2015]

[92a] Council Tax Reduction Schemes (Prescribed Requirements)(England) Regulations 2012 SI (2012/ 2885) and Council Tax Reduction Schemes (Prescribed Requirements)(Wales) Regulations 2012 (SI 2012/3144).
[103a] Pensions Act 2014 ss.30, 31.
[122a] Pensions Act 2014 s.2.

E.—RIGHTS TO RECOVER OVERPAYMENTS FROM ESTATES

Overpayments of DWP benefits

43–37   *[Add at end of the second sentence the following new text and fn.154a]*

On April 1, 2013 Council Tax Benefit was replaced by council tax reduction schemes administered by local authorities.[154a]

Overpayments from the social fund

43–41   *[Replace the first sentence with the following]*

Payments from the social fund such as funeral expenses payments may be recovered under the same rules as for other DWP benefits.

Overpayments of Housing Benefit and Council Tax Benefit

43–42   *[Add the following sentence at the beginning of this section]*

Although Council Tax Benefit was replaced with council tax reduction schemes on April 1, 2013 the details of the recovery of Council Tax Benefit remain unchanged for the time being.

43–43   *[Replace the last sentence in this section with the following new text and fn.196]*

The Limitation Act 1980 only applies to court proceedings for the recovery of Housing Benefit overpayments.[196]

F.—ARMED FORCES COMPENSATION SCHEME AND WAR PENSIONS

Introduction

43–49   *[Replace the website reference in fn.216 with the following]*

https://www.gov.uk/government/organisations/veterans-uk [Accessed April 6, 2015]

[Add at end of the second paragraph the following new text and fn.217a]

On April 8, 2013 a new benefit, the Armed Forces Independence Payment, was introduced for members and former members of the armed forces who have been

---

[154a] Council Tax Reduction Schemes (Prescribed Requirements)(England) Regulations 2012 (SI 2012/2885) and Council Tax Reduction Schemes (Prescribed Requirements)(Wales) Regulations 2012 (SI 2012/3144).
[196] WRA 2012 s.108.

seriously injured as a result of their service. It is paid in addition to the financial support received through the AFCS. Recipients of this new benefit cannot claim disability living allowance, personal independence payment or attendance allowance.[217a]

Claims

[Replace the third paragraph with the following. The footnotes are as per original but have been included here for ease of reference]   **43–54**

Under the AFCS, a claim for injury benefit must be made within seven years of the earliest of the following dates: the day on which the injury occurs or is exacerbated by service, the day on which medical advice is first sought in relation to an illness, or the date on which the service personnel leaves the service.[260] This seven-year period is extended by three years if a diagnosis is made only within the last year to end on the anniversary of the diagnosis.[261] Death benefits under the AFCS must be claimed within three years of death.[262] The times for making a claim may be extended in some circumstances if the service personnel suffers from a "late onset disease"[263] or is mentally incapacitated.[264]

[217a] The Armed Forces and Reserve Forces (Compensation Scheme) Order 2011 (SI 2011/517) arts 24A–24E inserted by the Armed Forces and Reserve Forces (Compensation Scheme) (Amendment) Order 2013 (SI 2013/436), arts 1(1), 2(4).

[260] CSO art.47(1).

[261] CSO art.47(3).

[262] CSO art.47(6).

[263] CSO art.48(1)(a).

[264] CSO art.49.

CHAPTER 44

THE DEVOLUTION OF CHATTELS

F.—TIMBER

44–06 *[In fn.44 replace "Lewin on Trusts, 18th edn (2011), para.37–251" with the following]*

Lewin on Trusts, 19th edn (2015), para.25–024

L.—CHATTELS ENTAILED, ETC.

44–20 *[In fn.115 replace "18th end (2011)" with the following]*

19th edn (2015)

O.—FIXTURES

44–23 *[Add at end of fn.123]*

See also *Brudenell-Bruce v Moore* [2012] EWHC 1024 (Ch); [2012] W.T.L.R. 931.

[Add at end of fn.124]

See also *Brudenell-Bruce v Moore* [2012] EWHC 1024 (Ch); [2012] W.T.L.R. 931.

CHAPTER 45

DEVOLUTION OF CLAIMS AND CHOSES IN ACTION

G.—EQUITABLE CLAIMS AND CLAIMS FOR CONTRIBUTION

Powers and discretionary trusts

[Add at end of fn.135]

45–31

; *Tasarruf Mevduati Sigorta Fonu v Merrill Lynch Bank and Trust Co (Cayman) Ltd* [2011] UKPC 17; [2012] 1 W.L.R. 1721 (PC) at paras [31] to [46].

M.—APPORTIONMENT OF SUMS DUE IN RESPECT OF CLAIMS

The Apportionment Act 1870

[Add at end of fn.297]

45–76

In respect of any entitlement to income under a trust created or arising on or after October 1, 2013, subject to any contrary intention that appears in the trust instrument or in any power under which the trust is created or arises, Apportionment Act 1870 s.2 does not apply; see below.

[Delete the last paragraph beginning with "If cl.(2) of the Trusts (Capital and Income) Bill [HL] 2012–13 is enacted in its present form" ending with "the trust is created or arises", including the footnote and footnote text.]

[Insert new heading, section 45–76A and fnn.309a–309d after para.45–76]

The Trusts (Capital and Income) Act 2013

Under the Trusts (Capital and Income) Act 2013 s.1, any entitlement to income under a trust that was created or arose on or after October 1, 2013[309a] is to income as it arises. Accordingly, subject to any contrary intention that appears in any trust instrument of such a trust or in any power under which the trust is created or arises, section 2 of the Apportionment Act 1870, which provides for income to accrue from day to day, does not apply in relation to the trust.[309b]

45–76A

Under Apportionment Act 1870 s.2, income is deemed to accrue at a uniform

---

[309a] That is the date that the section came into force: The Trusts (Capital and Income) Act 2013 (Commencement No.1) Order 2013 (SI 2013/676) art.4(a).
[309b] Trusts (Capital and Income) Act 2013 s.1(1).

rate so that each beneficiary is entitled only to the proportion of the income that is deemed to accrue during the period of his or her entitlement.[309c] In relation to any trusts created or arising after October 1, 2013, income arising on a particular date is allocated to the person who is entitled to income on that date. So, any income that arose before death but was not paid until afterwards would form part of the capital of the estate and be payable to his personal representatives; any income arising after death passes as appropriate.[309d]

The following paras 45–77 to 45–81 are subject to the operation of the provisions of the Trusts (Capital and Income) Act 2013.

Apportionment of dividends

45–77   *[Add to the beginning of the first sentence of the paragraph and replace "If" with "if"]*

Subject to the operation of the provisions of the Trusts (Capital and Income) Act 2013,

Apportionment of bonus issues or dividends of capital profits—capital or income

45–78   *[Add to the beginning of the first sentence of the paragraph and replace "Where" with "where"]*

Subject to the operation of the provisions of the Trusts (Capital and Income) Act 2013,

[Substitute the penultimate and last paragraphs with the following but retain the footnote at the end of the last paragraph]

By s.2 of the Trusts (Capital and Income) Act 2013, subject to any contrary intention that appears in "any trust instrument of the trust and any power under which the trust is created or arises", a receipt consisting of a "tax-exempt corporate distribution" is to be treated for the purposes of any trust (whenever created or arising) as a receipt of capital even if it would otherwise be treated for these purposes as a receipt of income. A "tax-exempt corporate distribution" is a distribution that is an exempt distribution by virtue of ss.1076, 1077 or 1078 of the Corporation Tax Act 2010 or any other distribution of assets in any form by a body corporate, where the distribution is of a description specified by an order made by the Secretary of State by statutory instrument. Section 1076 of the 2010 Act concerns the transfer to members of shares in certain subsidiaries. Sections 1077 and 1078 concern certain transfers of a trade, a part of a business or shares from one company to another and the issue of shares by the transferee to members of the transferor. Section 2(4) of the 2013 Act provides that the Secretary of State will be able to specify a description of distribution for the purposes of this provision only if neither income tax nor capital gains tax is chargeable in respect of it.

[309c] See para.45–76 above and para.6.31 of the Law Commission Report, *Capital and Income in Trusts: Classification and Apportionment* (Law Comm No 315).

[309d] See para.79–02 below.

By s.3 of the Trusts (Capital and Income) Act 2013, where a distribution is treated as a receipt of capital of a trust pursuant to s.2 of the 2013 Act and the trustees are satisfied that it is likely that, but for the distribution, there would have been a receipt from the body corporate that would have been a receipt of income, the trustees may make a payment out of the capital funds of the trust, or transfer any property of the trust, to an income beneficiary in order to place the income beneficiary so far as practicable in the position in which the trustees consider the beneficiary would have been had there been the receipt of income. Any such payment is to be treated as a payment or transfer of capital. For these purposes an "income beneficiary" is a person entitled to income arising under the trust, or for whose benefit such income may be applied.

Apportionment on a sale "cum dividend"

[Add new text before the existing paragraphs]   **45–79**

The following is now subject to the operation of the provisions of the Trusts (Capital and Income) Act 2013.

Apportionment of rent

[Add at end of the paragraph]   **45–81**

This is now subject to the operation of the provisions of the Trusts (Capital and Income) Act 2013.

CHAPTER 46

DEVOLUTION OF LAND

B.—REGISTERED LAND

Registration of representative as proprietor

When a representative can be registered as proprietor

46–03 *[Add at end of fn.10]*

; where there is an entry on the register to prevent registration on the basis of an alleged interest in the property and there is an application for the vacation of the entry, the court must proceed on the basis of an analogy with the position it would adopt if the beneficiary of the entry had, instead of registering that entry, applied for an interim injunction. "The court must therefore consider whether ... the respondents have a seriously arguable case that they will succeed at trial in obtaining ownership of or a proprietary interest in the real property held in the deceased's estate. If so, the court must consider whether either or both parties would be adequately compensated by an award of damages and, if neither can be adequately compensated in that way, where the balance of convenience lies." See per Richards J. in *Williams v Seals* [2014] EWHC 3708 (Ch) at [22]; *Nugent v Nugent* [2013] EWHC 4095 (Ch).

The application for registration

46–04 *[Add at end of fn.18]*

For applications to vacate an entry on the register to prevent registration, see *Williams v Seals* [2014] EWHC 3708 (Ch); *Nugent v Nugent* [2013] EWHC 4095 (Ch).

CHAPTER 47

INCIDENCE OF LIABILITIES OF THE DECEASED

C.—CONTRACT

Joint and several liability in contract

Joint liability only

[In fn.30 replace "Snell's Equity, 32nd edn (2010)" with the following]   **47–06**
Snell's Equity, 33rd edn (2015)

D.—TORT AND DEVASTAVIT

Tortious liability survives

[In fn.70 replace "20th edn (2010)" with the following]   **47–20**
21st edn (2014)

Joint and several liabilities in tort

[In fn.72 replace "20th edn (2010)" with the following]   **47–21**
21st edn (2014)

F.—COVENANTS IN RELATION TO LAND

[In fn.97 replace "(2012)" with the following]   **47–27**
(2013)

G.—COVENANTS IN LEASES

Representative liable under covenant to repair

[In fn.158 replace the last sentence with the following]   **47–45**
See also Woodfall, *Landlord and Tenant* (2014), para.16.232 onwards.

H.—PARTNERSHIP LIABILITIES

Liability of estate of deceased partner in respect of contractual claims

47–49 *[In fn.167 replace "(2010)" with the following]*
(2013)

47–49 *[In fn.169 replace "(2010)" with the following]*
(2013)

Remedies of creditor of partnership against estate of deceased partner

47–50 *[In fn.174 replace "(2010)" with the following]*
(2013)

Partnership debts postponed to separate debts

47–51 *[In fn.178 replace "(2010)" with the following]*
(2013)

[In fn.179 replace "(2010)" with the following]
(2013)

Duration of estate's liability

47–52 *[Add at end of fn.182]*
See also *Golstein v Bishop* [2014] EWCA Civ 10; [2014] Ch. 455.

[Add at end of fn.188]
See also *Golstein v Bishop* [2014] EWCA Civ 10; [2014] Ch. 455.

[In fn.189 replace "(2010)" with the following]
(2013)

I.—MISCELLANEOUS OTHER LIABILITIES

Contribution

47–55 *[In fn.196 replace "32nd edn (2010)" with the following]*
33rd edn (2015)

[In fn.197 replace "32nd edn (2010)" with the following]

33rd edn (2015)

Proprietary estoppel

[In fn.247 replace "32nd edn (2010)" with the following]   **47–66**

33rd edn (2015)

[In fn.248 replace the last sentence with the following]

and *Wright v Waters* [2014] EWHC 3614. See, generally, *Snell's Equity*, 33rd edn (2015), Ch.12 at para.12–016 onwards.

CHAPTER 48

PRELIMINARY MATTERS; DUTIES IN ADMINISTRATION

B.—THE FUNERAL

The corpse; right to possession; arrangements for funeral

The burial

48–05   *[In fn.34 replace the last sentence with the following]*

Re West Pennard Churchyard [1992] 1 W.L.R. 32 applied in *Re St Nicolas's Churchyard, Pevensey* [2012] P.T.S.R. 1207, but see *Re St Mary (Dodleston Churchyard)* [1996] 1 W.L.R. 451.

Disinterment

48–06   *[Add at end of fn.39]*

See also *Re St Mark's Churchyard, Fairfield* [2013] P.T.S.R. 953.

C.—INHERITANCE TAX ACCOUNT AND PAYMENT

48–16   *[In fn.108 replace "2006" with the following]*

2010

CHAPTER 49

ASSETS

A.—WHAT ARE ASSETS?

Statutory definition

[Add after first sentence of fn.12]   **49–02**

See also *Mertrux Ltd v Revenue and Customs Commissioners* [2012] UKUT 274 (TCC).

Goodwill of partnership

[In fn.25 replace "(2011)" with the following]   **49–05**

(2013)

D.—FOREIGN ASSETS

Right to ancillary grant (English domicile)

[In fn.147 replace "5th edn, (2009)" with the following]   **49–32**

6th edn (2013)

CHAPTER 49A

ADMINISTRATION OF DIGITAL INFORMATION

Introduction

49A–01 Information does not pass as property to a personal representative after the death of the deceased,[1] but rights associated with the information (which can be in digital form) can vest in the representative. Discovery and identification of those rights can be a challenge. The problem can be aggravated if the information is digital, existing as electrical signals. Digital information can exist both locally, on computing devices that were owned and/or used by the deceased, and in a cloud—on computing devices that are connected to the internet—having been transferred or copied by the deceased, pursuant to arrangements between him and the cloud

---

[1] See paras 49A–06 onwards below.

service provider. It is not sufficient to deliver a computing device to the relevant beneficiary without first investigating what digital information is stored on that device and whether the deceased stored any digital information in a cloud. In some cases, information stored on a local device can provide the only clue to the existence of cloud-stored information.

The personal representative's engagement with digital information associated with the deceased can be viewed as a process:

49A–02

(1)   The deceased's personal estate devolves on his personal representative, who must get in the estate of the deceased and administer it.[2] Where the deceased owned or controlled a computing device, the personal representative's duties will include an initial discovery of the deceased's communication or storage or other processing of information to, from or in a cloud. Once that has been done, the personal representative must identify what rights and obligations are associated with that information and have devolved on him by operation of law. This will include rights and causes of action relating to intellectual property[3] and to breach of confidence,[4] and rights and causes of action relating to contracts.[5]

(2)   The next step is for the personal representative to examine any terms of service agreements (to the extent that the agreement has survived the death of the deceased) that were in existence between the deceased and the providers of the various cloud services used by the deceased. These provisions will give rise to rights and obligations and, in addition, it is likely that they will have affected the operation of rights and obligations associated with the digital information transferred or copied by the deceased, pursuant to those service agreements, during his lifetime.[6]

(3)   Once the rights associated with that digital information have been identified and secured, their administration and appropriate distribution can be undertaken. Until the distribution of these rights, their administration might involve the processing of personal data, within the meaning of the Data Protection legislation.[7] Such processing might require the personal representative to register as a controller or processor under that legislation.[8]

(4)   The obligations of the personal representative relate only to assets that come into the representative's hands or, but for his wilful default, would have come into his hands. They do not apply to any assets that do not vest in the representative or in which the deceased or his estate have no interest.[9] Where information has been found by the representative to have been stored or otherwise processed by the deceased to, from or in a cloud but it does not

---

[2]   See para.49A–15 below.
[3]   See from para.49A–19 below.
[4]   See from para.49A–25 below.
[5]   See from para.49A–21 below.
[6]   See para.49A–23 below.
[7]   See the Data Protection Act 1998 and the Privacy and Electronic Communications (EC Directive) Regulations 2003 (SI 2003/2426) and paras 49A–42 onwards below.
[8]   See Pt III of the Data Protection Act 1998.
[9]   Paragraphs 49–26 and 49–27 above.

give rise to any property rights,[10] technically the personal representative has no business, as representative, to process it, but he may do so if the deceased has given directions about it. If the personal representative does process that information in the absence of any such direction, the question arises as to the recovery of the costs and expenses incurred.[11]

Nomenclature

49A–03   In books, articles and some will precedents that are currently in circulation, writers have begun to use the expression "digital assets".[12] Often that expression is not being used to refer to proprietary rights associated with digital information but rather to cloud services used by the deceased and to the rights that may potentially be associated with cloud services. Cloud services deal with digital information but the associated rights are not digital, they are contractual in nature[13]; and the digital information is not an asset under English law. So the terminology "digital assets" is misleading. As well as contractual rights, other rights associated with digital information are intellectual property rights and rights arising out of a duty of confidence, which are, or are in the nature of, choses in action.

49A–04   The Uniform Fiduciary Access to Digital Assets Act,[14] a draft statute adopted or in the course of being adopted by several US states, designed to deal with a problem of fiduciaries obtaining access to information relating to cloud services. It defines a digital asset as,[15]

> "... a record that is electronic. The term does not include an underlying asset or liability unless the asset or liability is itself a record that is electronic".

A record is defined as,

> "... information that is inscribed on a tangible medium or that is stored in an electronic or other medium and is retrievable in perceivable form".[16]

---

[10]   See from para.49A–06 below.

[11]   See paras 49A–40 onwards below.

[12]   See, for instance, *Butterworths Wills Probate and Administration Service*, para.[4.7]; *Butterworths Practical Will Precedents*, para.F5-1359 ("... so far as such asset or right may be lawfully transmissible or transferable ..."); McCallig, "Facebook after death: an evolving policy in a social network" (2014) 22(2) Int J Law Info Tech 107; Davies, "We are living in a virtual world", *Solicitors Journal* (2014) SJ 158/22; Currie, "Can a 'digital buddy' bring solace to our loved ones?", *Solicitors Journal* (2015) SJ 159/02; Ali, "£17bn of digital assets could be left in cyber space", *Solicitors Journal* (2014) SJ 159/09; Murray, "Digital life after death", *Solicitors Journal* (2014) SJ 158/36; Walsh and Teitell, "Protecting Clients' Digital Assets", *Trusts & Estates*, January 2014, p.32.

[13]   See paras 49A–21 onwards below.

[14]   It is known as "UFADAA" and is draft legislation prepared by the National Conference of Commissioners on Uniform State Laws in the United States and recommended for adoption by individual states for uniformity of state law. The Act has been enacted by Delaware and has been introduced in the legislatures of 23 other states.

[15]   UFADAA s.2(9).

[16]   UFADAA s.2(21).

This definition of digital asset therefore may include information that has no proprietary rights associated with it and the greater the adoption of UFADAA in the US and the more it is used as a model for legislation by other jurisdictions, the greater the potential confusion as to the meaning of the expression "digital assets". Indeed, any attempted nomenclature might give rise to confusion. For the sake of brevity and efficiency, however, the expression "digital property rights" is used in this chapter to refer only to proprietary rights that are associated with digital information, however they arose.[17]

Digital information

A printed book, a phonographic record and a cinematic film are examples of information (known as analog information) that is part of the containing media. The book, record and film are all chattels that devolve on the personal representative as personal property,[18] but the information—the words printed on the paper, the music etched onto the plastic disc and the images printed on the film—can be separated from the media and stored in a different way: processes can be applied to synthesise the information so that it is represented by numbers and the numbers can be reconverted back into analog form for enjoyment by the user. In the case of text, the characters are converted directly into numerical format. In the cases of sound and vision, the information is processed into small discrete chunks, or samples, that can be represented by numbers. The smaller the samples, the closer the fidelity to the original and the higher the quality when the numbers are reconverted back into sound or vision. The information represented by these numbers is commonly referred to as digital information. **49A–05**

This conversion of information into numbers is standardised so, with a binary numeral system (which is now the most common), the numerical representation uses different combinations of 0 and 1, whatever the source of the digital information. Once they have been digitised, images, words and music look very similar—a series of ones and zeros—and appear to be anonymous. Using logic processes known as software and suitable equipment the digital information can be stored on a magnetic or other medium that can accept an on (1) or off (0) signal, such as the application of higher and lower electrical signals, darkness and light or some other on-off pulse. Digital information can be copied easily between computing devices and, so long as the stream of ones and zeroes is not unexpectedly interrupted, perfect copies can generally be made, whatever the quality of the transmission.

The conversion of analog information to digital representations of it is limited only by human imagination and ingenuity. Examples of types of information that can now be converted into digital format are geographical information using GPS data; ordinary objects by two or three dimensional scanning; weather information from measurements by sensitive instrumentation; the operation of parts of a motor car engine or parts of high resolution space telescopes; measurements of heart beats and blood flow and motor traffic information. A converter to enable a

---

[17] See Murray, *Information Technology Law*, 2nd edn, Ch.5.
[18] See para.49A–18 above.

transfer of humans between distant galaxies may one day be achievable, although the restored being is unlikely to be the same person, it will likely be a copy.

Information as property

49A–06   In reports of cases, information has, not infrequently, been described as property.[19] The current state of the authorities shows, however, that information, in the sense of a fact or idea, is itself not capable of being owned and, without more, there are difficulties in characterising any enforceable rights in it. As will be seen later,[20] certain rights associated with the information, such as copyright and the rights arising out of a duty of confidence, can be identified as enforceable rights under English law, but there is no property in the information itself. In *National Provincial Bank Ltd v Hastings Car Mart Ltd*, Lord Wilberforce said[21]:

> "Before a right or an interest can be admitted into the category of property, or of a right affecting property, it must be definable, identifiable by third parties, capable in its nature of assumption by third parties, and have some degree of permanence or stability."

In *Fairstar Heavy Transport v Adkins*, Mummery L.J. said[22]:

> "Everybody knows that 'property' differentiates between things that are mine and things that are not mine. The law lays down criteria for determining the boundary between, on the one hand, those rights that are only enforceable against particular persons and, on the other hand, those rights attaching to things that are capable of being vindicated against the whole world. The claim to property in intangible information presents obvious definitional difficulties, having regard to the criteria of certainty, exclusivity, control and assignability that normally characterise property rights and distinguish them from personal rights."

One example of information that appears to be property is information gathered by cloud providers like Google, to sell to advertisers or others. Such information is received in circumstances of confidentiality and the sale is of confidential information, usually with the consent of the user, whom the information describes.[23] In Google's Terms of Service,[24] it is provided,

> "When you upload, submit, store, send or receive content to or through our Services, you give Google (and those we work with) a worldwide license to use, host, store, reproduce, modify, create derivative works (such as those resulting from translations, adaptations or other changes we make so that your content works better with our Services), communicate, publish, publicly perform, publicly display and distribute such content."

---

[19] See per Viscount Dilhorne in *Phipps v Boardman* [1967] 2 A.C. 46 at 91.
[20] See from para.49A–19 below.
[21] [1965] A.C. 1175 at 1248; adopted by Stephen Morris QC in *Armstrong GmbH v Winnington Networks Ltd* [2012] EWHC 10 (Ch); [2013] Ch. 156 at para.[50].
[22] [2103] EWCA Civ 886; [2013] 2 CLC 272 at para.[47]. For a full discussion of this decision, see para.49A–10 below. See also *Victoria Park Racing & Recreation Grounds Co. Ltd v Taylor* (1937) 58 C.L.R. 479; *RCA Mfg. Co. v Whiteman* 114 F.2d 86 (2d Cir. 1940); cf *News Service v Associated Press*, 248 U.S. 215, 39 S.Ct. 68, 63 L.Ed. 211, 2 A.L.R. 293.
[23] For a discussion about confidential information, see para.49A–25 below.
[24] *http://www.google.com/intl/en/policies/terms*.

The proprietary nature of information is now examined by reference to recent authorities.

Boardman v Phipps

In *Boardman v Phipps*,[25] trustees of a trust owned shares in a company. They **49A–07** received information about that company and the solicitor to the trustees learnt of that information. He and one of the remainder beneficiaries made a bid personally for shares in the company so as to gain control of it and acquire substantial benefits by liquidating its assets. During the course of the negotiations, in which they referred to themselves as representing the trust, the solicitor and beneficiary purchasers gained further detailed knowledge of the company. The purchase went through and they made a handsome profit. By this time the remainder interest had fallen into possession and one of the other beneficiaries sued for an account of profits made by the purchasers.

The court held that the purchasers had placed themselves in a special position that was of a fiduciary character in relation to the negotiations with the directors of the company relating to the trust shares. Out of that special position and in the course of the negotiations they had obtained the opportunity to make a profit out of the shares and knowledge that the profit was there to be made. They were accountable for their profits, although they were entitled to payment on a liberal scale for their work and skill.

One of the arguments made by the beneficiary plaintiff was that the information acquired by the purchasers was part of the trust estate. It is clear that, as a result of the information, the purchasers acquired an opportunity to use the resulting knowledge to obtain a profit. Although the language used in the various judgments in the courts below contemplated that the information and knowledge acquired was property of the trust,[26] that was rejected by a majority in the House of Lords. Lord Upjohn said[27]:

> "In general, information is not property at all. It is normally open to all who have eyes to read and ears to hear. The true test is to determine in what circumstances the information has been acquired. If it has been acquired in such circumstances that it would be a breach of confidence to disclose it to another then courts of equity will restrain the recipient from communicating it to another. In such cases such confidential information is often and for many years has been described as the property of the donor, the books of authority are full of such references; knowledge of secret processes, "know-how," confidential information as to the prospects of a company or of someone's intention or the expected results of some horse race based on stable or other confidential information. But in the end the real truth is that it is not property in any normal sense but equity will restrain its transmission to another if in breach of some confidential relationship."

---

[25] [1967] 2 A.C. 46.
[26] See per Wilberforce J. [1964] 1 W.L.R. 993 at 1011 and Lord Denning M.R. [1965] Ch. 992 at 1019.
[27] *Phipps v Boardman* [1967] 2 A.C. 46 at 127.

Viscount Dilhorne[28] and Lord Cohen[29] agreed. Lords Hodson[30] and Guest[31] dissented on this point.

Oxford v Moss

49A–08 In *Oxford v Moss*,[32] the defendant was a student who dishonestly obtained the proof of an examination paper and, after reading it, returned it, having no intention to retain the paper on which it was written. He was charged with the theft of confidential information from the university. The charges were dismissed by the magistrate on the ground that there had been no appropriation of intangible property within s.4(1) of the Theft Act 1968. On appeal to the Divisional Court, it was held that, although, "by any standards, it was conduct which is to be condemned, and to the layman it would readily be described as cheating", for the reasons set out by the magistrate it was not theft.[33]

Douglas v Hello! Ltd

49A–09 In *Douglas v Hello! Ltd*,[34] well-known film actors entered into an agreement with the publisher of an English celebrity magazine for the exclusive rights to publish approved photographs of their wedding. It was a term of the contract that all reasonable steps would be taken to restrict access to the wedding to prevent photographs being made available to others. Guests were informed accordingly and tight security measures were put in place but a freelance photographer surreptitiously, and without authority, took photographs of the wedding and sold them to a rival magazine. An injunction and damages were sought on the ground of breach of confidence to restrain publication of the unauthorised photographs and the action was successful.

---

[28] [1967] 2 A.C. 46 at 89: "While it may be that some information and knowledge can properly be regarded as property, I do not think that the information supplied by [the company] and obtained by [the purchasers] as to the affairs of that company is to be regarded as property of the trust in the same way as shares held by the trust were its property."

[29] [1967] 2 A.C. 46 at 103: "Information is, of course, not property in the strict sense of that word".

[30] [1967] 2 A.C. 46 at 106: "This information enabled him to acquire knowledge of a most extensive and valuable character"; and at 107: "... it is said on behalf of the appellants that information as such is not necessarily property and it is only trust property which is relevant. I agree ... I dissent from the view that information is of its nature something which is not properly to be described as property. We are aware that what is called " knowhow" in the commercial sense is property which may be very valuable as an asset. I agree with the learned judge and with the Court of Appeal that the confidential information acquired in this case which was capable of being and was turned to account can be properly regarded as the property of the trust."

[31] [1967] 2 A.C. 46 at 115: "I see no reason why information and knowledge cannot be trust property".

[32] [1979] 68 Cr. App. R. 183.

[33] See also per Sir Iain Glidewell in *St Albans City and District Council v International Computers Ltd* [1997] F.S.R. 251 at 266: "As I have already said, the [computer] program itself is not 'goods' within the statutory definition. Thus a transfer of the program ... does not, in my view, constitute a transfer of goods."

[34] [2007] UKHL 21; [2008] 1 A.C. 1.

Lord Hoffmann said,[35]

"There is in my opinion no question of creating an 'image right' or any other unorthodox form of intellectual property. The information in this case was capable of being protected, not because it concerned the [actors'] image any more than because it concerned their private life, but simply because it was information of commercial value over which the [actors] had sufficient control to enable them to impose an obligation of confidence."

Lord Walker[36] said that, "information, even if it is confidential, cannot properly be regarded as a form of property".

Fairstar Heavy Transport v Adkins

As to digital information, in *Fairstar Heavy Transport v Adkins*,[37] Fairstar, a **49A–10** Dutch company, was taken over and the new owners dispensed with the services of Mr Adkins. Those services had been supplied by a Jersey company that was controlled by him. A dispute arose and Fairstar tried to access Mr Adkins's emails in connection with the dispute. The difficulty for Fairstar and its new owner was that, as Mr Adkins was not an employee of Fairstar, all emails sent to him had been automatically forwarded by Fairstar's servers directly to his private address at his Jersey company and then deleted from the Fairstar's servers. Accordingly, Fairstar had no copies of these emails. Also, Mr Adkins sent emails directly from his own computer and they were not copied to Fairstar except on occasions when they were sent to individuals working there. Interim applications were made to the English court for an injunction against Mr Adkins and his English internet service provider to prevent them from deleting or interfering with the emails and for Fairstar's expert to be able inspect the emails (Mr Adkins's computer was by that time held by his English solicitors, pursuant to a court order). Mr Adkins claimed that Fairstar had no proprietary claim in relation to the content of the emails and so the orders should not be made.

At first instance, the judge commented that (para.43):

"... there is or may be an important distinction between the physical object which carries the information – for example, a letter – and the information which that object conveys. A letter, which consists of paper together with the ink of the writing which is on it, is clearly a physical object that can be owned. However, it does not follow from this that the information which the letter conveys is also property that is capable of being the subject of a proprietary claim (for this purpose I leave aside the possibility of any claim arising out of copyright in respect of the contents of the letter)."

---

[35] [2008] 1 A.C. 1 at paras [123] to [124].
[36] (Dissenting but not on this point) [2007] UKHL 21; [2008] 1 A.C. 1 at para.[275]. In *Phillips v News Group Newspapers Ltd* [2012] UKSC 28; [2013] 1 A.C. 1, Lord Walker said that, for the purposes of the Senior Courts Act 1981 s.72, "technical or commercial information" fell within the statutory definition of "intellectual property", notwithstanding that "... technical and commercial information ought not, strictly speaking, to be described as property (the majority view of the House of Lords in *Phipps v Boardman* [1967] 2 AC 46, 89—90, 103, 127—128; cf 107 and 115) cannot prevail over the clear statutory language. Whether or not confidential information can only loosely, or metaphorically, be described as property is simply irrelevant."
[37] [2012] EWHC 2952 (TCC); [2012] 2 CLC 795 at para.[58].

49A–11 Fairstar submitted that "logic and the circumstances of the modern world should encourage the court to hold that the content of an e-mail was a form of property ... it would be unrealistic for the courts not to recognise the proprietary right of an employer or principal in electronic materials that were created by or came into the possession of his employee or agent in the course of his employment or agency". This submission was rejected. The judge held:

> "69. ... I can find no practical basis for holding that there should be property in the content of an e-mail, even if I thought that it was otherwise open to me to do so. To the extent that people require protection against the misuse of information contained in e-mails, in my judgment satisfactory protection is provided under English law either by the equitable jurisdiction ... in relation to confidential information (or by contract, where there is one) or, where applicable, the law of copyright. There are no compelling practical reasons that support the existence of a proprietary right – indeed, practical considerations militate against it."

Fairstar's appeal was allowed, but for different reasons; the Court of Appeal said that the judge had asked the wrong question, and the correct one had nothing to do with the ownership of the content of the emails; the real issue was one of principal and agent and the duty of the former agent to allow inspection of the emails.[38]

Your Response Limited v Datateam Business Media Ltd

49A–12 In *Your Response Limited v Datateam Business Media Ltd*,[39] the defendant, a publishing company, engaged the claimant, a database management company, to hold and maintain its subscribers' records in an electronic database. A dispute arose about the service that was being provided by the claimant and the defendant purported to terminate the contract. The defendant asked for the database to be released to it and the claimant sent an invoice for fees due, refusing to release the database or give the defendant access to it until payment. The claimant brought a claim for fees due and damages for repudiation of the contract and the defendant counterclaimed for damages for breach of contract. The claimant sought to exercise a lien over the database pending payment of its fees and this was upheld at first instance but not on appeal. On the question of whether information is property, Floyd L.J. said[40]:

> "I would add only one observation in connection with the wider implications of [counsel for the claimant's] submission that the electronic database was a type of intangible property which, unlike choses in action, was capable of possession and thus of being subject to a lien. An electronic database consists of structured information. Although information may give rise to intellectual property rights, such as database right and copyright, the law has been reluctant to treat information itself as property. When information is created and recorded there are sharp distinctions between the information itself, the physical medium on which the information is recorded and the rights to which the information gives rise. Whilst the physical medium and the rights are treated as property, the information itself has never been ... If [counsel for the claimants] were right that the database could be possessed and could be the subject of a lien and that its possession could be withheld until payment and released or transferred on payment, one would be coming close to treating information as property."

---

[38] See the dictum of Mummery L.J. in para.49A–06 above.
[39] [2014] EWCA Civ 281; [2015] Q.B. 41.
[40] [2015] Q.B. 41 at para.[42].

Conclusion

Information, including digital information, is therefore not recognised as property in English law. The medium on which information is written, such as paper, a strip of film, a magnetic disk or silicon chip, is a chattel capable of ownership but the ownership of that medium does not necessarily carry with it the ownership of the recorded information. Certain rights associated with the information can, however, be enforced, as explained above.   **49A–13**

A.—THE PERSONAL REPRESENTATIVE

In England and Wales the personal representative must in general have a grant of representation before being able properly to administer the estate of a deceased person.[41] Certain assets are vested automatically in the representative under statute and the common law,[42] and powers are conferred on him, either by statute or by testamentary instrument, in order to administer and distribute the estate.   **49A–14**

The personal representative's duties

The duties of a personal representative in the administration of the assets of the deceased's estate, insofar as they are relevant to the present topic, are dealt with in more detail elsewhere in this work.[43] Under s.25(1)(a) of the Administration of Estates Act 1925, the personal representative of a deceased person is required to collect and get in the real and personal estate of the deceased and administer it according to law. This collection of duties involves getting in debts owed to the estate, calling in assets and their conversion into money and a duty to preserve and protect the estate once it has been collected and got in.[44]   **49A–15**

Where the personal property of the deceased is in the form of money or debts, the manner of getting in the assets is relatively simple: money can be taken into possession and proceedings may be brought for debts if payment is not duly made. In the case of a chose in action or property in the nature of a chose in action, ultimately it is enforceable by court action.

The obligations of the personal representative relate only to assets that come into his hands or, but for his wilful default, would have come into his hands.[45] They do not apply to any assets that do not vest in the representative or in which the deceased or his estate have no interest.[46] Furthermore, where the personal representative has a duty to get in assets, he is exonerated and never required to make good any loss if he has done all he can to do so but his efforts have not proved successful. This is the case even if he has taken no steps at all where it appears   **49A–16**

---

[41] See para.4–02 above.
[42] See para.4–07 above.
[43] Paragraph 48–17 above.
[44] Paragraph 48–18 above.
[45] In this context "wilful default" results from the personal representative having "been guilty of a want of ordinary prudence", see per Millett L.J. in *Armitage v Nurse* [1998] Ch. 241 at 252.
[46] Paragraphs 49–26 and 49–27 above.

that, if he had done so, they would have been, or there is reasonable ground for believing that they would have been, ineffectual.[47]

49A–17 The personal representative has a duty to preserve and protect assets that have been collected and got in.[48] In performing these duties, a representative must act with due diligence. If he does use all reasonable care and could not avoid the loss, the representative will not be liable.[49] Personal representatives are also in certain circumstances subject to a statutory duty of care and skill under the Trustee Act 2000 s.1.[50]

Devolution and vesting

49A–18 A deceased's personal estate devolves on his personal representative.[51] This does not apply to any interests that cease on death, such as a joint beneficial interest that accrues in favour of the surviving joint tenant or tenants and not on the representative[52]; nor does it apply to any rights arising out of a cause of action that does not survive the deceased's death, although the personal representative is entitled to sue in respect of rights that accrued before death.[53]

The deceased's personal estate includes the "... personal estate, whether legal or equitable, of a deceased person, to the extent of his beneficial interest therein, and the ... personal estate of which a deceased person in pursuance of any general power (including the statutory power to dispose of entailed interests) disposes by his will".[54] The expression "choses in action" is used to describe all personal rights of property that can only be claimed or enforced by action, and not by taking physical possession.[55]

Under the Law Reform (Miscellaneous Provisions) Act 1934 s.1(1), "on the death of any person ... all causes of action subsisting against or vested in him shall survive against, or, as the case may be, for the benefit of, his estate", apart from defamation.

---

[47] See per Sir John Romilly M.R. in *Clack v Holland* (1854) 19 Beav 262 at 271–272.
[48] Paragraph 48–18. A higher standard is required of a paid representative: para.57–07 below.
[49] *Jones v Lewis* (1751) 2 Ves. Sen. 240.
[50] See also s.35(1) of that Act.
[51] Paragraphs 41–28 and 41–29 above; if there is an intestacy, the estate vests in the Public Trustee until the appointment of an administrator: para.41–03 above.
[52] Paragraph 41–30 above.
[53] *Stubbs v The Holywell Railway Company* (1867) LR 2 Ex 311.
[54] Section 32(1) Administration of Estates Act 1925; see para.49–02. For the purposes of the Wills Act 1837, personal estate "extends to leasehold estates and other chattels real, and also to monies, shares of government and other funds, securities for money (not being real estates), debts, choses in action, rights, credits, goods, and all other property whatsoever which by law devolves upon the executor or administrator, and to any share or interest therein": Wills Act 1837 s.1.
[55] See per Channell J. in *Torkington v Magee* [1902] K.B. 427 at 430 (reversed on another ground: [1903] 1 K.B. 644); *Your Response Ltd v Datastream Business Media Ltd* [2014] EWCA Civ 281; [2014] 3 W.L.R. 887; [2014] 2 All E.R. (Comm) 899; [2014] C.P. Rep. 31; *Colonial Bank v Whinney* (1886) 11 App Cas 426.

Intellectual property

Copyright is transmissible by testamentary disposition or by operation of law as personal property,[56] as is database right.[57] A patent is personal property (without being a thing in action) and vests by operation of law in the same way as any other personal property and may be vested in a beneficiary by an assent of personal representatives.[58] In addition, the following rights are also personal property, in the nature of choses in action: unregistered design right[59] and performer's property rights.[60] A registered trade mark is personal property,[61] and is transmissible by testamentary disposition.[62] Other intellectual property rights are not assignable inter-vivos but are transmissible on death: moral rights[63] and a performer's non-property rights.[64] There is no ownership in the information itself.[65]

49A–19

Digital information brings complications to the law of intellectual property. For instance, it is a common feature of viewing pages on the world wide web that they might contain one or more of text, images, videos, sound or music, or even a database. Each of these might constitute a copyright work within section 1 of the Copyright, Designs and Patents Act 1988. The page will have a title that might be classed as a copyright work,[66] and any hyperlinks might also satisfy the test.[67] Computer games offer similar issues. Each work could be protected under the 1988 Act and the whole web page or game might be classified as a film.[68] Another added complexity is the ability of a user to prepare works using cloud computing tools, such as Google Docs.[69]

Where there has been infringement of intellectual property rights, the normal remedies are injunctive relief, delivery up of infringing materials,[70] seizure and damages or an account of profits. The court also has an inherent jurisdiction to make declaratory orders as to the respective rights of the parties.[71]

49A–20

---

[56] Copyright, Designs and Patents Act 1988 s.90(1).
[57] Copyright and Rights in Databases Regulations 1997 (SI 1997/3032) reg.23.
[58] Patents Act 1977 s.30.
[59] Paragraph 45–49 above.
[60] Paragraph 45–56 above.
[61] Trade Marks Act 1994 s.22; see also arts 16–24 of Council Regulation (EC) No 207/2009 for Community Trade Marks.
[62] Trade Marks Act 1994 s.24.
[63] Paragraph 45–53 above.
[64] Paragraph 45–56 above.
[65] See from para.49A–06 above.
[66] *Shetland Times Limited v Dr Jonathan Wills* [1997] F.S.R. 604.
[67] *The Newspaper Licensing Agency Ltd v Meltwater Holding BV* [2012] RPC 1.
[68] Copyright, Designs and Patents Act 1988 s.5B. See generally, Ch.2, Stokes, *Digital Copyright, Law and Practice*, 4th edn.
[69] A Software as a Service (SaaS) system offered by Google to its account holders.
[70] This can be ordered under the court's inherent jurisdiction or under, for instance, Copyright, Designs and Patents Act 1988 s.99 for copyright. The claimant has no proprietary rights in these materials: *Vavasseur v Krupp* (1878) 9 Ch D 351.
[71] See generally, Pt VI in *Copinger and Skone James on Copyright*, 16th edn.

Contract

49A–21 Cloud computing has been defined as "access to computing resources, on demand, via a network".[72] The network may be a private network whose use is limited to employees of a company or it may comprise a public network such as the internet, for the use of such members of the public as wish to enter into arrangements with a cloud provider for particular services. Many different kinds of service are offered, including information storage facilities, social networking opportunities, business opportunities and operations, email and messaging services, world wide web services and banking operations.[73] Some of the services are provided for a fee and some for no monetary fee but in return for the collection of private information about users to pass on, at a fee, to others, such as advertisers. The cloud services are generally governed by terms of service agreed between the service provider and the service user. The deceased may during his lifetime have been a provider or a user of a particular cloud service.

Agreements, particularly those providing services without charge, are often made between users and providers following an affirmative act by the user, such as clicking or tapping on some part of an e-commerce web page, such as an item on an electronic store or an application to join a social networking operation. This act will usually constitute an offer, following an invitation to treat displayed on the web page.[74] Generally, cloud providers seek to include standard terms and conditions in the agreement and will generally be successful, provided it is reasonable (such as where the web page contains an express reference to the terms and a hyperlink for the user to read before clicking or tapping) for the user to expect there to be contractual conditions.[75]

49A–22 For the purposes of the Unfair Terms in Consumer Contracts Regulations 1999,[76] where one of the parties to the agreement is a "natural person" acting outside his trade, business or profession, he will be contracting as a consumer, whereas a person (including a company) acting for purposes relating to his trade, business or profession will be contracting as a supplier.[77] The 1999 Regulations require that certain terms of a contract between a seller or supplier and a consumer be fair and that the language of any written terms should be plain and intelligible. The Unfair Contract Terms Act 1977 also provides relief for certain terms excluding liability for negligence and other matters. The Consumer Rights Act 2015 has passed through Parliament but is not yet in force; Chapter 3 deals with provisions

---

[72] See the Information Commissioner's Office Guidance on the use of cloud computing, para.12. The guidance provides a full introduction to cloud computing. See generally, Millard, *Cloud Computing Law.*

[73] Chapter 3, Millard, *Cloud Computing Law.*

[74] See *Fisher v Bell* [1961] 1 Q.B. 394; *Pharmaceutical Society of Great Britain v. Boots Cash Chemists (Southern) Ltd* [1953] 1 Q.B. 401; *Chitty on Contracts* (31st edn), Ch.2, Section 2. See also Electronic Commerce (EC Directive) Regulations 2002 (SI 2002/2013).

[75] *Parker v South Eastern Ry* (1877) 2 C.P.D. 416; *Thornton v Shoe Lane Parking Ltd* [1971] 2 Q.B. 163; *Chitty on Contracts* (31st edn), para.12–013.

[76] "The 1999 Regulations".

[77] Regulation 3(1) of the 1999 Regulations.

concerning, amongst other things, quality, fitness for purpose and description of content in relation to digital content.[78] Other relevant legislation includes the Consumer Protection from Unfair Trading Regulations 2008[79] and the Consumer Contracts (Information, Cancellation and Additional Charges) Regulations 2013.[80]

Common terms imposed by standard terms of service in cloud computing agreements include[81]: **49A–23**

(1)   Governing, or applicable law clauses, which might subject the agreement to the law of a jurisdiction within or outside the UK;

(2)   Choice of forum (very often expressed to be exclusive) for settling disputes between provider and user, which might be in a jurisdiction within or outside the UK;

(3)   Termination clauses in the event of breaches by the user of the terms of service[82];

(4)   Terms as to acceptable use by the user, for the prevention of fraud, hacking, obscenity and defamation;

(5)   Reservation by the service provider of a right to vary the terms of service;

(6)   Provisions relating to data confidentiality and integrity and a prohibition on disclosure to others of password information.[83] For instance, the sentiment in this clause in the Facebook Statement of Rights and Responsibilities is common[84]:

> "You will not share your password . . . let anyone else access your account, or do anything else that might jeopardize the security of your account."

(7)   Location of stored information[85];

(8)   Access and deletion of stored information after termination of the agreement;

(9)   Disclosure of stored information to third parties;

(10) The effect of the agreement on the respective rights of the user associated with information transferred by him to the provider. For instance, the Facebook Statement of Rights and Responsibilities provides:

> "For content that is covered by intellectual property rights, like photos and videos (IP content), you specifically give us the following permission, subject to your privacy and application settings: you grant us a non-exclusive, transferable, sub-licensable, royalty-free, worldwide license to use any IP content that you post on or in connection with Facebook (IP License). This IP License ends when you delete your IP content or your account unless your content has been shared with others, and they have not deleted it."

---

[78] Digital content is defined as "data which are produced and supplied in digital form": s.2(9) of the Bill.

[79] SI 2008/1277.

[80] SI 2013/3134.

[81] See Ch.3, Millard, *Cloud Computing Law*.

[82] A provision terminating the agreement on the death of the user is rarely, if ever, to be found.

[83] See discussion about the Computer Misuse Act 1990 in para.49A–31 below.

[84] See s.4(8).

[85] See para.49A–75 on how this issue relates to data protection.

Other terms apply to the rights associated with digital information transferred or copied by the service provider to the user. For instance, in relation
to digital versions of music purchased by a user from the iTunes Store, the
iTunes Store Terms and Conditions provide that the user has no rights of
ownership in any such music[86]:

> "You agree that the iTunes Products are provided to you by way of a license only ... You
> shall be authorised to use iTunes Products only for personal, noncommercial use."

(11) Warranties given by provider and user, including exclusion and limitation of
liability provisions.[87]

49A–24 The contractual rights pass automatically to the personal representative as part of
the personal estate of the deceased. Any causes of action for breaches incurred
before death also pass under the Law Reform (Miscellaneous Provisions) Act
1934 s.1(1).[88] The position may be different if the service agreement is governed
by the law of a country outside the UK.[89] The remedies for default in performance
or breach of the contract include an order for specific performance or an award of
damages.

Confidential information

49A–25 In the digital age there is considerable scope for information to be obtained
covertly or by illegal means, such as by hacking. Such information may well be
confidential. Also, commercially confidential information might have been
legitimately received, but in circumstances that imported an obligation of confidentiality and with some notice that it was confidential.[90] In such cases, the
person bound by the confidentiality owes a duty of confidence,[91] for breach of
which the person owed the duty can turn to the court for equitable remedies.
Contracts might include terms that restrict the use of information; information may
be obtained in the course of a confidential relationship, such as between spouses[92];
it may be received by accident or mistake; or it may be received under an express
duty of confidence.[93] In the context of an application for disclosure by an NHS
Trust under the Freedom of Information Act 2000, the duty of confidence is
capable of surviving the death of the deceased.[94]

---

[86] See Section B, "Use of Content".
[87] Exemption provisions will be construed contra proferentem, so that any doubt or ambiguity will be resolved against the party who made the document and seeks to rely on it: *John Lee (Grantham) Ltd v Ry Executive* [1949] 2 All E.R. 581.
[88] See Pt 8, Beale, *Chitty on Contracts*, 31st edn.
[89] See para.49A–23 above and the Uniform Fiduciary Access to Digital Assets Act: *http://www.uniformlaws.org/shared/docs/Fiduciary%20Access%20to%20Digital%20Assets/UFADAA%20E-nactment%20Kit%20October%202014.zip* [Accessed January 5, 2015].
[90] See generally, Toulson and Phipps, *Confidentiality*, 3rd edn; *Snell's Equity*, 32nd edn, Ch.9.
[91] *Douglas v Hello! Ltd* [2007] UKHL 21 (HL); [2008] 1 A.C. 1.
[92] *Argyll v Argyll* [1967] 1 Ch. 302.
[93] This includes medical records and information of a like nature: *Campbell v MGN Ltd* [2004] UKHL 22; [2004] 2 A.C. 457.
[94] *Bluck v The Information Commissioner*, Information Tribunal [2008] W.T.L.R. 1.

If the information is such as to warrant an obligation of confidentiality and there is **49A–26** no public interest in its disclosure,[95] the court may make an order for an injunction to prevent a misuse of the information. Compensation for any loss caused by a breach of confidence may be awarded in lieu of an injunction,[96] or by way of equitable compensation for breach of a duty of confidence. Alternatively, the person to whom the duty was owed could recover an amount equal to the benefit gained by the defendant by the breach.[97] The court can grant declaratory relief where appropriate.

In November 2013 the European Commission published a proposal for a Directive on the protection of undisclosed know-how and business information (trade secrets) against their unlawful acquisition, use and disclosure.[98] Article 2(1) of the proposed Directive defines a "trade secret" as "information which meets all of the following requirements: (a) is secret in the sense that it is not, as a body or in the precise configuration and assembly of its components, generally known among or readily accessible to persons within the circles that normally deal with the kind of information in question; (b) has commercial value because it is secret; (c) has been subject to reasonable steps under the circumstances, by the person lawfully in control of the information, to keep it secret." The final Directive is expected to be published in summer 2015.

Other Assets

The estate might contain other digital property rights that do not fit neatly into one **49A–27** or other of the above categories. An example is cryptocurrency, such as bitcoin. This is a complex peer-to-peer service,[99] using cryptography to validate and protect the security of transactions. It can be described as a species of documentary intangibles, which are "rights to money, goods or securities which are 'locked up' in a document to the extent that the document is considered to represent the right, which thus becomes transferable by transfer of the document itself".[100] Here the "document" is the electronic "wallet" held by each owner of bitcoin to identify his ownership.

---

[95] There is also a tension between confidentiality, including the right to privacy conferred by art.8 of the European Convention on Human Rights, and the right to freedom of expression, protected by art.10 of the Convention: *Campbell v MGN Ltd* [2004] 2 A.C. 457; see also per Lord Nicholls in *Douglas v Hello! Ltd* [2007] UKHL 21 (HL); [2008] 1 A.C. 1 at para.[255].

[96] Senior Courts Act 1981 s.50.

[97] *Force India Formula One Team Ltd v 1 Malaysia Racing Team* [2013] EWCA Civ 780; [2013] R.P.C. 36.

[98] The text can be found at *http://eur-lex.europa.eu/legal-content/EN/TXT/PDF/?uri=CELEX: 52013PC0813&from=EN.*

[99] Users can transact directly with each other, without the need for an intermediary, such as a cloud service provider or a central bank.

[100] See per Stephen Morris QC in *Armstrong GmbH v Winnington Networks Ltd* [2012] EWHC 10 (Ch); [2013] Ch. 156 at para.[47]; Taylor, "Give me back my bitcoins", C&L (2013), *http:// www.scl.org/site.aspx?i=ed34546.*

Intermeddling

49A–28 If someone who has not been lawfully appointed a personal representative and has no entitlement to a grant intermeddles in the affairs of the deceased, he may be treated for some purposes as having assumed the executorship and he will be known as an executor de son tort.[101] Activities that have given rise to such treatment include carrying on the deceased's trade, taking a Bible or a bedstead. In principle even the slightest intermeddling with goods is sufficient. Where a person who does not have or is not entitled to a grant exercises the contractual rights between the deceased and a cloud service provider by typing in a username and password to log in to the deceased's account, that person is likely to be an executor de son tort. Whether or not he will be chargeable as executor will depend on whether or not he has taken control of any digital property rights[102]; for instance if an online banking account was accessed and funds transferred.

If access to the account has been obtained after discovery that the account was insecure in some way, for instance if there was evidence that unauthorised attempts had been made to log in to the account, action taken to make the account secure would not result in treatment as executor do son tort.[103]

Discovery

49A–29 An initial item in the personal representative's task list in relation to digital property rights[104] is the discovery of the information that is stored on the computing devices left by the deceased as well as identifying the various cloud services that the deceased used during his lifetime. This will include banking accounts that have online access.[105] It may not be sufficient for the representative just to give possession of the computing device to the relevant beneficiary, or even to put it aside pending determination of the rightful beneficiary. The representative must do all that he can reasonably do to discover whether there are any digital property rights,[106] associated with information in a cloud, that are part of the estate of the deceased. If the deceased has left a list of cloud services, the task will be relatively simple. If there is no convenient list, the information may be discoverable locally on a device. The personal representative may need to seek professional advice on accessing the device and the cloud services.

Once the various cloud accounts have been discovered, the personal representative should not automatically go on to access the accounts, even if he knows the usernames and passwords used by the deceased to access them, without ascertaining whether or not he is permitted to do so under the terms and conditions

---

[101] Paragraph 7–01 above.
[102] Section 28 of the Administration of Estates Act 1925; for the meaning of "digital property rights", see para.49A–03 above.
[103] Paragraph 7–11 above.
[104] For the meaning of "digital property rights", see para.49A–03 above.
[105] Some modern bank accounts are accessible only online.
[106] For the meaning of "digital property rights", see para.49A–03 above.

of the cloud service.[107] He may need to contact the service providers armed with the grant of representation to obtain authority from them to do so.

Security

A common problem with cloud computing is security. Accessing a cloud account is generally achieved by entering a username and a password into specified regions of a web page. There may be further security measures to overcome, such as what is known as "two factor authentication", which requires additional information to be entered after entering the correct username and password. To the extent that the personal representative is authorised to do so, he should ascertain the strength of the existing security for all cloud service accounts and, if it is insecure, he should improve it. If the personal representative is not authorised to access the service to test or improve the account's security, he should contact the service provider.

49A–30

Computer Misuse Act 1990

As mentioned above,[108] it is a common feature in terms of service applicable to agreements between cloud service providers and users of their services that disclosure of usernames and passwords by the user is prohibited. The issue here is whether a person, who has received a username and password from the user of a cloud service, is himself authorised to access that service. Section 1 of the Computer Misuse Act 1990[109] provides that a person is guilty of an offence if (a) he causes a computer to perform any function with intent to secure access to any program or data held in any computer, or to enable any such access to be secured; (b) the access he intends to secure, or to enable to be secured, is unauthorised; and (c) he knows at the time when he causes the computer to perform the function that that is the case. This knowledge may be lacking in many cases. His intent need not be directed at (a) any particular program or data; (b) a program or data of any particular kind; or (c) a program or data held in any particular computer. It is necessary (unless the charge is of conspiracy to commit the offence) that, at the relevant time, either the person, or the computer holding the program or data he was accessing, was in England and Wales.[110] Other jurisdictions have similar legislation.[111]

49A–31

Securing access to any program or data held in a computer includes altering or erasing the program or data; copying or moving it to any storage medium other than that in which it is held or to a different location in the storage medium in which it is held; using it; or outputting it to a display or in some other manner.[112]

49A–32

---

[107] For a discussion on the terms and conditions of cloud services see para.49A–23 above. For a discussion on the criminal aspects of unauthorised access to cloud services, see para.49A–31 below.
[108] See para.49A–23.
[109] "The 1990 Act".
[110] Sections 4 and 5 of the 1990 Act.
[111] See, for instance, the Computer Fraud and Abuse Act, 18 U.S.C. § 1030.
[112] Section 17(2) of the 1990 Act.

Access is unauthorised if the person is not himself entitled to control access of the kind in question to the program or data; and he does not have consent to access by him of the kind in question to the program or data from any person who is so entitled.[113]

49A–33 Accordingly, if a user in England of a cloud service gives out password information, without the authority of the service provider (who owns or controls the computing device providing the service) to someone, including a personal representative, who then accesses the service, that someone might be committing an offence. Subject to a proper construction of the terms of service, however, after the deceased's death the personal representative, who will have succeeded to the contractual rights of the user,[114] including the right to log in to the account, will stand in his place in relation to the agreement and will be authorised,[115] and no offence will be committed by accessing the cloud account. If the governing law of the service agreement is not that of England and Wales or the service is provided using a computing device situated outside the UK, the position might be different and appropriate advice should be taken.

Foreign assets

49A–34 Property of the deceased that is situate in England at the time of death vests in the English executors on death or in the administrators on grant.[116] Assets outside England do not automatically vest in the English representative[117]; his entitlement will depend on the law of the country in which they are situate. If the English representative actually obtains possession of any foreign assets as such representative, he is accountable for them in England, as if they were part of the English estate.[118]

49A–35 A user's digital information may be stored on one or more computing devices located outside England and the service provider of a cloud service may be resident or domiciled in a different jurisdiction from those computing devices.

As to the situs of the assets of the deceased,[119] the law of the country in which an asset is situate determines whether it (or any rights or obligations connected

---

[113] Section 17(5) of the 1990 Act; this does not apply to powers of search and seizure under any enactment.

[114] See para.49A–18 above; a testator could, for instance, leave a sealed envelope with his solicitor, not to be opened until after his death—the contents of the letter should be kept up to date with periodical changes in passwords.

[115] An executor derives title from the will and the deceased's property vests in him from the moment of death (see para.5–02 above) but not an administrator, who takes title after the grant (see para.5–10 above).

[116] An executor derives title from the will and the deceased's property vests in him from the moment of death (see para.5–02 above) but not an administrator, who takes title after the grant (see para.5–10 above).

[117] See para.54–02.

[118] See per Neville J. in *Re Scott* [1916] 2 Ch. 268; this issue was not appealed.

[119] From August 17, 2015, the rules governing the applicable to succession to the estate of a deceased person will in most states of the EU be governed by the Succession Regulation, (EU) 650/2012. The UK has not adopted the Regulation but the administration of an English estate may be affected by it.

with it) is movable or immovable.[120] In general, choses in action or property in the nature of choses in action, are movables and are situate in the country where they are properly recoverable.[121] Of relevance to this chapter are rights of action in contract, intellectual property rights,[122] and rights of action for breach of a duty of confidence.

In relation to contracts, the proper law is generally governed by the provisions of the Rome I Regulation.[123] Any express or implied choice of law applies[124] and, in the absence of choice, the governing law depends on the type of contract or the country with which the contract is most closely connected.[125] A contract for the provision of services is governed by the law of the country where the service provider has his habitual residence.[126] Special provisions apply to certain consumer contracts (as defined)[127]: the governing law is the country where the consumer has his habitual residence if the other, non-consumer,[128] party directs his commercial activities to the country where the consumer has his habitual residence. This would be the case if the services of a non-UK provider are promoted or advertised on the provider's website, inviting consumers to enter into contracts through the site or by direct mail or fax. The parties may still choose the governing law provided that it does not deprive the consumer of protection afforded to him by the local law.[129] As to the jurisdiction of the UK courts, Brussels 1 applies.[130]

49A–36

Claims for infringement in the UK of UK intellectual property rights may be brought in the UK courts. For certain unregistered rights (such as copyright), proceedings may be brought in UK courts for infringements of intellectual property rights taking place in other EU Member States if jurisdiction is conferred on the UK courts by Brussels I.[131] For instance, if the defendant is domiciled within the UK, he should generally be sued in the UK.[132] The law to be applied to

49A–37

---

[120] See generally Dicey, Morris and Collins, *The Conflict of Laws*, 15th edn, Ch.22.

[121] *Alloway v Phillips (Inspector of Taxes)* [1980] 1 W.L.R. 888.

[122] Ownership of the intellectual property right should be properly ascertained. A purchaser of digital works from a cloud service provider may acquire only a licence to use the work, rather than a property right actionable at law. In addition, cloud service agreements may affect the ownership or value of any intellectual property rights stored in the cloud: see para.49A–23 above.

[123] Regulation (EC) 593/2008 on the law applicable to contractual obligations. Rome I applies whether or not the governing law is the law of a Member State of the EU: art.2. See generally *Chitty on Contracts*, 31st edn, Ch.30.

[124] Article 3.

[125] Article 4.

[126] Article 4.1(b).

[127] Article 6.

[128] Known as "the professional".

[129] Article 6.2.

[130] Regulation (EC) 1215/2012 on jurisdiction and the recognition and enforcement of judgments in civil and commercial matters (recast) (also known as the Judgments Regulation). See also the Lugano Convention 2007. See generally Dicey, Morris and Collins, *The Conflict of Laws*, 15th edn, Ch.11.

[131] See para.49A–36 above; see also Lugano Convention 2007; *Pearce v Ove Arup Partnership Ltd* [2000] Ch. 403.

[132] See art.2 of the Judgments Regulation. For an exception, see art.5(3), concerning matters relating to tort: see *Pinckney v KDG Mediatech AG* (Case C-170/12, ECJ).

the infringement is that of the country for which protection is claimed.[133] Where infringements of unregistered rights in the nature of copyright take place outside the EU, claims can be brought in the UK courts, provided they have in personam jurisdiction over the defendant.[134]

49A–38 A claim for breach of confidence in circumstances where there was no prior contract between the parties is characterised as a restitutionary claim and the applicable law is determined under the common law.[135] In *Douglas*, English law (the place where the defendant had been enriched) was applied to determine whether the information was private and whether there had been a breach of duty but New York law (where the photographs were taken) was held to be relevant to the question of whether or not the claimants had a reasonable expectation of privacy.[136]

Business property

49A–39 One aspect of the administration of digital information concerns the administration of businesses of the deceased.[137] Very often digital property rights will need administration, either as the product around which the business is based or as part of the management of the business. For instance, the product of the business might be the sale of e-books or music files and the management of the business might involve the use of databases and the collection and analysis of personal information of customers and other persons accessing the business website. The significance of this power is that, while administering that business, the representative may have duties under the Data Protection legislation.[138]

The general rule is that the representatives of a deceased person have no authority in law to carry on the trade of the deceased although such authority might be conferred expressly or impliedly by the terms of his will or in order to enable them to sell it to the best advantage of the estate.[139] If the representatives do carry on the deceased's business, they will be personally liable for all debts that they contract in so doing after the death of the deceased,[140] although, if they have authority to do so, they will have a right to indemnity as against the beneficiaries out of the part of the estate that they are authorised to employ in the business.[141]

---

[133] See art.8(1) of Regulation (EC) No.864/2007 on the law applicable to non-contractual obligations (Rome II); Dicey, Morris and Collins, *The Conflict of Laws*, 15th edn, para.35R–073; *Pearce v Ove Arup Partnership Ltd* [2000] Ch. 403 at 423F.
[134] *Lucasfilm Ltd v Ainsworth* [2011] UKSC 39; [2012] 1 A.C. 208; see Dicey, Morris and Collins, *The Conflict of Laws*, 15th edn, paras 34–025—34–027.
[135] *Douglas v Hello! Ltd (No 3)* [2005] EWCA Civ 595; [2006] Q.B. 125 (partly reversed on other grounds: [2007] UKHL 21; [2008] 1 A.C. 1). Choice of law rules for tort claims can be found in Pt III of the Private International Law (Miscellaneous Provisions) Act 1995 and Rome II.
[136] [2006] Q.B. 125 at para.100; See paras 34–091—34–092, Dicey, Morris and Collins, *The Conflict of Laws*, 15th edn.
[137] See para.57–85.
[138] See paras 49A–42 onwards below.
[139] See generally, paras 57–85 to 57–89. The court may be able to extend the powers of the personal representatives under the Trustee Act 1925 s.57.
[140] See para.57–94.
[141] See para.57–95.

The personal representatives have a duty to do whatever is required to be done to preserve the business as an asset and can avoid liability for breach resulting in loss by acting in good faith and to the best of their judgment.

Non-proprietary information

As was previously stated, information is not an asset that passes to the personal representative.[142] Accordingly, the personal representative owes no duty to the beneficiaries in respect of it, nor does he have any entitlement or obligation to deal with it. Any stored information will almost inevitably be a copy and there is no right under English law to retrieve it unless its existence is as a result of some infringement of copyright. Such information might consist of message text that does not qualify for copyright protection or photographs or videos that are not original. The representative can call on the service provider to delete it, unless the service agreement denies him that right.

49A–40

Where contractual rights are personal to the deceased and do not survive his death the personal representative would fail if he sought to recover them. Section 1 of the Law Reform (Miscellaneous Provisions) Act 1934, which provides for the survival of causes of action subsisting against or vested in the deceased, specifically excludes causes of action for defamation.[143] A person's reputation, dignity and integrity are not items of property. Private information about an individual has, however, become much more important since the incorporation into English law of the European Convention on Human Rights and, as has been seen,[144] a duty of confidence may well survive the death of a deceased.

If, for instance, the deceased posted messages on Facebook or Twitter, those messages might not have sufficient originality or independent skill or intellectual endeavour on the part of the deceased for copyright protection. Photographs or documents uploaded by the deceased to a cloud server may have been copies themselves. Music uploaded by the deceased to a cloud storage device may have been purchased by him from the iTunes Store and he may have been a licensee without any right to claim copyright in the files.[145]

A question therefore arises as to whether the personal representative is entitled to recover the cost and expense (and remuneration) for administering information that has no rights associated with it. If the will contains specific directions for the representative to deal with matters that do not come into his hands as property, the expense to the representative of dealing with those matters should come out of the estate. Otherwise, and in the case of an intestacy, there must be some doubt as to

49A–41

---

[142] See para.49A–06 above.
[143] Other instances are: an applicant's right to apply under the Inheritance (Provision for Family and Dependants) Act 1975 comes to an end on his death and any pending proceedings abate at that time; proceedings for a divorce order cannot be brought or continued after the death of one of the parties to the marriage; the interest of a deceased person under a joint tenancy where another joint tenant survives him does not survive his death and does not devolve on the representative.
[144] See para.49A–25 above.
[145] See para.49A–23 above.

whether the expenses will have been properly incurred by the representative in the conduct of his office within s.31(1) of the Trustee Act 2000.[146]

B.—DATA PROTECTION

49A–42 Certain information is sensitive and legislation has been enacted to regulate the "processing of information relating to individuals, including the obtaining, holding, use or disclosure of such information".[147] The legislation is "underpinned by a set of eight straightforward, common-sense principles" that are designed to ensure complicity with the law.[148] The Data Protection Act 1998 (DPA 1998) is the UK's implementation of the Data Protection Directive,[149] which was designed to harmonise legislation relating to data protection throughout the European Union.[150] The EU Commission Regulation No. 611/2013 provides for the processing of personal data and the protection of privacy in the electronic communications sector. The administration of the digital information with which the estate is concerned might involve the use of databases and the collection and analysis of personal information of beneficiaries, creditors, debtors and other persons. This might impose on the representative duties under the Data Protection legislation.

Definitions[151]

Data

49A–43 "Data", for the purposes of the DPA 1998, essentially constitute information that is held on a computer and information recorded on paper if it is intended to be put on a computer.[152]

Personal data

49A–44 "Personal data" is data that relate to a living individual who can be identified from that data or from that data and other information that is in the possession of, or is likely to come into the possession of, a data controller. It includes any expression

---

[146] It may be that the court will be able to grant power to the representative to administer the information under the Trustee Act 1925 s.57.

[147] See the long title of the Data Protection Act 1998 (the "DPA 1998"). See generally, Jay, *Data Protection, Law and Practice*, 4th edn and Millard, *Cloud Computing Law*, Chs 7 to 10.

[148] DPA 1998 s.4(1) and Pt I of Sch.1. See the Information Commissioner's Office, *Guide to Data Protection*, Part A1, para.1. The Guide can be found at *https://ico.org.uk/for-organisations/guide-to-data-protection/*. For the data protection principles see paras 49A–66 onwards below. For data and processing that are exempt from the data principles, see paras 49A–54 onwards below.

[149] European Parliament and Council Directive (EC) 95/46.

[150] "EU".

[151] DPA 1998 s.1(1).

[152] See the Information Commissioner's Office, *Guide to Data Protection*, Part A3, para.3. See also the guide published by the ICO for determining what is data for the purposes of the DPA 1998: *https://ico.org.uk/media/for-organisations/documents/1609/what_is_data_for_the_purposes_of_the_dpa.pdf*.

of opinion about the individual and any indication of the intentions of the data controller or any other person in respect of the individual.[153]

Sensitive personal data

"Sensitive personal data" is personal data consisting of "information as to (a) the racial or ethnic origin of the data subject,[154] (b) his political opinions, (c) his religious beliefs or other beliefs of a similar nature, (d) whether he is a member of a trade union (within the meaning of the Trade Union and Labour Relations (Consolidation) Act 1992), (e) his physical or mental health or condition, (f) his sexual life, (g) the commission or alleged commission by him of any offence, or (h) any proceedings for any offence committed or alleged to have been committed by him, the disposal of such proceedings or the sentence of any court in such proceedings."[155]   **49A–45**

Data controller

A "data controller" is a person who (either alone or jointly or in common with other persons) determines the purposes for which and the manner in which any personal data are, or are to be, processed.   **49A–46**

Data processor

A "data processor", in relation to personal data, means any person (other than an employee of the data controller) who processes the data on behalf of the data controller.[156]   **49A–47**

Processing

"Processing", in relation to information or data, means obtaining, recording or holding the information or data or carrying out any operation or set of operations on the information or data, including organisation, adaptation or alteration of the information or data; retrieval, consultation or use of the information or data; disclosure of the information or data by transmission, dissemination or otherwise making available; or alignment, combination, blocking, erasure or destruction of the information or data.[157]   **49A–48**

---

[153] *Durant v FSA* [2003] EWCA Civ 1746; [2004] F.S.R. 28; *Johnson v The Medical Defence Union Ltd* [2004] EWHC 347 (Ch); *Common Services Agency v Scottish Information Commissioner* [2008] 1 W.L.R. 1550. The ICO have issued a quick guide to personal data at *https://ico.org.uk/media/for-organisations/documents/1549/determining_what_is_personal_data_quick_reference_guide.pdf.*
[154] *Campbell v MGN* [2003] Q.B. 633.
[155] DPA 1998 s.2.
[156] For a guide published by the ICO on data controllers and data processors and the difference between them, see *https://ico.org.uk/media/for-organisations/documents/1546/data-controllers-and-data-processors-dp-guidance.pdf.*
[157] *Johnson v Medical Defence Union* [2007] EWCA Civ 262; *Campbell v MGN* [2003] Q.B. 633.

Data subject

49A–49 A "data subject" means an individual who is the subject of personal data.

The Information Commissioner

49A–50 Information rights in the UK are upheld by the Information Commissioner, who is a corporation sole and the independent authority that promotes data privacy for individuals. He is responsible for "promoting good practice in handling personal data, and giving advice and guidance on data protection; keeping a register of organisations that are required to notify him about their information-processing activities; helping to resolve disputes by deciding whether it is likely or unlikely that an organisation has complied with the [DPA 1998] when processing personal data; taking action to enforce compliance with the [DPA 1998] where appropriate; and bringing prosecutions for offences committed under the Act".[158] He acts through the Information Commissioner's Office.[159] There is a wealth of information about data protection on the ICO website.[160]

Registration

49A–51 Personal data must not be processed unless the data controller is registered in a register maintained by the Commissioner for the purpose.[161] The register must contain the "registrable particulars", which include his name and address; if he has nominated a representative for the purposes of the Act, the name and address of the representative; a description of the personal data being or to be processed by or on behalf of the data controller and of the category or categories of data subject to which they relate; a description of the purpose or purposes for which the data are being or are to be processed; and a description of any recipient or recipients to whom the data controller intends or may wish to disclose the data.[162]

Application

49A–52 Apart from international obligations of the Information Commissioner,[163] the DPA 1998 applies to a data controller in respect of any data only if the data controller is established in the UK and the data are processed in the context of that

---

[158] Information Commissioner's Office Guide to Data Protection, Part A2, para.3. In Scotland the Procurator Fiscal brings prosecutions.

[159] The "ICO".

[160] *http://www.ico.org.uk.*

[161] DPA 1998 ss.17(1) and 19. There is a procedure for application to be registered and adjudication by the Commissioner as to the suitability for registration: see DPA 1998 ss.22 onwards. Contravention of s.17(1) is an offence: DPA 1998 s.21(1).

[162] See generally DPA 1998 s.16(1).

[163] See DPA 1998 s.54.

establishment or, if he is not established within the UK, or any EEA State,[164] but uses equipment in the UK for processing data otherwise than for the purposes of transit through the UK.[165] For the purposes of the administration of an estate, the following are treated as established in the UK: an individual (which would include an individual personal representative) who is ordinarily resident in the UK, a body incorporated under the law of any part of the UK, a partnership or other unincorporated association formed under the law of any part of the United Kingdom, and (d) any person other than those previously described who maintains in the United Kingdom an office, branch or agency through which he carries on any activity, or a regular practice.[166]

Right of access

Provided a data controller has received a request in writing and, in certain cases, a fee, with certain exceptions and limitations,[167] an individual is entitled to be informed by any data controller (i) whether personal data of which that individual is the data subject are being processed by or on behalf of that data controller and, if so, to be given by the data controller a description of those data, the purposes for which they are being or are to be processed, and the recipients or classes of recipients to whom they are or may be disclosed; (ii) to have the information constituting those data and available information as to their source communicated to him in an intelligible form; and (iii) where the processing by automatic means of personal data of which that individual is the data subject for the purpose of evaluating matters relating to him such as, for example, his performance at work, his creditworthiness, his reliability or his conduct, has constituted or is likely to constitute the sole basis for any decision significantly affecting him, to be informed by the data controller of the logic involved in that decision-taking.[168] An individual has a right to prevent the processing or limit the use of personal data in respect of which he is the data subject.[169] The court has power to order a data controller to rectify, block, erase or destroy any personal data that are inaccurate and any expression of opinion that appears to be based on that inaccurate data.[170]

49A–53

---

[164] "EEA State" means a State which is a contracting party to the Agreement on the European Economic Area signed at Oporto on May 2, 1992 as adjusted by the Protocol signed at Brussels on March 17, 1993. It includes EU countries and Iceland, Liechtenstein and Norway, but not Switzerland: see *https://www.gov.uk/eu-eea*.

[165] DPA 1998 s. 5(1).

[166] DPA 1998 s.5(3); the reference to establishment in any other EEA State has a corresponding meaning.

[167] See, for instance, where the controller is a credit reference agency (s.9) and personal data held by public authorities (s.9A).

[168] DPA 1998 s.7.

[169] DPA 1998 ss.10, 11 and 12.

[170] DPA 1998 s.14.

Exemptions

49A–54 There are certain exemptions, set out in Part IV of the DPA 1998, which limit the operation of the data protection principles and references to personal data or the processing of personal data.[171] If an exemption is required for the purpose of the safeguarding national security, personal data are exempt[172]; personal data processed for the prevention or detection of crime are exempt to a limited extent[173]; and certain processing undertaken with a view to the publication by any person of any journalistic, literary or artistic material are also exempt to a limited extent. Certain other limited exemptions might apply, such as confidential references,[174] negotiations with the data subject,[175] and legal professional privilege.[176]

The Domestic Purposes exemption

49A–55 The most relevant exemption to consider for the purposes of this Chapter is that in s.36 of the DPA 1998:

> "Personal data processed by an individual only for the purposes of that individual's personal, family or household affairs (including recreational purposes) are exempt from the data protection principles and the provisions of Parts II and III".[177]

This is sometimes referred to as the "domestic purposes" or "Christmas card list" exemption. Recital 12 of the Data Protection Directive provides[178]:

> "Whereas the protection principles must apply to all processing of personal data by any person whose activities are governed by Community law; whereas there should be excluded the processing of data carried out by a natural person in the exercise of activities which are exclusively personal or domestic, such as correspondence and the holding of records of addresses"

Section 36 was enacted to implement art.3(2) of Data Protection Directive, which provides:

> "This Directive shall not apply to the processing of personal data:
> . . .
> – by a natural person in the course of a purely personal or household activity."

---

[171] DPA 1998 s.27.
[172] DPA 1998 s.28.
[173] DPA 1998 s.29.
[174] DPA 1998 Sch.7, para.1.
[175] DPA 1998 Sch.7, para.7.
[176] DPA 1998 Sch.7, para.10.
[177] In other words, the obligations giving rise to the right of access to personal data (Part II) and the requirement of registration (Pt III): DPA 1998 s.36.
[178] Directive 95/46.

ICO Guides

The ICO Guide to Data Protection provides little further analysis of this exemption, apart from two examples[179]:

      49A–56

> "An individual keeps a database of their friends' and relatives' names, addresses and dates of birth on their PC. They use the database for keeping track of birthdays and to produce address labels for Christmas cards. The domestic purposes exemption applies to this type of processing."

and

> "An individual records the highlights of their summer holiday on a digital camcorder. The recording includes images of people they meet on holiday. Although those digital images are personal data, the domestic purposes exemption applies."

In the ICO guidance on Social Networking and Online Forums, para.9 provides:

> "The section 36 exemption is based on the purposes for which the personal data is being processed, not on the nature or content of the data itself. It applies whenever someone uses an online forum purely in a personal capacity for their own domestic or recreational purposes. It doesn't apply when an organisation or an individual uses an online forum for corporate, business or non-domestic purposes."[180]

And para.21:

> "The section 36 exemption only applies when an individual is processing personal data for their own personal, family or household affairs (including recreational purposes). This means that even when the processing is clearly done by an individual rather than a group or organisation, if the purpose of the processing is non-domestic then the exemption won't apply."

Law Society v Kordowski

In *Law Society v Kordowski*,[181] the defendant was the founder, operator and publisher of a website known as "Solicitors from Hell", which published "name and shame" comments about solicitors from members of the public. The Law Society and some solicitors brought proceedings in the High Court to require the defendant to cease publication of the website, relying on, amongst other things, the DPA 1998.[182] The Commissioner formed the view that he could not intervene, because of the domestic purposes exemption; he considered that the exemption was,[183]

      49A–57

---

[179] Part C2 para.43; *https://ico.org.uk/media/for-organisations/documents/1607/the_guide_to_data_protection.pdf.*

[180] *https://ico.org.uk/media/for-organisations/documents/1600/social-networking-and-online-forums-dpa-guidance.pdf.*

[181] [2011] EWHC 3185 (QB); [2014] E.M.L.R. 2.

[182] The claim was for an order under DPA 1998 s.10(4) for compliance with a notice under s.10(1).

[183] See [2014] E.M.L.R. 2 at para.[96]; the quotation is an extract from a letter written by the Commissioner.

"... intended to balance the individual's rights to respect for his/her private life with the freedom of expression. These rights are equally important and I am strongly of the view that it is not the purpose of the DPA to regulate an individual right to freedom of expression—even where the individual uses a third party website, rather than his own facilities, to exercise this ... Although solicitorsfromhell / Mr Kordowski may well be a data controller, and is indeed is registered as such, the instigators of the website content are generally private individuals expressing their own views. Their activity attracts the s.36 exemption, which emanates ultimately from Article 10 of the European Convention on Human Rights. In giving due weight to freedom of expression in cases like this we have to accept that enforcing the data protection principles in respect of the activities of the website owner is likely to entail a disproportionate level of interference with the rights of the contributors, however unpleasant their contributions might be."

The judge, Tugendhat J., disagreed. He said[184]:

"... I do not understand how it could be said that s.36 has any application to the present case. It is true that s.36 gives protection to art.10 rights limited to personal, family and household affairs ... Those who drafted the directive and the DPA omitted to address generally the relationship between the art.8 rights which the Directive sought to implement, and the art.10 rights which must also be respected, in accordance with both EU and English law."

He held that the defendant had no tenable defence to the data protection claim.

Criminal Proceedings against Lindqvist

49A–58 In *Criminal Proceedings against Lindqvist*,[185] the defendant, who was a religious teacher in Sweden, set up a website using her home computer containing information for parishioners who were preparing for their confirmation. The website also contained information about parish colleagues, including their names, their employment, their hobbies and in many cases telephone numbers and family circumstances. She did not inform her colleagues about these pages on the website or obtain their consent. She did not inform the Swedish equivalent of the Commissioner and was prosecuted for offences under the equivalent of the DPA 1998. One of the questions referred to the ECJ was whether the act of referring, on an internet page, to various persons and identifying them by name or by other means, for instance by giving their telephone number or information regarding their working conditions and hobbies, was within the domestic purposes exemption of Directive 95/46.[186] It was held that,[187]

"That exception must ... be interpreted as relating only to activities which are carried out in the course of private or family life of individuals, which is clearly not the case with the processing of personal data consisting in publication on the internet so that those data are made accessible to an indefinite number of people."

---

[184] See [2014] E.M.L.R. 2 at para.[99].
[185] Case C-101/01; [2004] Q.B. 1014; [2004] All E.R. (EC) 561.
[186] [2004] Q.B. 1014 at para.[29].
[187] [2004] Q.B. 1014 at para.[47].

František Ryneš

In *František Ryneš*,[188] the defendant installed and used a camera system located **49A–59** under the eaves of his family home in the Czech Republic. It was installed in a fixed position and recorded the entrance to his home, the public footpath and the entrance to the house opposite. A visual recording was stored on a hard disk drive. No monitor was installed on the recording equipment, so the images could not be studied in real time. Only the defendant had direct access to the system and the data. It was installed to protect the property, health and lives of the defendant and his family from attacks that had occurred in the past. The system was used to identify suspects of these offences but one of the suspects that was identified claimed that the system was unlawful. One of the questions for the court was whether the video recordings were within the domestic purposes exemption of the Czech data protection legislation.[189] It was held by the ECJ that, to the extent that the video surveillance covered, even partially, a public space and was generated outwards from the private setting of the person processing the data, it could not be regarded as an activity that was a purely personal or household activity for the purposes of the legislation.

Other jurisdictions The Isle of Man Data Protection Supervisor issued gui- **49A–60** dance in 2014 on the effect that the IoM data protection legislation[190] had on the requirement to inform a beneficiary about the details of a will or trust when it is made, or to permit a beneficiary to find out about such details. His guidance was[191]:

> "Wills
>
> Wills are created by individuals to manage their own 'personal, family or household affairs'. The 'domestic purposes' exemption applies to personal data processed for this purpose.
>
> Family trusts
>
> The 'domestic purposes' exemption will also apply to Trusts created by an individual for their own 'personal, family or household affairs', i.e. a 'family trust'.
>
> In the above circumstances the Act does not provide individuals with any rights to find out whether they are beneficiaries of a will or trust, or to be informed whether their personal data is being processed for that purpose."

Reform There are proposals for the reform of data protection legislation in the **49A–61** EU. A draft Regulation was published in January 2012. Paragraph (15) of the recitals to that draft provided:

---

[188] ECJ, Case C-212/13; *http://curia.europa.eu/juris/document/document.jsf?text=&docid=160561& pageIndex=0&doclang=EN&mode=lst&dir=&occ=first&part=1&cid=12.*

[189] Paragraph [26] of the judgment.

[190] Section 33 of the Data Protection Act.

[191] *http://www.gov.im/lib/docs/odps/tgn_trusts_and_wills.pdf.* For a discussion about the equivalent provision in New Zealand (s.56 of the Privacy Act), see from para.5.43 in *http://www.lawcom.govt.nz/ sites/default/files/publications/2010/03/Publication_129_460_Part_8_Chapter-5-Exclusions%20and% 20Exemptions.pdf.* See also the Australian Law Reform Commission discussion about s.7B(1) of the Privacy Act 1988, where the exemption is for acts and practices done "other than in the course of business": *http://www.alrc.gov.au/publications/43.%20Other%20Private%20Sector%20Exemptions/ personal-or-non-business-use.*

"This Regulation should not apply to processing of personal data by a natural person, which are exclusively personal or domestic, such as correspondence and the holding of addresses, and without any gainful interest and thus without any connection with a professional or commercial activity. The exemption should also not apply to controllers or processors which provide the means for processing personal data for such personal or domestic activities."

Article 28.4 of the draft Regulation provides:

"The obligations referred to in paragraphs 1 and 2 shall not apply to the following controllers and processors:
(a) a natural person processing personal data without a commercial interest ...".

The personal representative's data processing

49A–62   In the course of the administration of the deceased's estate a personal representative might carry out certain types of data processing. Any of these could be achieved electronically and is capable of constituting the processing of personal data.

The deceased's activities

49A–63   During his lifetime, the deceased may have been involved in the processing of personal information for various purposes.

(1)   He may have had a collection of names and addresses of friends, acquaintances and business contacts in an electronic address book on his computer or mobile phone. This would be within the domestic purposes exemption and the representative's processing of that data for the purposes of administering the estate would likewise be exempt.

(2)   He may have published a website that collected names and addresses of individuals who registered as account holders to take advantage of information available to registered users of the site. This would not have been exempt and the representative's processing of that data for the purposes of administering the estate would not be exempt.

(3)   He may have run a business (whether online or not) that involved, either directly or indirectly, the digital processing of personal data, such as the names and addresses and the buying history of customers or the names and addresses and historic appraisals of employees. He may have carried out marketing operations using email addresses held electronically.[192] These would not have been exempt and the representative's processing of that data for the purposes of administering the estate would not be exempt.

(4)   If he had installed a CCTV system to identify individuals accessing his premises, those images may have been personal data and may not have been exempt.[193]

---

[192] This activity would in addition have been restricted by the provisions of the Privacy and Electronic Communications (EC Directive) Regulations 2003, as amended, implementing the EU Privacy and Electronic Communications Directive 2002/08/EC.

[193] See *František Ryneš,* ECJ, Case C-212/13; para.49A–59 above.

(5) If the deceased had been a doctor, the records relating to his patients would be sensitive personal data.[194] He would have been authorised to process that information if it was necessary for medical purposes,[195] but the representative would not be entitled to do so.

(6) If the deceased had been the owner of an application, or program, that was sold to users of personal computers, mobile phones or tablet devices, that application might collect personal data in the course of its operation and send that data to a server that was controlled by the deceased. For instance, the application might send photographs that contain metadata such as the location where the image was taken and the names of the individuals in the photos. Processing by the deceased would not have been exempt and the representative's processing of that data for the purposes of administering the estate would not be exempt.

(7) If the deceased had been operating a news blog, that might have been exempt under the journalism exemption conferred by s.32 of the 1998 Act.[196] Continuation of that blog by the representative might also be exempt.

Estate accounting

The personal representative catalogues the deceased's estate and, for that purpose, might list the assets and liabilities and documents that are associated with them. Some of the documents will identify the deceased. Some of the information might lead to the identification of the deceased and other individuals who are living, such as joint bank account statements, joint property title deeds and partnership documents and any wills executed by the deceased. Yet other information could lead to the identification of individuals; for instance the deceased may have owed money to an individual or he may have been owed money by an individual. These would likely have been exempt under the domestic purposes exemption and the representative's processing of that data for the purposes of administering the estate would likewise be exempt.

49A–64

Administration processing

The personal representative might process personal data about individuals in the course of administering the estate. For instance, the representative might keep records of the names and addresses of individuals who are contacted about the assets and liabilities making up the estate and about the identification of beneficiaries mentioned in the will or entitled on an intestacy. He might also process names and addresses of beneficiaries so that the proper documentation can be prepared and executed. This would be exempt under the domestic purposes exemption.

49A–65

If the personal representative organises, retrieves, alters, discloses or destroys

---

[194] See reg.5 of the Data Protection (Notification and Notification Fees) Regulations 2000 for notifications by partnerships.
[195] Paragraph 8, Sch.3 to the DPA 1998.
[196] See *BBC v Sugar (No 2)* [2012] UKSC 4; [2012] 1 W.L.R. 439.

any personal data that had been processed by the deceased during his lifetime, that might be exempt under the domestic purposes exemption, depending on the data.

If the personal representative wishes to sell a business that had been owned by the deceased and processing of personal data was involved in the running of the business, he might need to share those personal data with a potential purchaser during negotiations or a process of due diligence. That would not be exempt under the domestic purposes exemption.

The data protection principles

49A–66   The DPA 1998 sets out eight data protection principles. Unless there is some exemption, it is the duty of a data controller to comply with the data protection principles in relation to all personal data with respect to which he is the data controller.[197] The eight principles are set out below.

First principle

49A–67   Personal data must be processed fairly and lawfully[198] and, in particular, must not be processed unless at least one of the conditions in Sch.2 is met, and, in the case of sensitive personal data, at least one of the conditions in Sch.3 is also met.[199]

In determining for the purposes of the first principle whether personal data are processed fairly, regard is to be had to the method by which they are obtained, including in particular whether any person from whom they are obtained is deceived or misled as to the purpose or purposes for which they are to be processed. Data are to be treated as obtained fairly if they consist of information obtained from a person who (a) is authorised by or under any enactment to supply it, or (b) is required to supply it by or under any enactment or by any convention or other instrument imposing an international obligation on the United Kingdom.[200]

Except where the provision of information would involve a disproportionate effort, or the recording of the information or the disclosure of the data by the data controller is necessary for compliance with any legal obligation to which the data controller is subject, other than an obligation imposed by contract, personal data are not to be treated as processed fairly unless the data subject has, is provided with, or has made readily available to him, the identity of the data controller or of any nominated representative of his for the purposes of the DPA 1998, the purpose or purposes for which the data are intended to be processed, and any further information which is necessary, having regard to the specific circumstances in which the data are or are to be processed, to enable processing in respect of the data subject to be fair.[201]

---

[197] DPA 1998 s.4(4).
[198] Data published in breach of a right to respect for privacy may be held to have been processed unlawfully: *Murray v Express Newspapers plc* [2008] EWCA Civ 4546; [2009] Ch. 481 at para.[62].
[199] DPA 1998 Sch.1, Part I, para.1.
[200] DPA 1998 Sch.1, Part II, para.1.
[201] DPA 1998 Sch.1, Part II, paras 2–4.

The conditions in Sch.2 include the giving of consent by the data subject; **49A–68** enforcement of contractual rights or other legal obligations; the protection of the vital interests of the data subject; and where the processing is necessary for the purposes of legitimate interests pursued by the data controller or by the third party or parties to whom the data are disclosed,[202] except where the processing is unwarranted in any particular case by reason of prejudice to the rights and free-doms or legitimate interests of the data subject.[203] The conditions in Sch.3 include the data subject giving his explicit consent to the processing of the personal data; the protection of the vital interests of the data subject or another person where there are difficulties in obtaining consent; publication of the personal data by the data subject; processing to do with legal, judicial or parliamentary process; and the prevention of fraud.[204]

Second principle

Personal data must be obtained only for one or more specified and lawful pur- **49A–69** poses, and must not be further processed in any manner incompatible with that purpose or those purposes.[205] The purpose or purposes for which personal data are obtained may in particular be specified in a notice given by the data controller to the data subject, or in a notification given to the Commissioner. In determining whether any disclosure of personal data is compatible with the purpose or pur-poses for which the data were obtained, regard is to be had to the purpose or purposes for which the personal data are intended to be processed by any person to whom they are disclosed.[206]

Third principle

Personal data must be adequate, relevant and not excessive in relation to the **49A–70** purpose or purposes for which they are processed.[207]

Fourth principle

Personal data must be accurate and, where necessary, kept up to date.[208] This **49A–71** principle is not to be regarded as being contravened by reason of any inaccuracy in personal data that accurately record information obtained by the data controller from the data subject or a third party where (a) having regard to the purpose or purposes for which the data were obtained and further processed, the data

---

[202] See *South Lanarkshire Council v Scottish Information Comr* [2013] UKSC 55; [2013] I.R.L.R. 899.
[203] DPA 1998 Sch.2. Consent is defined in art.2(h) of the Data Protection Directive as "any freely given, specific and informed indication of his wishes by which the data subject signifies his agreement to personal data relating to him being processed."
[204] DPA 1998 Sch.3.
[205] DPA 1998 Sch.1, Pt I, para.2.
[206] See DPA 1998, Sch.1, Pt II, paras 5 and 6.
[207] DPA 1998 Sch.1, Pt I, para.3.
[208] DPA 1998 Sch.1, Pt I, para.4.

controller has taken reasonable steps to ensure the accuracy of the data, and (b) if the data subject has notified the data controller of the data subject's view that the data are inaccurate, the data indicate that fact.[209]

Fifth principle

49A–72 Personal data processed for any purpose or purposes must not be kept for longer than is necessary for that purpose or those purposes.[210]

Sixth principle

49A–73 Personal data must be processed in accordance with the rights of data subjects under the DPA 1998.[211] A person is to be regarded as contravening this principle if, but only if[212] (a) he fails to provide a right of access of a data subject to information about the processing of personal data[213]; (b) he fails to comply with a notice against processing that is likely to cause substantial and unwarranted damage or distress (to the extent that it is held by a court to be justified) or to give a notice of compliance or challenging justification[214]; (c) he fails to comply with a notice against processing for the purposes of direct marketing[215]; or (d) he fails to comply with a notice, or to provide required information, in relation to automated decision-taking.[216]

Seventh principle

49A–74 Appropriate technical and organisational measures must be taken against unauthorised or unlawful processing of personal data and against accidental loss or destruction of, or damage to, personal data.[217] Having regard to the state of technological development and the cost of implementing any measures, the measures must ensure a level of security appropriate to (a) the harm that might result from such unauthorised or unlawful processing or accidental loss, destruction or damage as are mentioned in this principle, and (b) the nature of the data to be protected.[218] The data controller must take reasonable steps to ensure the reliability of any employees of his who have access to the personal data.[219]

Where processing of personal data is carried out by a data processor on behalf of a data controller, the data controller must, in order to comply with the seventh principle, choose a data processor providing sufficient guarantees in respect of the

---

[209] DPA 1998 Sch.1, Pt II, para.7.
[210] DPA 1998 Sch.1, Pt I, para.5.
[211] DPA 1998 Sch.1, Pt I, para.6.
[212] DPA 1998 Sch.1, Pt II, para.8.
[213] See DPA 1998 s.7.
[214] See DPA 1998 s.10.
[215] See DPA 1998 s.11.
[216] See DPA 1998 s.12.
[217] DPA 1998 Sch.1, Pt I, para.7.
[218] DPA 1998 Sch.1, Pt II, para.9.
[219] DPA 1998 Sch.1, Pt II, para.10.

technical and organisational security measures governing the processing to be carried out, and take reasonable steps to ensure compliance with those measures. Furthermore, in such a case the data controller is not to be regarded as complying with this principle unless the processing is carried out under a contract made or evidenced in writing, requiring the data processor to comply with obligations equivalent to those imposed on a data controller by this principle, and under which the data processor is to act only on instructions from the data controller.[220]

Eighth principle

Personal data must not be transferred to a country or territory outside the EEA unless that country or territory ensures an adequate level of protection for the rights and freedoms of data subjects in relation to the processing of personal data.[221]   **49A–75**

An adequate level of protection is one which is adequate in all the circumstances of the case, having regard in particular to (a) the nature of the personal data, (b) the country or territory of origin of the information contained in the data, (c) the country or territory of final destination of that information, (d) the purposes for which and period during which the data are intended to be processed, (e) the law in force in the country or territory in question, (f) the international obligations of that country or territory, (g) any relevant codes of conduct or other rules which are enforceable in that country or territory (whether generally or by arrangement in particular cases), and (h) any security measures taken in respect of the data in that country or territory.[222]

This principle does not apply in certain circumstances, including where the data subject has given his consent to the transfer; the transfer is necessary in relation to contractual matters or for reasons of substantial public interest, legal proceedings or advice; the transfer is necessary in order to protect the vital interests of the data subject; the transfer is made on terms which are of a kind approved by the Commissioner as ensuring adequate safeguards for the rights and freedoms of data subjects and the transfer has been authorised by the Commissioner as being made in such a manner as to ensure adequate safeguards for the rights and freedoms of data subjects.[223]   **49A–76**

In the *Lindqvist* case,[224] although the defendant had placed personal data on her website, which was hosted within the EU but could be viewed by anyone, anywhere in the world with free access to the internet, it was held that there was no transfer to a third country in breach of the local equivalent of the eighth principle.   **49A–77**

---

[220] DPA 1998 Sch.1, Pt II, paras 11 to 12.
[221] DPA 1998 Sch.1, Pt I, para.8. See the US–EU and EU–US Safe Harbor Framework, *http:// ec.europa.eu/justice/policies/privacy/thridcountries/adequacy-faq1_en.htm* (stet). See also *In re Warrant to Search a Certain Email Account Controlled & Maintained by Microsoft Corp*, 15 F. Supp. 3d 466 (S.D.N.Y. 2014) and *Maximillian Schrems v Data Protection Commissioner*, Case C-362/14 (ECJ).
[222] DPA 1998 Sch.1, Pt II, para.13.
[223] DPA 1998 Sch.1, Pt II, para.14 and Sch.4.
[224] *Criminal Proceedings against Lindqvist*, Case C-101/01; [2004] Q.B. 1014; [2004] All E.R. (EC) 561; see above, para.49A–58.

Enforcement

49A–78 The Commissioner has a wide range of powers and remedies for enforcement of the rights and duties in the DPA 1998 and the Privacy and Electronic Communications (EC Directive) Regulations 2003.[225] He has civil enforcement powers and powers to prosecute and apply for warrants of entry.

The Commissioner's civil powers include the following:

(i) the Commissioner may require data controllers to provide him with information by means of the service of an information notice[226];
(ii) the Commissioner may serve assessment notices on certain data controllers[227];
(iii) the Commissioner may serve enforcement notices on data controllers who have contravened or are contravening any of the data protection principles[228];
(iv) the Commissioner may serve monetary penalty notices on data controllers where there have been serious contraventions of the data protection principles that are of a kind likely to cause substantial damage or substantial distress.[229]

The Commissioner also has powers to prosecute for certain offences.

---

[225] 2003/2426.
[226] DPA 1998 s.43.
[227] DPA 1998 s.41A.
[228] DPA 1998 s.40.
[229] DPA 1998 s.55A.

CHAPTER 50

TAXATION OF PERSONAL REPRESENTATIVES

B.—INHERITANCE TAX

The transfer of value on death

[Add at end of fn.12]

50–04

Section 1 of the Presumption of Death Act 2013 (which came into force on October 1, 2014) applies where is a person who is missing is thought to have died or has not been known to have been alive for a period of at least seven years. The High Court may make a declaration that a missing person is presumed to have died at a particular date and time.

The deceased's estate

[Add to fn.16 following "O'Neill v IRC 1998 S.T.C. (S.C.D.) 110"]

50–05

; *Matthews v HMRC* [2013] W.T.L.R. 99.

Excluded property

[Add at end of fn.22]

50–06

The draft Finance Bill 2015 extends this exemption, for transfers of value made on or after December 3, 2014, to all medals and decorations awarded to the armed services or to emergency services personnel, and to awards made by the Crown for achievements and service in public life, provided that they do not consist of money.

The value of a person's estate

[Add at end of fn.29]

50–07

The severable joint interest that the deceased had, immediately before her death, in a terminal illness benefit under a life insurance policy that she had taken out with her husband had no value immediately before her death because it would cease to exist if (as happened) death occurred without a claim to that benefit being made: *Lim v Walia* [2014] EWCA Civ 1076.

50–09   *[Add at end of fn.32]*

The costs of settling a probate action in respect of the deceased's will are not deductible as the deceased would have been under no liability to make such a payment before his death (*Silber v HMRC* [2013] W.T.L.R. 113).

[Add at end of the paragraph the following new text and fnn.42a–42h]

50–09A   The Finance Act 2013 amended the Inheritance Tax Act 1984 to restrict the deduction of the following liabilities for Inheritance Tax purposes with effect in relation to transfers of value made, or treated as made, on or after July 17, 2013:

(a)   a liability attributable to financing directly or indirectly the acquisition of any excluded property, or the maintenance, or an enhancement of, the value of any such property, or property which has become excluded property, unless specified exceptions apply[42a];

(b)   a liability incurred on or after April 6, 2013 attributable to financing directly or indirectly the acquisition of property attracting business property, agricultural property, or woodlands, relief, or an enhancement of the value of such property: the liability is taken, so far as possible, to reduce the value of the relievable property before relief applies, so that only the excess value can be set against other assets[42b]; and

(c)   a liability, affecting the deceased's estate on death, unless the liability is discharged on or after death, out of the estate or from excluded property owned by the deceased immediately before the death, in money or money's worth, or, if it is not so discharged, there is a real commercial reason for the liability not being discharged, and securing a tax advantage is not the main purpose, or one of the main purposes, of leaving the liability undischarged.[42c]

The Finance Act 2014 introduced a further limitation on the deduction of liabilities in relation to transfers of value made, or treated as made, on or after July 17, 2014. A liability which is attributable, in whole or in part, to finance, directly or indirectly, a balance on a UK bank account, denominated in a foreign currency, held by an individual who is neither domiciled, nor resident in the UK,[42d] can only be taken into account so far as the liability exceeds the relevant balance, and only so far as the excess does not arise for a tax avoidance purpose or to increase the value of the liability.[42e]

Consequential amendments apply to provide a deemed order of discharge, in respect of transfers of value made or treated as made on or after July 17, 2013, where a liability has been partially discharged (a) before death when determining the value of a person's estate immediately before death[42f]; (b) in any other case

---

[42a] Inheritance Tax Act 1984 s.162A.

[42b] Inheritance Tax Act 1984 s.162B.

[42c] Inheritance Tax Act 1984 s.175A.

[42d] The value of such a bank account is left out of account in determining the value of a person's estate on death: Inheritance Tax Act 1984 s.157.

[42e] Inheritance Tax Act 1984 s.162AA.

[42f] Inheritance Tax Act 1984 s.162C(1A).

where a liability is discharged in part before the time in relation to which the question as to whether or how to take it into account arises[42g]; and (c) on or after death out of the estate or from excluded property owned by a deceased person immediately before death, in money or money's worth.[42h]

The Inheritance Tax (Delivery of Accounts) (Excepted Estates) Regulations 2004 were amended by the Inheritance Tax (Delivery of Accounts) (Excepted Estates) (Amendment) Regulations 2014 with effect in relation to deaths occurring on or after April 1, 2014 to take into account the above changes to the rules on deducting liabilities. Fewer estates will now qualify as excepted from the obligation to submit a full IHT 400. HMRC has also published updated IHT400 Notes.

Exempt transfers and other reliefs

[Add after first sentence of fn.55]   **50–14**

From March 13, 2014 a reference in legislation to a person who is married includes a reference to a person who is married to a person of the same sex: Marriage (Same Sex Couples) Act 2013 s.11, Sch.3, para.1.

[Add after second sentence of fn.55 (following "s.18(2)")]

On or after April 6, 2013 the exemption is increased from £55,000 to the amount of the prevailing nil rate band less any amounts previously taken into account for the purposes of the spouse exemption. A written election may now be made in writing to HMRC by a non-domiciled person or by his or her personal representatives (within two years of death or such longer period as HMRC may allow) whose spouse or civil partner is or was domiciled in the UK on a specified date, for that person to be treated as domiciled in the UK for IHT purposes, provided that certain conditions are satisfied: see Inheritance Tax Act 1984 s.267ZA and 267ZB.

[Add at end of fn.67]   **50–16**

HMRC have with effect from January 23, 2013 revised Inheritance Tax Manual IHTM 33026, relating to IHTA 1984 s.191 (sale of land within four years of death) to make clear that a claim to substitute a higher sale price where the estate is taxable must be rejected as being invalid.

Alterations of dispositions on death

[In fn.70. replace "McCutcheon on Inheritance Tax, 5th edn (2009), paras 8–115   **50–18**
to 8–173. See paras 8–132 and 8–166" with the following]

McCutcheon on Inheritance Tax, 6th edn, paras 8–115 to 8–174. See paras 8–132 and 8–167

[42g] Inheritance Tax Act 1984 s.162C(2).
[42h] Inheritance Tax Act 1984 s.175A(7).

[In fn.71, replace "McCutcheon on Inheritance Tax, 5th edn (2009), paras 8–175 to 8–184" with the following]

McCutcheon on Inheritance Tax, 6th edn, paras 8–176 to 8–175

[In fn.72, replace "McCutcheon on Inheritance Tax, 5th edn (2009), paras 8–185 to 8–187" with the following]

McCutcheon on Inheritance Tax, 6th edn, paras 8–186 to 8–188

[In fn.73, replace "McCutcheon on Inheritance Tax, 5th edn (2009), paras 8–188 to 8–204" with the following]

See *McCutcheon on Inheritance Tax*, 6th edn, paras 8–189 to 8–205 The draft Finance Bill 2015 amends IHTA 1984 s.144 so as to provide that the provisions of s.65(4) which prevent a charge to tax arising in the first three months after a settlement commenced, or within a 10-year anniversary, shall not apply to appointments out of property settled by will, in respect of deaths on or after December 10, 2014.

[In fn.74, replace "McCutcheon on Inheritance Tax, 5th edn (2009), paras 8–205 to 8–206" with the following]

McCutcheon on Inheritance Tax, 6th edn, paras 8–206 to 8–207.

[In fn.75, replace "McCutcheon on Inheritance Tax, 5th edn (2009), paras 8–205 to 8–206" with the following]

McCutcheon on Inheritance Tax, 5th edn (2009), paras 8–208 to 8–215

Transferable nil rate band

50–27 *[Add at end of fn.91]*

A legacy giving "such sum as is at the date of my death the amount of my unused nil rate band for Inheritance Tax" included the transferable nil rate band of the testatrix's husband which had been claimed by her personal representatives, since the statutory consequence of claiming the nil rate band is to increase the nil rate band retrospectively to death: *The Woodland Trust v Loring* [2014] EWCA Civ 1314. In *RSPCA v Sharp* [2011] 1 W.L.R. 980 a gift of the maximum amount the testator could give without inheritance tax being payable was construed as a gift of only the unused nil rate band after deducting the value of a property given under other provisions in the will, rather than of the entire nil rate band. In *Brooke v Purton* [2014] EWHC 547 a nil rate band legacy which had been drafted in such a way as to exclude property attracting business property relief was construed, with the aid of extrinsic evidence pursuant to s.21 of the Administration of Justice Act 1982, as if it included business assets. All these cases proceed on the basis that the nil rate band legacy extends to the maximum amount (no more, and no less) that can be given without any Inheritance Tax liability. For comments on *RSPCA v*

Sharp, see (2011) *Private Client Business* 95; (2011) 9 *Trust Quarterly Review* Issue 3 (Sept) 13; Issue 4 (Dec) 9.

Recovery and appeals

[Add in the first paragraph following "determination.[194]"]   **50–62**

However, the draft Finance Bill 2015 includes provisions allowing HMRC to recover tax and tax credit debts of £1,000 or more directly from taxpayer bank and building society accounts subject to certain safeguards.

Penalties

[Add at end of fn.201]   **50–63**

Executors were not liable for filing an inaccurate return, which omitted to contain details of certain gifts made by the deceased within seven years prior to his death, where they had made suitable enquiries, but the relevant information had been withheld: *Hutchings v HMRC* [2015] UKFTT 0009 (TC). However, the beneficiary who had withheld the relevant information was liable for a penalty pursuant to Finance Act 2007 Sch.24, para.1A.

C.—CAPITAL GAINS TAX ON DEATH

Death not a chargeable event for CGT

[Add at end of fn.219]   **50–68**

The tax-free uplift on death applies to a disabled person's interest, which is a deemed interest in possession for the purposes of IHTA 1984 s.89B(1)(a) or (b), in relation to deaths on or after December 5, 2013: IHTA 1984 s.72(6). Generally, there is no uplift if the settled property reverts to the original settlor on the death of the life tenant. The deemed disposal on death will be at no gain and no loss: TCGA 1992 s.73(1)(b).

Disposals by personal representatives

[Delete "ordinary residence" and "or ordinarily resident" from this paragraph]   **50–71**

[Add at end of fn.229]

as amended by the Finance Act 2013 s.219(1) and Sch.46, Pt 3, so as to exclude any reference to the deceased's ordinary residence, in relation to a person's liability to CGT for the tax year 2013–14 or any subsequent year. Section 2(1A)(b) TCGA 1992 provides that the residence condition is, in the case of personal representatives of a deceased person, that the single and continuing body mentioned in s.62(3) is resident in the United Kingdom. The residence of the personal representatives is, in turn, dependent upon the residence of the deceased at the date of death: s.62(3). In relation to deaths on or after April 6, 2013 the statutory residence test contained in Sch.46 of the Finance Act 2014 applies to determine the residence of the deceased and, therefore, of the personal representatives.

50–72   *[Add at end of paragraph the following new text and fn.232a]*

Executors are entitled to claim that there has been a deemed disposal and reacquisition at market value, where an asset has become of negligible value, thereby crystallising an allowable loss.[232a]

[232a] Under Taxation of Chargeable Gains Act 1992: see *Drown v HMRC* [2014] UKFIT 892 (TC).

CHAPTER 51

THE PAYMENT OF DEBTS

C.—SOLVENT ESTATES

Debts charged on property—s.35 Administration of Estates Act 1925

Section 35—applies subject to documented evidence of a contrary intention

[Add new fn.66a after the word "will"]

51–17

⁶⁶ᵃ See, e.g. *Re Ross (Deceased)* [2013] EWHC 2724 (Ch).

D.—INSOLVENT ESTATES

Meaning of insolvent estate

[Add at end of fn.190]

51–41

And see also *Joint Stock Co Aeroflot – Russian Airlines v Berezovsky* [2013] EWHC 4348 (Ch) where the court declined to make orders for access to the estate's information and documents on the applications of receivers and an administrator appointed for limited purposes until the court had decided whether the estate was solvent or insolvent (and who should represent it).

Choice of method of administration

Challenging transactions

[Add at end of fn.240]

51–50

; as to ratification, see also *National Westminster Bank PLC v Lucas* [2013] EWHC 770 (Ch) where payments were subsequently ratified under s.284(4) of the Act. The payments related to funeral expenses, legal expenses and inheritance tax liabilities made before and after the executor became aware that the estate of the television personality Jimmy Savile might become insolvent due to incoming and prospective personal injury claims.

[Add at end of fn.245]

As to the scope and remedies under s.423 of the Act, as well as its inter-relationship with s.10 of the Inheritance (Provision for Family and Dependants)

Act 1975 and s.37 of the Matrimonial Causes Act 1973, see *B v IB* [2013] EWHC 3755 (Fam).

The valuation of future and contingent liabilities

51–54   *[Add at end of fn.272]*

See also *National Westminster Bank PLC v Lucas* [2014] EWHC 653 (Ch) and *National Westminster Bank PLC v Lucas* [2014] EWCA Civ 1632 where the court approved a scheme agreed between the executor and creditors to facilitate the resolution and quantification of a large number of personal injury claims against the estate of Jimmy Savile. Court approval of distributions under the scheme would exhaust the estate, so that the scheme effectively replaced the rights of claimants to bring court proceedings.

CHAPTER 53

DEBTS DUE TO AND FROM REPRESENTATIVES AND BENEFICIARIES

B.—LEGACY BY A CREDITOR TO HIS DEBTOR

Rule in *Cherry v Boultbee*—contribution and set-off

[Add at end of fn.53]

; *In re Lehman Bros International (Europe) (in administration) (No 4)* [2014] EWHC 704 (Ch); [2015] Ch. 1.

Qualification: mutual claims

[Add at end of fn.69]

; In *re Lehman Bros International (Europe) (in administration) (No 4)* [2014] EWHC 704 (Ch); [2015] Ch. 1.

[Insert after first sentence of fn.70]

, see also *In re Lehman Bros International (Europe) (in administration) (No 4)* [2014] EWHC 704 (Ch); [2015] Ch. 1.

B.—APPOINTMENT OF DEBTOR AS EXECUTOR OR ADMINISTRATOR

Rule in *Strong v Bird*

[Insert after first sentence of fn.100]

See also *Day v Royal College of Music and another* [2014] Ch. 211.

53–10

53–12

53–20

CHAPTER 55

POWERS OF THE REPRESENTATIVE

A.—INTRODUCTION

Bases of a representative's powers

Statute

55–04 *[In the final paragraph, add new fn.18a after the words "Trustee Act 1925"]*

[18a] Sections 31 and 32 of the Trustee Act 1925 have been amended by ss.8, 9, and 10 of the Inheritance and Trustees' Powers Act 2014 to which reference should be made.

55–05 *[In fn.19 replace "Lewin on Trusts, 17th edn (2000)" with the following]*

Lewin on Trusts, 19th edn (2015)

Structure of this chapter

55–06 *[Delete the second paragraph but retain the bullet point list]*

B.—GETTING IN AND VALUING THE ESTATE

Power to compromise and compound

55–09 *[In fn.38 replace the final sentence with the following]*

See *Lewin on Trusts*, 19th edn (2015), para.36–091 onwards

[In fn.42 delete the full stop at the end of the third sentence and insert the following]

; but not to all claims by beneficiaries: see *Lewin on Trusts*, 19th edn (2015), para.36–097 onwards.

Power to value property

55–10 *[Replace the first sentence of the paragraph with the following]*

A representative has power from time to time by duly qualified agents to ascertain and fix the value of any property in the estate in such manner as he thinks proper.

[Insert the following at the beginning of fn.47]

Trustee Act 1925

Powers as to reversionary interests

[Replace the first paragraph with the following new text and fn.49]   **55–11**

Where the estate includes any share or interest in property that is not presently vested in the representative, or the proceeds of the sale of any such property, or any other thing in action, the representative has power, upon the same falling into possession or becoming payable or transferable, to:

(a) agree or ascertain the amount or value thereof or any part thereof in such manner as he thinks fit;
(b) accept any authorised investments in or towards satisfaction thereof at the market or current value or upon a valuation or estimate of value which he may think fit;
(c) allow deductions for such duties, costs, charges and expenses as they think proper and reasonable; and
(d) execute any release so as effectually to discharge all accountable parties from all liability within the scope of the release.[49]

C.—GENERAL ADMINISTRATIVE POWERS

Power of investment

[Replace text in fn.73 with the following]   **55–17**

See, e.g. *Lewin on Trusts*, 19th edn (2015). See also *Snell's Equity*, 33rd edn (2015), para.29-007 onwards.

D.—POWER TO SELL, GRANT OPTIONS, MORTGAGE AND LEASE

Power to mortgage

Common law

[In fn 141 replace "Megarry & Wade: Law of Real Property, 7th edn (2008), para.24–041" with the following]   **55–30**

Megarry & Wade: Law of Real Property, 8th edn (2012), para.24-041.

Representative may not become lessee of the estate

[In fn.167 delete all the text after Re Edwards [1982] Ch. 30]   **55–36**

---

[49] Trustee Act 1925 s.22(1) (which applies to a representative, see s.68(17) of that Act).

Representative may in certain circumstances purchase the reversion

55-37   *[In fn.178 replace "Lewin on Trusts, 18th edn (2011), paras 20–01 and 20–27" with the following]*

Lewin on Trusts, 19th edn (2015), para.20–001 onwards.

E.—PROTECTION AFFORDED TO PURCHASERS FROM A REPRESENTATIVE

Overreaching equitable interests on sale of land

55-50   *[In fn.234 replace the final sentence with the following]*

See also *Megarry & Wade: Law of Real Property*, 8th edn (2012), para.6-052 onwards.

F.—POWERS RELATING TO DISTRIBUTION AND BENEFICIARIES

Power to permit possession before assent

55-52   *[In the first sentence of para.55–52 replace "prejudging" with the following]*

prejudicing

Power to appropriate

Statutory power

55-56   *[Replace the text of para.(iv) with the following]*

(iv) no consent is required where no deputy has been appointed for a person who lacks capacity to consent and where the appropriation is of an investment authorised by law or by the will, if any;

[Replace the text of fn.253 with the following]

Under s.41(1)(ii) of the Administration of Estates Act 1925 (as amended), if the person whose consent is required is an infant or lacks capacity (within the meaning of the Mental Capacity Act 2005) to give the consent, it shall be given on his behalf by his parents or parent, testamentary or other guardian, or a person appointed as deputy for him by the Court of Protection, or if, in the case of an infant, there is no such parent or guardian, by the court on the application of his next friend (now referred to as litigation friend: CPR 1998, Pt 21).

I.—POWERS WHERE THERE ARE JOINT REPRESENTATIVES

General rule—acts of one joint representative are binding

[Add at end of fn.304]

55–69

This paragraph was accepted as a statement of the law in *Birdseye and Cooke v Roythorne & Co. and Ors* [2015] EWHC 1003 (Ch.).

[Replace the text of fn.318 with the following]

See *Hammersmith L.B.C. v Monk* [1992] 1 A.C. 478; and there is no breach of trust as between the joint tenants: *Crawley B.C. v Ure* [1996] Q.B. 13; *Notting Hill Housing Trust v Brackley* [2002] H.L.R. 10. As will be seen from these cases, this principle applies to all joint tenants, not merely to personal representatives. The notice to quit must comply with the terms of the tenancy and any applicable statutory provisions: *Hounslow London Borough Council v Pilling* [1993] 1 W.L.R. 1242; *Osei-Bonsu v Wandsworth London Borough Council* [1999] 1 W.L.R. 1011.

Acts binding on the co-representative

[At the end of the paragraph (after fn.338) add the following sentence and new fn.338a]

55–72

The act of one co-representative in disclosing privileged documents may be sufficient to waive the representatives' privilege in those documents.[338a]

K.—DELEGATION OF POWERS

[Replace the text in fn.395 with the following]

55–85

See also *Lewin on Trusts*, 19th edn (2015), para.29–093 onwards (Delegation of Powers) and para.36–009 onwards. (Power to Employ Agents).

The general rule against delegation

[Replace the second sentence of fn.400 with the following]

55–86

As to the employment of agents, see *Lewin on Trusts*, 19th edn (2015), para.36–009 onwards.

Short-term delegation by an individual representative

[In fn.404 replace "Lewin on Trusts, 18th edn (2011), para.29–95" with the following]

55–87

Lewin on Trusts, 19th edn (2015), para.29–095.

[338a] *Birdseye and Cooke v Roythorne & Co. and Ors* [2015] EWHC 1003 (Ch.).

Delegation by representatives collectively under the Trustee Act 2000 (since January 2001)

Power to appoint agents

55–90 *[In fn.420 replace "Lewin on Trusts, 18th edn (2011), para.36–13 et seq" with the following]*

Lewin on Trusts, 19th edn (2015), para.36–013 onwards.

Duty to review

55–94 *[In fn.434 replace "Lewin on Trusts, 18th edn (2011)" with the following]*

Lewin on Trusts, 19th edn (2015).

CHAPTER 56

REMUNERATION AND PAYMENTS

A.—REMUNERATION

The rule in equity

[Remove reference in fn.1 to Lewin on Trusts]   **56–02**

[Replace text in fn.3 with the following]

For more on the remuneration of trustees, see *Lewin on Trusts*, 19th edn (2015), para.20–192 onwards.

Authorisation by will

[Replace last sentence of fn.13 with the following]   **56–05**

For more on clauses permitting a representative to charge, see *Lewin on Trusts,* 19th edn (2015), para.20–204 onwards.

Remuneration under the express authority of the court

[Add at end of fn.42]   **56–09**

In *Perotti v Watson* [2002] EWCA Civ 771; [2002] W.T.L.R. 913 a personal representative had been allowed remuneration but at a reduced rate to reflect both the fact that a professional executor who takes a grant of a will with no charging clause can expect a degree of irrecoverable costs, and the executor's ineptitude. Permission to appeal the judge's decision to allow remuneration in those circumstances at all was refused.

In *Brudenell-Bruce v Moore* [2014] EWHC 3679 (Ch) at [225] to [236], the court referred to the guidance in Lewin on Trusts (18th edn) at 20–175, and refused retrospectively to authorise remuneration for a lay trustee despite the role proving far more onerous than he had anticipated. Interestingly, his professional co-trustee was not overtly criticised for allowing the remuneration to be paid at the time.

Statutory authority for remuneration

Trustee Act 2000

56–13 *[Replace fn.64 with the following]*

See para.56–06, above.

Other statutory provision

56–14 *[Add new section 56–14A after para.56–14]*

Quantum of remuneration

56–14A The quantum of remuneration allowed may depend on the basis on which it is allowed. Where it is allowed under the will itself, it is a matter of construction of the charging clause in question. Under the Trustee Act 2000, "reasonable remuneration" is defined as such remuneration as is reasonable in the circumstances for the provision of those services to or on behalf of that estate.

In *Pullan v Wilson* [2014] EWHC 126 (Ch); [2014] W.T.L.R. 669 the court considered how it should approach assessment of what remuneration would be reasonable. Although much of the case related to the assessment of hourly rates, the court (at [58]) ultimately eschewed reliance on strict mathematic formulae in favour of an evaluative assessment. Expert evidence of what is reasonable for an accountant to charge was admitted. In that case, the beneficiaries were held to have acquiesced in the rates being charged by the defendant trustee, and were therefore debarred from challenging them. The judge emphasised (at [54]) that professional trustees would be well advised to identify their charging rates clearly before accepting their office, which in the case of personal representatives may mean at the time the will is drafted.

Questions of remuneration will be often be determined by the Master: see *Brudenell-Bruce v Moore* [2014] EWHC 3679 (Ch) at [238].

CHAPTER 57

THE LIABILITY FOR A REPRESENTATIVE'S OWN ACTS

A.—LIABILITY FOR WASTE (*DEVASTAVIT*)

Devastavit, breach of trust and the liability to account

Representatives as trustees; representatives distinguished from trustees

[Replace fn.15 text with the following]   **57–06**

See *Snell's Equity*, 33rd edn (2015), para.21-048, Parry and Kerridge, *Law of Succession*, 12th edn, para.24–50 onwards and Hanbury & Martin, *Modern Equity*, 19th edn (2012), para.2–014 onwards.

Time for assessing the loss to the estate

[Add at end of fn.35]   **57–08**

See also *AIB Group (UK) plc v Mark Redler & Co Solicitors* [2014] UKSC 58; [2014] 3 W.L.R. 1367.

Unauthorised or unnecessary payments

Examples

[Add at end of fn.88]   **57–15**

; see also *National Westminster Bank v Luke Lucas, Roger Bodley, PI, Denise Coles, Amanda McKenna, Secretary of State for Health BBC* [2014] EWHC 1683.

Conversion of estate into money

Neglect to convert

[Add at end of fn.122]   **57–21**

See also *AIB Group (UK) plc v Mark Redler & Co Solicitors* [2014] UKSC 58; [2014] 3 W.L.R. 1367.

Remedies against the representative

57–39   *[Add at end of fn.199]*

See also *AIB Group (UK) plc v Mark Redler & Co Solicitors* [2014] UKSC 58; [2014] 3 W.L.R. 1367.

B.—ACCOUNTABILITY FOR PROFITS

Representative's liability to account for breaches of duty

57–41   *[Replace fn.207 text with the following]*

See *Regal (Hastings) Ltd v Gulliver* [1942] 1 All E.R. 378. *Phipps v Boardman* [1967] 2 A.C. 46; *Tito v Waddell* (No.2) [1977] Ch. 106 at 225, 240. *Re Thompson* [1986] Ch. 99; and *Bristol & West Building Society v Mothew* [1998] Ch. 1 at 18. See also *FHR European Ventures LLP v Cedar Capital Partners LLC* [2014] Ch. 1; *Brudenell-Bruce v Moore* [2012] W.T.L.R. 9311. For detailed discussions of the nature of fiduciary duties (including the rules against unauthorised profits and conflicts of interest), see *Lewin on Trusts*, 19th edn, Ch.20 and *Snell's Equity*, 33rd edn (2015), Ch.7.

I.—LIABILITY IN CRIMINAL LAW

Theft by dishonestly appropriating property

57–104   *[Add at end of fn.480]*

overruled by *FHR European Ventures LLP and others v Cedar Capital Partners LLC* [2014] UKSC 45; [2015] A.C. 250 on a separate point.

[Add at end of fn.489]

See also *O'Kelly v Davies* [2014] EWCA Civ 1606.

J.—ANTI-MONEY LAUNDERING AND COUNTER TERRORIST FINANCING

Money laundering in relation to the administration of estates

Money laundering; the distribution of the estate

57–123   *[Replace fn.539 text with the following]*

www.hm-treasury.gov.uk/fin_sanctions_index.htm [Accessed February 1, 2015].

CHAPTER 58

FAMILY PROVISION: THE PURPOSE AND EXTENT OF THE LEGISLATION

C.—THE FUTURE

[Replace para.58–03 with the following new text and fn.20]

58–03

Following a wide-ranging consultation the Law Commission published its report on *Intestacy and Family Provision Claims on Death*.[20] This report set out its proposals for reforming the law, inter alia, on family provision and included two draft bills: The Inheritance and Trustees' Powers Bill and the Inheritance (Cohabitants) Bill. The relevant parts of the former contain revisions to the law on family provision intended to permit those treated as children of the deceased outside a marriage or civil partnership to apply and to make it easier for dependants to succeed. In addition, it was proposed that awards may be made against assets governed by the English law of succession of those domiciled elsewhere than in England and Wales. These were seen as fairly uncontroversial. The second draft bill contained significant revisions of the law on intestacy and family provision as it relates to cohabitants. Undoubtedly correctly, the Law Commission anticipated that the latter were likely to be much more controversial: it was for this reason they were included in a separate bill so that the other revisions would not be delayed or remain unimplemented as a result of such controversy. As trailed in the consultation paper, the proposals are that "qualifying" cohabitants should have the same rights on intestacy as spouses.

As anticipated, a new Act, the Inheritance and Trustees' Powers Act 2014 (the "2014 Act") came fully into force on October 1, 2014 albeit with some changes to the draft bill. The changes to the 1975 Act are all found in Sch.2 of the 2014 Act save for the revised provisions on the determination of when a grant is first taken out for the purposes of time limits: this is found in Sch.3, para.2. Many of the changes simply make explicit the current practices of the courts. The changes, in brief, include the following (references to paragraph numbers are to those in Sch.2 of the 2014 Act unless otherwise stated):

i)   Widening the category of children who may apply pursuant to s.1(d) of the 1975 Act to include any child in relation to whom the deceased stood as a parent and who was treated as a child of the family whether or not the deceased was married to, or in a civil partnership with, that child's parent (para.2). This extends the class of applicants to non-biological children of

---

[20] Law Com. No.331.

cohabiting couples who could previously have claimed only as dependants. It also extends the class to any case where the deceased was the sole carer of a non-biological child;

ii) For the purposes of claims by dependants (s.1(1)(e) of the 1975 Act) maintenance now includes any substantial contribution in money or money's worth unless made pursuant to a commercial arrangement. This avoids the need for arid arguments over whether or not the applicant's contributions to the household matched or exceeded those of the deceased (para.3);

iii) The power of the court to vary will or intestacy trusts is now express (para.4(2)) and the court, when considering the value of the estate net of all liabilities including inheritance tax, may assume that the order has already been made (para.4(3)). This reflects current usual practice when ascertaining what everyone would get in the light of a particular order;

iv) In claims by surviving spouses the court is now expressly directed that the amount that such a spouse might have received had the marriage ended in divorce rather than death places neither an upper nor a lower limit on what may be awarded reflecting the principle set out in *P v P* [2004] EWHC 2944 (Fam); [2006] 1 F.L.R. 431 and applied in *Lilleyman v Lilleyman* [2012] EWHC 821 (Ch); [2013] Ch. 225 (para.5(2));

v) As far as applications by children of the deceased or those treated as children are concerned, the court is now directed to have regard to whether or not the deceased had in fact maintained the applicant and the extent and basis of that maintenance as well as the extent to which the deceased had assumed responsibility for the applicant's maintenance (para.5(3)(a)). It remains to be seen whether this change of emphasis results in a substantive change in awards.

vi) In claims made by dependants, the additional matters to which the court is to have regard are amended in similar terms to the amendments in relation to applications by children (para.5(4));

vii) Section 4 (time limits) is amended to permit applications to be made prior to the grant of representation with respect to the subject estate being issued. This gives statutory effect to the decision in *Re Searle* [1949] Ch. 73 which held that the lack of a grant when the claim was commenced did not render the proceedings a nullity or otherwise invalidate them while removing the need to establish waiver (para.6).

viii) The final amendment in Sch.2 is to s.9 of the 1975 Act which deals with property held on a joint tenancy. The amendment disposes of the difficulty of valuing the deceased's interest in jointly owned property by providing that its value should be determined on the basis that the joint tenancy was severed immediately before death. This is discussed in more detail below.

A significant change that was not adopted was the proposal to allow orders to be made against property within the jurisdiction irrespective of the deceased's domicile.

58–12   *[Replace from "As stated above" to the end of that paragraph with the following text and fn.61]*

As stated above,[61] the Law Commission's proposal that awards could be made out of assets governed by the English law of succession irrespective of domicile has not been adopted in the 2014 Act.

E.—PRELIMINARY REQUIREMENTS

(c) Time for application

[Replace the first paragraph with the following new text and fnn.63–66]   **58–13**

An application for an order must not, except with the permission of the court,[63] be made[64] after the end of the period of six months from the date on which representation with respect to the estate of the deceased is first taken out. The purpose of this condition is to avoid delay in the administration and distribution of estates where there might be doubts as to whether an application is likely to be made. It thus affords some protection to the principle of the executor's year.[65] Section 23 of the 1975 Act, which deals with the determination of when a grant is first taken out has been amended by Sch.3, para.2 of the 2014 Act. In addition to i) the exclusion of grants limited to settled land or to trust property and ii) grants limited to real estate or to personal estate unless a grant limited to the remainder of the estate has previously been made or is made at the same time[66] being left out of account for these purposes, the 2014 Act provides that any grant that prevents the estate from being distributed and any grant or equivalent made outside of the United Kingdom should also be left out of account unless, in the latter case, the overseas grant is one sealed under s.2 of the Colonial Probates Act 1892 which counts as a grant made in the United Kingdom for the purposes of the 1975 Act. The amendment should prevent arid arguments about when a relevant grant has been taken out.

[Replace paragraphs 3, 4 and 5 with the following]

The question as to whether or not an effective grant is a precondition of making a claim has, not before time, been resolved by the 2014 Act: para.4 of Sch.2 adds the following words to the end of s.4 of the 1975 Act "(but nothing prevents the making of an application before such representation is first taken out)". Parties and practitioners need no longer trouble themselves with the cases of *Re Searle* and *Re McBroom*.

---

[61] See para.58–03, above.
[63] See *Hanbury v Hanbury* [1999] 2 F.L.R. 253 (delay may affect the substantive order).
[64] An application is made when it is issued, not when it is served: *Re Chittenden* [1970] 1 W.L.R. 1618.
[65] See Ch.69, below. The time-limit is not merely procedural. It is substantive. See *Re Salmon* [1981] Ch. 167 at 175.
[66] 1975 Act s.23, as unamended. It is submitted that, by analogy, other limited grants, for example those *ad colligenda bona* or *pendente lite*, do not count either: *Re Johnson* [1987] C.L.Y. 3882. Cf. *Re Bidie* [1949] Ch. 121. These grants are known as preservation grants under the Draft Probate Rules.

F.—EXTENSION OF TIME

58-14   *[Add at the end of the penultimate paragraph the following text and fn.84a]*

To those who have considered that time will usually be extended if the claim has merit, sufficient funds remain in the estate and no prejudice will be suffered by the beneficiaries, the Court of Appeal decision in *Berger v Berger*[84a] is a salutary reminder that excessive delay will not be tolerated. In that case, a claim by a surviving spouse, the Court of Appeal held that the claim had significant merit, the estate had not been fully distributed and there were sufficient funds remaining in it to satisfy the claim but refused permission to proceed out of time on the basis that the claim was six years out of time and there was no good reason for the delay. This suggests that the third guideline above carries significant weight, more than had previously been thought.

G.—FAILURE TO MAKE REASONABLE PROVISION

(c) Intestacy

58-17   *[Add the following at end of the paragraph]*

The changes to the rules on intestacy effected by the 2014 Act (covered elsewhere in this supplement) should reduce the number of claims by surviving spouses when the deceased left no issue. The changes may reduce the number of such claims even when there are issue as the surviving spouse will take an absolute interest in 50 per cent of the residue after provision for the fixed capital sum, rather than merely a life interest (s.1(1) of the 2014 Act).

H.—PERSONS ENTITLED TO APPLY

58-18   *[Replace (d) with the following]*

(d) any person (not being a child of the deceased) *who in relation to any marriage or civil partnership to which the deceased was at any time a party, or otherwise in relation to any family in which the deceased at any time stood in the role of a parent, was treated by the deceased as a child of the family*; the words in italics have replaced the previous provisions to permit claims by those treated as children by the deceased whatever the relationship between the deceased and the claimant or the latter's parent (para.2(2) of Sch.2 to the 2014 Act);

[Add at end of fn.97]

Of course, the term "spouse" now includes parties to same-sex marriages following the coming into force of the Marriage (Same Sex Couples) Act 2013.

[84a] [2013] EWCA Civ 1305.

(c) Cohabitants

[Add at end of fn.130]

Re Watson was recently applied in *Kaur v Dhaliwal* [2014] EWHC 1991 (Ch).

(e) A person treated by the deceased as a child of the family

[Replace the first sentence of the first paragraph with the following text and fn.140]

The concept of a "child of the family" had been imported from the matrimonial law.[140] However, the amendment introduced by the 2014 Act has significantly extended the permitted category of claimants to include those treated as children by the deceased whatever the relationship between the deceased and the claimant or the latter's parent (para.2(2) of Sch.2 to the 2014 Act). The addition of a new subs.(2A) makes it clear that a family can consist of only two people, the deceased and the applicant.

[Add the following words to the end of the second paragraph, following "marriage[142]"]

, where relevant.

[Replace subparagraph (a) in the third paragraph with the following]

"(a) to whether the deceased maintained the applicant and, if so, to the length of time for which and basis on which the deceased did so, and to the extent of the contribution made by way of maintenance;
(aa) to whether and, if so, to what extent the deceased assumed responsibility for the maintenance of the applicant;"

[In subparagraph (b) in the third paragraph replace the words "assuming and discharging that responsibility" with the following]

"maintaining or assuming responsibility for maintaining the applicant"

(f) A person maintained by the deceased

[Replace the second paragraph with the following text and fnn.145–150]

A significant amendment introduced by the 2014 Act will greatly improve the situation for some claimants in this category. The 2014 Act has amended s.1(3) of the Act so that it now reads as follows (the italicised words make the significant change):

---

[140] Matrimonial Causes Act 1973 s.52(1), although under that Act the child must have been treated as a child of the family by both parties to the marriage.

"For the purposes of subsection (1)(e) above, a person is to be treated as being maintained by the deceased (either wholly or partly, as the case may be) only if the deceased was making a substantial contribution in money or money's worth towards the reasonable needs of that person, other than a contribution made for full valuable consideration *pursuant to an arrangement of a commercial nature.*"

The applicant must establish, first, that the deceased was making a substantial contribution in money or money's worth towards the reasonable needs of the applicant, and secondly, that the deceased was so doing otherwise than for full valuable consideration pursuant to an arrangement of a commercial nature.[145] Prior to its amendment the Act had created difficulties for those in a mutually dependent relationship with the deceased as the unqualified reference to "full valuable consideration" was not merely intended to exclude maintenance provided under a contract.[146] This resulted in fine balancing computations involving the value of the normal exchange of support in the domestic sense, which was unsatisfactory.[147] Thus, where there had been mutual and financial interdependence between cohabitants the contribution of one of them had been held to be substantial[148] but where love and affection formed the primary motive there was no question of full valuable consideration.[149] The Court of Appeal did try to mitigate this by advocating a common sense approach in purely domestic situations.[150] Fortunately, such exercises will no longer be necessary.

[Replace paragraph 8 to the end inclusive with the following]

All these three situations are not only capable of coming within this category but now, without doubt, do so following the amendment, irrespective of whether or not the applicant was contributing to the deceased's maintenance also.

---

[145] *Jelley v Iliffe* [1981] Fam. 128; *Bishop v Plumley* [1991] 1 W.L.R. 582. *Re Wilkinson* [1978] Fam. 22 with the new amendment. The provision of accommodation may be a substantial contribution to needs: *Jelley, Bishop.*
[146] *Re Beaumont* [1980] Ch. 444; *Jelley v Iliffe* [1981] Fam. 128 notes; (1978) 94 L.Q.R. 175; (1978) 41 M.L.R. 352.
[147] *Bishop v Plumley* [1991] 1 W.L.R. 582; *Graham v Murphy* [1997] 1 F.L.R. 860; *Re B* [2000] Ch 662 CA.
[148] *Re Kirby* (1981) 11 Fam. Law. 210. This was prior to the introduction of the separate class of cohabitant applicant and the question of dependency, as such, does not arise in such cases today.
[149] *Bishop v Plumley* [1991] 1 W.L.R. 582 at 588.
[150] *Bishop v Plumley* [1991] 1 W.L.R. 582; *Graham v Murphy* [1997] 1 F.L.R. 860; *Re B* [2000] Ch 662 CA.

CHAPTER 59

FAMILY PROVISION: EXERCISE OF DISCRETION

A.—INTRODUCTION

[Add the following at the end of the first sentence]   **59-01**

and Sch.2 of the Inheritance and Trustees' Powers Act 2014 ("the 2014 Act")).

D.—PARTICULAR GUIDELINES: SURVIVING SPOUSES AND CIVIL PARTNERS

[Add the following at end of the paragraph]   **59-09**

The 2014 Act has added the words "but nothing requires the court to treat such
provision as setting an upper or lower limit on the provision which may be made
by an order under section 2" to the end of each of the final two sentences in s.1(3).
This gives statutory effect to the current practice of the courts (see *P v G, P v P*
[2004] EWHC 2944 (Fam); [2006] Fam 178 & *Lilleyman v Lilleyman* [2012]
EWHC 821 (Ch); [2013] Ch. 225).

The particular guidelines and the general guidelines

[Add at end of the last paragraph the following]   **59-10**

This principle has now been enshrined in the Act by the addition of the words
"but nothing requires the court to treat such provision as setting an upper or lower
limit on the provision which may be made by an order under section 2" to s.3(3)
(para.5(2) of Sch.2 to the 2014 Act).

G.—A CHILD OR PERSON TREATED AS A CHILD

[Replace the third paragraph with the following new text and fnn.125–126]   **59-19**

The Act, as amended by para.5(3) of Sch.2 to the 2014 Act, specifies four further
guidelines for applications by persons who were not children of the deceased, but
were treated as such.[125] The court is to have regard: (a) to whether the deceased
had in fact maintained the applicant and, if so, to the length of time for which and
basis on which the deceased did so, and to the extent of the contribution made by
way of maintenance; (aa) to whether and, if so, to what extent the deceased
assumed responsibility for the maintenance of the applicant; (b) to whether in

---

[125] 1975 Act s.3(3).

assuming and discharging that responsibility the deceased did so knowing that the applicant was not his own child; and (c) to the liability of any other person to maintain the applicant. These guidelines broadly correspond with those laid down for the matrimonial jurisdiction by the Matrimonial Causes Act 1973.[126]

[Replace the first sentence of the fourth paragraph with the following]

The introduction of the category of persons treated as children, as now further extended by the amendments introduced by the 2014 Act, raises the question whether their claims will be weaker than those of true children; in other words whether the blood (or adoptive) tie is of itself significant.

H.—A person maintained by the deceased

59–20 *[Replace the second sentence of the first paragraph with the following new text and fnn.137–138]*

However, as has already been mentioned,[137] its operation is restricted by its, formerly one and now, two particular guidelines,[138] whereby the court is directed to have regard to (a) the length of time for which and basis on which the deceased maintained the applicant, and to the extent of the contribution made by way of maintenance; and (b) to whether and, if so, to what extent the deceased assumed responsibility for the maintenance of the applicant. What practical effect this will have remains to be seen.

I.—Orders that the court can make

59–21 *[Add the following new text and fn.148a after subparagraph (f)]*

(g) an order varying any settlement i) made during the subsistence of a civil partnership formed by the deceased or ii) made in anticipation of the formation of such a civil partnership on the civil partners (including one made by will). The variation must be for the benefit of the surviving partner or any child of them both or any person treated as a child of the family by the deceased in relation to that civil partnership;

(h) an order varying for the applicant's benefit the trusts on which the deceased's estate is held (whether arising under the will or the law relating to intestacy, or both).[148a]

[Add the following new paragraph to the end of the section]

The 2014 Act has added a new subsection of s.2 of the 1975 Act. It provides as follows:

---

[126] Matrimonial Causes Act s.25(4), as amended.
[137] See para.58–24, above.
[138] As amended by para.5(4) of Sch.2 to the 2014 Act.
[148a] Added by para.4 of Sch.2 to the 2014 Act.

"(3A) In assessing for the purposes of an order under this section the extent (if any) to which the net estate is reduced by any debts or liabilities (including any inheritance tax paid or payable out of the estate), the court may assume that the order has already been made."

This gives statutory effect to the current practice of the court which is to take into account the effect on the net estate of any additional inheritance tax payable (or recoverable) as a result of monies being moved from (or to) a spouse or civil partner to (or from) an applicant in another category.

Variation of settlements

[Add at end of the first paragraph]   **59–27**

The provisions relating to variations of settlements in respect of civil partnerships effectively mirror those relating to anti- and post-nuptial settlements.

[Add the following new paragraph to the end of the section]

The new power to vary trusts arising on the deceased's death applies in relation to all categories of applicant. It provides the court with greater flexibility in that it is no longer necessary to create new trusts whether for minors or others as, presumably, beneficiaries can be added or removed, the trust fund subdivided and interests altered. See also fn.185.

J.—VARIATION OF ORDERS

[Add at end of fn.190]   **59–29**

A variation may be ordered even when the original order was made by consent: *Taylor v Bell* LTL March 12, 2015.

CHAPTER 60

FAMILY PROVISION: PROPERTY AVAILABLE FOR PROVISION

D.—STATUTORY NOMINATIONS

60–04   *[Add at end of fn.13]*

In *Goenka v Goenka* [2014] EWHC 2966 (Ch), the deceased had nominated his father to receive any death in service benefit payable as a result of his employment by the National Health Service. The sum subsequently paid to the father (£201,000) was held to fall within s.8(1) of the 1975 Act and was treated as part of the net estate. The court held that the term "any enactment" included regulations (the National Health Service Pension Scheme Regulations 1995) made under primary legislation, the Superannuation Act 1972.

F.—PROPERTY HELD ON JOINT TENANCY

60–06   *[Add the following text and fn.25a at end of the second paragraph]*

Nevertheless, the value attributable to the deceased's interest in jointly held property has continued to provide work for lawyers, particularly in relation to life policies: see *Lim v Walia*.[25a]

An amendment introduced by para.7(3) of Sch.2 to the 2014 Act seeks to address these difficulties. It introduces a new subs.(1A) to s.9 of the 1975 Act. This provides that where an order is made in respect of the deceased's interest in jointly held property, the share is to be treated as if the interest had been severed immediately before death and valued at the value it would have had at the date of the hearing of the application unless the court orders otherwise. This may not fully address the problem in *Lim v Walia* where the question was whether or not a half interest in a joint life policy had any value immediately prior to death. The Court of Appeal did not speak with one voice and this area of the law is ripe for resolution in the Supreme Court but may have much less effect in the light of the amendment to s.9.

[Delete the last two sentences of the fourth paragraph and replace them with the following text and fn.27]

The provisions preventing the court from extending time for such claims beyond the six-month post-grant period have been removed.[27]

[25a] [2014] EWCA Civ 1076.
[27] By para.7(3) of the 2014 Act.

CHAPTER 62

ADMINISTRATION PROCEEDINGS

B.—The history of the procedure

[Add new fn.2a at end of sentence "Because of these developments, full admin-istration orders became virtually obsolete."]

62–02

[2a] See per Patten L.J. in *Re Savile's Estate* [2014] EWCA Civ 1632 at para.[51]: "... a full administration order is a comparatively rare beast not least because after the making of the order the personal representatives can only exercise their powers with the sanction of the Court. Where an administration order is sought by a creditor or beneficiary as a means of coercing a recalcitrant or ineffective personal representative or trustee into action, the Court will usually seek to resolve the difficulty by appointing a new administrator."

C.—Types of application

Applications to the court by the personal representative

[Add the following new text and fnn.12a–12d after the paragraph beginning "References to trustees in CPR Pt 64 ... " and ending "... this procedure is described below.[12]"]

62–04

In *Public Trustee v Cooper*,[12a] Hart J. categorised the types of case in which the court is likely to be invited to express its own views on a trustee's proposed course of action:

"... when the court has to adjudicate on a course of action proposed or actually taken by trustees, there are at least four distinct situations (and there are no doubt numerous variations of those as well).

(1) The first category is where the issue is whether some proposed action is within the trustees' powers. That is ultimately a question of construction of the trust instrument or a statute or both. The practice of the Chancery Division is that a question of that sort must be decided in open court and only after hearing argument from both sides. It is not always easy to distinguish that situation from the second situation that I am coming to ...

(2) The second category is where the issue is whether the proposed course of action is a proper exercise of the trustees' powers where there is no real doubt as to the nature of the trustees' powers and the trustees have decided how they want to exercise them but, because the decision is particularly momentous, the trustees wish to obtain the blessing of the court for the action on which they have resolved and which is within their powers. Obvious examples of that, which

---

[12a] [2001] W.T.L.R. 901; the dictum was adopted from the unreported decision of Robert Walker J. in *Re Egerton Trust Retirement Benefit Scheme*.

are very familiar in the Chancery Division, are a decision by trustees to sell a family estate or to sell a controlling holding in a family company. In such circumstances there is no doubt at all as to the extent of the trustees' powers nor is there any doubt as to what the trustees want to do but they think it prudent, and the court will give them their costs of doing so, to obtain the court's blessing on a momentous decision. In a case like that, there is no question of surrender of discretion and indeed it is most unlikely that the court will be persuaded in the absence of special circumstances to accept the surrender of discretion on a question of that sort, where the trustees are prima facie in a much better position than the court to know what is in the best interests of the beneficiaries.

(3) The third category is that of surrender of discretion properly so called. There the court will only accept a surrender of discretion for a good reason, the most obvious good reasons being either that the trustees are deadlocked (but honestly deadlocked, so that the question cannot be resolved by removing one trustee rather than another) or because the trustees are disabled as a result of a conflict of interest. Cases within categories (2) and (3) are similar in that they are both domestic proceedings traditionally heard in Chambers in which adversarial argument is not essential though it sometimes occurs. It may be that ultimately all will agree on some particular course of action or, at any rate, will not violently oppose some particular course of action. The difference between category (2) and category (3) is simply as to whether the court is (under category (2)) approving the exercise of discretion by trustees or (under category (3)) exercising its own discretion.

(4) The fourth category is where trustees have actually taken action, and that action is attacked as being either outside their powers or an improper exercise of their powers. Cases of that sort are hostile litigation to be heard and decided in open court."

These categories apply also to the decisions and proposed decisions of personal representatives.[12b]

As to applications for an order under category 2, the court must be satisfied, after a scrupulous consideration of the evidence, that the representatives have in fact formed the opinion that they should act in the particular way relevant to that case; that the opinion of the representatives is one that a reasonable representative properly instructed as to the meaning of the relevant clause could properly arrive at; and that the opinion is not vitiated by any conflict of interest under which any of the representatives is labouring.[12c] The representatives must put the court in possession of all relevant facts so that it may be satisfied that the decision of the representatives is proper and for the benefit of the beneficiaries. Moreover, it must be demonstrated that the exercise of their discretion is untainted by any collateral purpose. The representatives have the burden of proof and must, therefore, give the court all the information and disclosure that it requires to be satisfied that approval can be granted. If they fail to do so, they will not obtain the approval they seek. But the court may, in such a case, send the representatives away to produce more evidence. Whilst the process is not inquisitorial, it is part of the inherent jurisdiction of the court to supervise personal representatives.[12d]

Applications for directions whether to bring or defend legal proceedings (*Beddoe* applications)

62–11 *[Add at end of fn.52]*

See also *Williams v Seals* [2014] EWHC 3708 (Ch) at [41] to [43].

12b See per Patten L.J. in *Re Savile's Estate* [2014] EWCA Civ 1632 at para.[83].
12c See per Hart J. at [2001] W.T.L.R. 901 at 925.
12d See per Vos L.J. in *Earl of Cardigan v Moore* [2014] EWHC 3679 (Ch) at para.[61].

[Add at end of fn.58]

In the general Practice Direction as to Pre-Action Conduct, para.2.2(3) provides that the principles set out in the Practice Direction do not apply to "most applications for directions by a trustee or other fiduciary". The representative's evidence is not required to do more than state whether any relevant Pre-Action Protocol has been complied with as regards the proposed proceedings for which the representative seeks directions: see generally per Lloyd L.J. in *Davies v Watkins* [2012] EWCA Civ 1570; [2013] CP Rep. 10; [2013] 1 P& CR DG14, at paras [41]–[45].

Lloyd's names—potential creditors

[Add at end of fn.68]

See also *Ingrey v King*, February 11, 2015, Judge Walden-Smith.

62–13

Claims against personal representatives

[In the second paragraph replace "Ch.[ ]" with the following]

Ch.63

62–14

Removal of representative

[Add at end of fn.78]

62–15

In *Re Goodman, decd* [2013] EWHC 758 (Ch); [2014] Ch. 186; [2013] W.T.L.R. 1181, Newey J. held that s.50 applied to a named executor who has not proved. The executor derives title from the will and the property of the deceased vests in him from the moment of the testator's death; the definition of "will" is not limited to a document of which probate has already been granted (see s.56 of the Act); it cannot be inferred that Parliament did not intend there to be an overlap between s.50 and s.116 of the Senior Courts Act 1981 (see [2014] Ch. 186 at para.[15]); see also 57PD.13.1(1) and 57PD 14.3.

[Add at end of fn.83]

Muckian v Hoey [2014] N.I. Ch. 11; [2014] W.T.L.R. 1255 (Northern Ireland; application successful); *Re Savile's Estate* [2014] EWHC 653 (Ch); [2014] B.P.I.R. 551; [2014] W.T.L.R. 637 (appeal dismissed [2014] EWCA Civ 1632) (application unsuccessful; applicants had failed to show that there was any real risk that the representative would not act fairly and conscientiously as executor: "... the direct intervention by the Court in the administration of a trust or an estate by the removal of the trustee or personal representative has, for the most part, to be justified by evidence that their continuation in office is likely to prove detrimental to the interests of the beneficiaries. A lack of confidence or feelings of mistrust are not therefore sufficient in themselves to justify removal unless the breakdown in relations is likely to jeopardise the proper administration of the trust or estate. This is something which requires to be objectively demonstrated and considered on a case-to-case basis having regard to the particular circumstances"; see per Patten L.J. at [2014] EWCA Civ 1632 at para.[83]); Where an application is made for a full administration order (see para.62–01 above), "... as a means of coercing a recalcitrant or ineffective personal representative or trustee into action, the Court will usually seek to resolve the difficulty by appointing a new administrator": see per Patten L.J. in *Re Savile's Estate* [2014] EWCA Civ 1632 at para.[51]; *Earl of Cardigan v Moore* [2014] EWHC 3679 (Ch) (application successful).

[Add new fn.90a at the end of the paragraph ending with "(see para.5–02 above)"]

[90a] See *Re Goodman, dec'd* [2013] EWHC 758 (Ch); [2014] Ch. 186; [2013] W.T.L.R. 1181.

D.—BINDING ABSENT PARTIES

County court jurisdiction

62–17　*[Add at end of fn.102]*

For the procedure see 2CPD1: Practice Direction 2C – Starting proceedings in the County Court.

E.—RECTIFICATION OF WILLS

62–18　*[Add at end of fn.107]*

See also *Marley v Rawlings* [2014] UKSC 2; [2015] A.C. 157; T & T 2014, 20(9), 966–970 (Ham); (2014) Conv 357 (Drummond); (2014) Tru LI 38 (Thomas); [2014] 130 LQR July p.360 (Häcker). See paras 13–39 et seq.

CHAPTER 63

OTHER PROCEEDINGS IN ADMINISTRATION

[Add at end of the paragraph]

63–01

; and (7) applications under the Presumption of Death Act 2013.

A.—APPOINTMENT OF RECEIVER OR JUDICIAL TRUSTEE RECEIVERS

Judicial trustees

[In fn.22, replace "Lewin on Trusts, 18th edn (2011), para.19–01 et seq." with the following]

63–06

Lewin on Trusts, 19th edn (2015), paras 19–01 onwards

B.—PAYMENT INTO COURT: COMMITTAL

Payment into court on admission of assets

[In fn.31, replace "Lewin on Trusts, 18th edn (2011), para. 38-13 et seq." with the following]

63–08

Lewin on Trusts, 19th edn (2015), paras 38–016 onwards

C.—DOCUMENTS: ACCOUNTS: ACCOUNTING FOR WILFUL DEFAULT: IMMEDIATE ORDER FOR PAYMENT: ADMISSION OF ASSETS

Grounds for objection to produce documents

[Add at end of fn.86]

63–22

No order should be made to provide for a receiver, which was appointed over an estate that might be insolvent, to have access to privileged information, the privilege belonging to the estate, where the information is not needed for the purpose of preserving or safeguarding assets: *Aeroflot v Berezovsky* [2013] EWHC 4348 (Ch).

Just allowances

63–26   *[Add at the end of the second paragraph]*

In *Re Savile's Estate*; *National Westminster Bank v Lucas*,[118a] the executor of the estate of the television personality Jimmy Savile applied to the court for validation orders for the purposes of the Insolvency Act 1986 s.284. A validation order was made for the funeral expenses, even though they were relatively high. For legal expenses incurred before it became clear that the estate was probably insolvent, they were given limited validation so that a challenge could be made at a later date. For expenses payable after notice of probable insolvency, a rigorous test for validation was to be applied. A validation order was made for inheritance tax already paid but not for income tax due from the deceased to HM Revenue and Customs. The validation orders were upheld on appeal: *Re Savile's Estate* [2014] EWCA Civ 1632.

D.—VESTING AND SIMILAR ORDERS

Realty

63–38   *[In fn.167, replace "Lewin on Trusts, 18th edn (2011), Ch. 18" with the following]*

Lewin on Trusts, 19th edn (2015), Ch.18

[In fn.172, replace "Lewin on Trusts, 18th edn (2011), para. 18-04 onwards" with the following]

Lewin on Trusts, 19th edn (2015), para.18–04 onwards

Personalty

63–40   *[In fn.177, replace "Lewin on Trusts, 18th edn (2011), para. 18-12" with the following]*

Lewin on Trusts, 19th edn (2015), para.18–014

Trusts of land

63–43   *[In fn.190, replace "Lewin on Trusts, 18th edn (2011), para. 18-04 onwards" with the following]*

Lewin on Trusts, 19th edn (2015), para.18–003 onwards

[118a] [2013] EWHC (Ch).

The powers of trustees of land and trustees for sale

[In fn.192, replace "Lewin on Trusts, 18th edn (2011), para. 37-66 et seq" with the following] **63–44**

Lewin on Trusts, 19th edn (2015), paras 37–066 onwards

Other similar orders

[In fn.203, replace "Lewin on Trusts, 18th edn (2011), 18-16" with the following] **63–50**

Lewin on Trusts, 19th edn (2015), para.18–018

[In fn.208, replace "Lewin on Trusts, 18th edn (2011), para 31-43" with the following]

Lewin on Trusts, 19th edn (2015), para.31–049

F.—FREEZING ORDERS AND SEARCH ORDERS

[Add at end of fn.232] **63–54**

See also *Tadros v Barratt* [2014] EWHC 2860 (Ch), where the application was for an anti-suit injunction in the course of proceedings in England and in Holland concerning challenges to the validity of the English and Dutch wills of the deceased.

[Add new section G and fnn.233–241 after para.63–54]

G.—APPLICATIONS UNDER THE PRESUMPTION OF DEATH ACT 2013[233]

The Presumption of Death Act 2013 (the "2013 Act") confers on the court power **63–55**
to make a declaration that a person with a sufficient connection to England and Wales, who is missing and either is thought to have died or has not known to be alive for a period of at least seven years, is presumed dead.[234] Although any person may apply under the 2013 Act to the High Court for a declaration that a missing person is presumed to be dead, the court must refuse to hear an application made by someone other than the missing person's spouse, civil partner, parent, child or sibling unless the court considers that the applicant has a sufficient interest in the determination of the application.[235] This means that there will need to be good reason for a personal representative, who is not within one of those categories, to make an application under the 2013 Act.

If a trust arises, or property becomes held on trust, as a result of a declaration, the court may direct the trustee (which term includes a personal representative)[236]

---

[233] For the procedure under this Act see generally CPR 57.17-23 and 57BPD.1.
[234] Sections 1 and 2 of the 2013 Act.
[235] Section 1(5) of the 2013 Act.
[236] Section 20(1) of the 2013 Act.

as soon as reasonably practicable to take out an insurance policy in respect of any claim that might arise if the declaration is varied or revoked.[237]

63–56 Ordinarily, an application will be made so that the process for obtaining a grant can begin; this will, of course, be before administration of the estate has begun and there will be no need for the involvement of a personal representative, unless the missing person has left no relative to make an application. A declaration under the 2013 Act will, however, be effective against all persons and for all purposes, including for the purposes of the acquisition of an interest in any property,[238] and, when making the declaration, the court will have power to determine questions relating to interests in property arising as a result of the declaration.[239] A personal representative might, therefore, have a sufficient interest to make an application under the 2013 Act if there is a question whether a beneficiary of the deceased is alive or dead.

A declaration that has already been made under the 2013 Act may be varied or revoked (a "variation order") on an application by any person who is considered by the court to have a sufficient interest in the determination of the application.[240] A personal representative might in certain circumstances have a sufficient interest if he is administering the will of a person who was missing and declared to be presumed dead under s.2 of the 2013 Act but is later discovered to be alive.

If an application is made for a declaration or a variation order, any person may intervene but only with the permission of the court if not the missing person's spouse, civil partner, parent, child or sibling.[241]

---

[237] Section 13 of the 2013 Act.
[238] Section 3(2) of the 2013 Act.
[239] Section 4(1) of the 2013 Act.
[240] Section 5 of the 2013 Act.
[241] Section 11 of the 2013 Act.

CHAPTER 64

THE REPRESENTATIVE AS CLAIMANT

A.—Claims Begun by the Deceased in his Lifetime

Writ of fi. fa.

[Add at end of the paragraph the following text and fn.2a]   **64–15**

Writs of fieri facias have been renamed writs of control. Their validity, and so the
right of the enforcement agent to take control of goods, is determined by a period
specified in reg.9 of the Taking Control of Goods Regulations 2013, which
generally apply to applications for permission for the issue of writs or warrants
after April 6, 2014.[2a]

D.—Procedure

Executor refusing to join

[Add at end of fn.133]   **64–35**

Paragraph cited in *Kicks v Leigh* [2014] EWHC 3926 (Ch), per Stephen Morris
QC (sitting as a Deputy High Court Judge), in para.[177].

Beneficiaries not necessary parties

[In fn.137, replace "Lewin on Trusts, 18th edn (2011), paras 21–113–21–115"   **64–37**
with the following]

Lewin on Trusts, 19th edn (2015), para.27–046

[2a] See CPR 83 to 85.

CHAPTER 65

THE REPRESENTATIVE AS DEFENDANT

B.—PARTIES IN ACTION AGAINST PERSONAL REPRESENTATIVES

Where deceased defendant is a personal representative

65–12   *[Add at end of fn.51]*
Rule 48 of the Draft Probate Rules is to the same effect as r.52.

CHAPTER 66

LIMITATION OF ACTIONS

C.—CLAIMS AGAINST PERSONAL REPRESENTATIVES

Action for waste (*devastavit*)

[Add new text and fnn.68a–68b after paragraph beginning "Where a repre-
sentative has committed waste . . . "]

66–13

There is a 12-year limitation period for beneficiaries to make a claim against the
personal representatives for the due administration of the estate, in respect of
personalty.[68a] As to realty, if ss.21(1) or 21(2) do not apply, no other period is
prescribed by the Act and the limitation period will accordingly be six years.[68b]

Personalty

[Add at end of fn.83]

66–16

; *Davies v Sharples* [2006] EWHC 362 (Ch); [2006] W.T.L.R. 839.

[Add at the end of the paragraph beginning "The 12-year period applies not only
to actions . . . " the following text and fnn.83a–83b]

Section 22 of the Act does not apply in respect of any breaches of trust committed
after the administration of the estate is complete[83a] and the personal representative
has become a trustee.[83b]

[Delete the paragraph: "The Court of Appeal also decided that an application to
remove a personal representative was subject to the same rule.[89] "]

Account

Where no limitation exists

[In fn.102, substitute "Lewin on Trusts, 18th edn (2011), paras 44–04 et seq" with
the following]

66–20

Lewin on Trusts, 19th edn (2015), paras 44–004 onwards

[68a] *Davies v Sharples* [2006] EWHC 362 (Ch); [2006] W.T.L.R. 839 at para.[34]; West T.E.L. & T.J.
2007, (Dec) 12.
[68b] Limitation Act 1980 s.21(3).
[83a] *Davies v Sharples* [2006] EWHC 362 (Ch); [2006] W.T.L.R. 839.
[83b] See para.81–02 below.

Executor de son tort

Executor after completion of the administration (functus officio)

66–22 *[In fn.113, substitute "Lewin on Trusts, 18th edn (2011), Ch 44" with the following]*

Lewin on Trusts, 19th edn (2015), Ch.44

CHAPTER 67

JUDGMENTS AGAINST REPRESENTATIVES

J.—EXECUTION FOLLOWING JUDGMENT OF FUTURE ASSETS

[Add at end of the second paragraph the following new text and fn.53a]   **67–10**

After April 6, 2014 writs and warrants of control, execution, delivery and possession must not be issued without the permission of the court where any change has taken place, whether by death or otherwise, in the parties entitled to enforce the judgment or order or liable to have it enforced against them; or the judgment or order is against the assets of a deceased person coming into the hands of that person's executors or administrators after the date of the judgment or order, and it is sought to issue execution against such assets.[53a]

[53a] CPR 83.2(3)(b) and (c); the procedure for such enforcement is in CPR 83–85, which generally apply to applications for permission for the issue of writs or warrants after April 6, 2014.

CHAPTER 68

COSTS IN ADMINISTRATION PROCEEDINGS

A.—INTRODUCTION

In litigation with outsiders

68–01   *[Add at end of fn.2]*

For the effect on costs of a Part 36 offer, see *Jopling v Leavesley* [2013] EWCA Civ 1605; [2014] W.T.L.R. 807; see also the changes made to Pt 36, as set out in Sch.1 of the Civil Procedure (Amendment No. 8) Rules 2014 (SI 2014/3299), taking effect on April 6, 2015. For a discussion on the court's discretion under CPR r.38.6, on a claimant's discontinuance of proceedings, see *Al-Sadi v Al-Sadi* [2013] EWHC 2379 (Ch). See also *Flint v Verma*, February 19, 2015, Henderson J.

In administration proceedings

68–02   *[Add at end of fn.11]*

This paragraph was cited with approval by Vos J. in *Abdullah v Abdullah* [2013] EWHC 4281 (Ch) at para.[22].

[Delete final paragraph, beginning with "CPR48.4 provides that" and ending with "identifies some circumstances relevant to propriety.¹⁴" and add new text and fnn.14–14d]

CPR r.46.3 provides that, where a person is a party to any proceedings in the capacity of trustee or personal representative, and CPR r.44.5 (costs payable pursuant to a contract) does not apply, the general rule is that he is entitled to be paid the costs of those proceedings out of the relevant trust or estate, insofar as they are not recovered from or paid by any other person, and that those costs will be assessed on the indemnity basis. Practice Direction 46PD1 restricts the right to costs properly incurred, which depends on all the circumstances of the case, including whether the trustee or personal representative (a) obtained directions from the court before bringing or defending the proceedings; (b) acted in the interests of the fund or estate or in substance for a benefit other than that of the estate, including the trustee's own; and (c) acted in some way unreasonably in bringing or defending, or in the conduct of, the proceedings. The trustee or personal representative is not to be taken to have acted for a benefit other than that of the fund by reason only that the trustee has defended a claim in which relief is sought against the trustee or personal representative personally.[14]

Section II of Practice Direction 3F, "Costs Capping in Relation to Trust Funds" applies to proceedings relating to property that is the subject of a trust or the estate of a deceased person (referred to as a "trust fund"). Any party to such proceedings who intends to apply for an order for the payment of costs out of the trust fund must file and serve on all other parties written notice of that intention together with a budget of the costs likely to be incurred by that party.[14a] The notices must be filed and served (a) in a Part 7 claim, with the first statement of case; and (b) in a Part 8 claim, with the evidence (or, if a defendant does not intend to serve and file evidence, with the acknowledgement of service).[14b] When proceedings first come before the court for directions the court may make a costs capping order of its own initiative whether or not any party has applied for such an order.[14c] In addition, the court may order that the costs management provisions of CPR Pt 3 will apply to any proceedings begun under CPR Pt 8.[14d]

C.—INDEMNITY COSTS

[In fn.18 replace "48.4(3)" with the following]   **68–04**

46.3(3)

D.—COSTS OF THIRD PARTY OUT OF ESTATE

[Add new text and fn.18a before the existing paragraphs]   **68–05**

There are three main types of dispute in which personal representatives might be involved: a dispute as to the how they must administer and distribute the estate; a dispute with one or more of the beneficiaries as to the propriety of any action which the representatives have taken or omitted to take or may or may not take in the future; and a dispute with persons, otherwise in the capacity of beneficiaries, in respect of rights or liabilities, such as in contract or tort, that are assumed by the representatives as such in the course of administration of the estate.[18a] This section concerns the first two types of dispute. The third type involves litigation with outsiders and is considered at para.68–01 above.

[In fn.19, substitute "Lewin on Trusts, 18th edn (2011), para 21–79" with the following]

Lewin on Trusts, 19th edn (2015), paras 27–139 onwards

---

[14] See *Abdullah v Abdullah* [2013] EWHC 4281 (Ch), where it was unsuccessfully argued that the trustee acted unreasonably in defending or in the conduct of the proceedings.

[14a] Paragraphs 3FPD 5.1 to 5.4.

[14b] Paragraph 3FPD 5.5.

[14c] Paragraph 3FPD 5.6.

[14d] CPR r.3.12.

[18a] See per Lightman J. in *Alsop Wilkinson v Neary*, a case involving trustees.

[Insert new fn.19a at the end of the paragraph numbered (1)]

[19a] "... necessary parties to such an application ...": *Re Savile deceased* [2014] EWCA Civ 1632 at para.[108].

[Insert into the last paragraph, between "... amongst the parties.[21]" and "Where the Public Trustee ..." the following new text and fnn.21a–21c]

Where a beneficiary's unreasonable conduct led to substantial costs being incurred by a personal representative in applying to the court, it was appropriate for that beneficiary to bear those costs rather than them falling on the estate and therefore the beneficiaries generally. Such a case was closer to hostile litigation, in which the other beneficiaries supported the personal representative, who had faced sustained hostility and opposition from the one beneficiary who had opposed the claim.[21a] In an application by a representative to construe a clause in a will, the respondent notified the representative that it was treating the proceedings as hostile litigation and expected the costs to follow the event and sought an assurance from the representative that it would not seek to recover costs from the estate without an order of the court. The representative was ultimately successful and, in the circumstances, costs were ordered against the respondents, rather than out of the estate.[21b] In a Part 64 application, where both sides acted largely in good faith but were "blinded by their personal dispute" but it could not be said that the claimant wholly succeeded or that the defendant wholly failed, no order for costs was made.[21c]

E.—REPRESENTATIVE GUILTY OF MISCONDUCT

68–06 *[In fn.23, substitute "Lewin on Trusts, 18th edn (2011), para 21-64 et seq" with the following]*

Lewin on Trusts, 19th edn (2015), paras 27–112 onwards and 27–141 onwards

[Add at end of fn.23]

See also *Re Bogusz (deceased)* [2013] EWHC 1449 (Ch); [2014] Ch. 271; [2013] W.T.L.R. 1095, where a costs order was made against a genealogist, who took a grant as attorney in the hope of financial gain, and unsuccessfully opposed a *donatio mortis causa* claim. See also *Flint v Verma*, February 19, 2015, Henderson J.

Q.—PROFESSIONAL EXECUTOR

68–19 *[In fn.74, substitute "Lewin on Trusts, 17th edn (2000), para.20–141 onwards" with the following]*

Lewin on Trusts, 19th edn (2015), paras 20–227 onwards

[21a] *Green v Astor* [2013] EWHC 1857 (Ch); [2013] 6 Costs L.O. 911; [2013] W.T.L.R. 1489.
[21b] *Loring v Woodland Trust (Costs)* November 28, 2013 Asplin J. (permission to appeal refused; appeal against substantive decision dismissed: [2014] EWCA Civ 1314).
[21c] *Abdullah v Abdullah* [2013] EWHC 4281 (Ch).

S.—Beneficiaries' costs

[Add at end of the paragraph numbered (1) the following new text and fnn.79a–79b]   **68–21**

Even strong opposition by a beneficiary to a proposed course of action by a personal representative "is not, without more, sufficient to justify a departure from the general rule that the costs of all necessary parties to a *Buckton* class 1 or class 2 application should be borne by the trust fund or estate."[79a] In an action that includes an application for the removal of a representative, any parties not necessary to that application might not be entitled to the costs of being heard on it unless there is otherwise some justification in making a costs order against the estate in favour of non-parties to the application.[79b]

[In fn.80, substitute "Lewin on Trusts, 17th edn (2000), para.21–80" with the following]

Lewin on Trusts, 19th edn (2015), paras 27–139 onwards

[Add at end of fn.80]

See also *Green v Astor* [2013] EWHC 1857 (Ch); [2013] 6 Costs L.O. 911; [2013] W.T.L.R. 1489, where a beneficiary's unreasonable conduct led to substantial costs being incurred by a personal representative in applying to the court, so that it was appropriate for that beneficiary to bear those costs rather than them falling on the estate and therefore the beneficiaries generally.

X.—Costs under the Variation of Trusts Act 1958

[In fn.97, substitute "Lewin on Trusts, para. 45-102" with the following]   **68–27**

Lewin on Trusts, 19th edn (2015), paras 45–117 onwards

[79a] Per Patten L.J. in *Re Savile deceased* [2014] EWCA Civ 1632 at para.[112].
[79b] Per Patten L.J. in *Re Savile deceased* [2014] EWCA Civ 1632 at paras [123 to 125].

CHAPTER 70

PROBLEMS OF DISTRIBUTION

A.—COMPLETING THE ADMINISTRATION

Alteration of dispositions

70–01   *[Replace text in fn.1 with the following]*

See para.50–18, above. Inheritance Tax Act 1984 ss.142, 143. *Dymond's Capital Taxes*, para.8.109 onwards; *McCutcheon on Inheritance Tax*, 6th edn (2013), para.8–114 onwards; *Brighouse's Precedents of Wills*, 14th edn (2007), Pt 9; *Potter & Monroe's Tax Planning with Precedents*, Ch.8. For general trust precedents (which may guide the form of a variation) see J. Kessler QC, *Drafting Trusts and Will Trusts*, 12th edn (2014), and Withers LLP, *Practical Trust Precedents*.

Disclaimer

70–02   *[Replace last sentence of fn.4 with the following]*

See *McCutcheon on Inheritance Tax*, 6th edn (2013), para.8–182.

[In fn.15 replace "para.8–100 et seq." with the following]

para.8.109 onwards.

C.—DISTRIBUTION BY THE TRUSTEE

Obligation to distribute

70–10   *[Replace last sentence of fn.50 with the following]*

See further *Lewin on Trusts*, 19th edn (2015), Ch.35.

[In fn.51, replace "Snell's Equity, 31st edn (2005), para.6–001 et seq." with the following]

Snell's Equity, 33rd edn (2015), para.6-001 onwards

A *"Benjamin"* order

[Replace text in fn.69 with the following]   **70–18**

An application for a declaration of presumed death must now be made under s.1 of the Presumption of Death Act 2013 if the conditions specified as to the domicile or habitual residence in England and Wales of the missing person or the applicant are met. The Act contains nothing affecting the jurisdiction of the court to give directions to a personal representative or trustee to proceed on the footing that a person is dead, and s.16(4) of the Act expressly preserves any power or duty that a court or tribunal has other than under the Act to determine a question relating to the death of a missing person: see also *Lewin on Trusts*, 19th edn (2015), para.26–078. For the common law principles, which will continue to apply to cases outside the Act, see *Chard v Chard* [1956] P. 239.

[Replace text in fn.70 with the following]

See now the Presumption of Death Act 2013 and fn.69 above. Applications for a *Benjamin* order to distribute on the footing of a beneficiary's death and for a declaration of presumed death were often combined. In *Re Green's Will Trusts* [1985] 3 All E.R. 455, Nourse J. left open the question of what distinctions might exist between the two jurisdictions, commenting that the modern practice is to make a *Benjamin* order where there is no need to make a declaration. It remains to be seen what difference the Act will make.

[Add new fn.70a at the end of the sentence following fn.70]

70a It is to be noted that if an applicant under the Presumption of Death Act 2013 is not the missing person's spouse, civil partner, parent, child or sibling and cannot show that he has "sufficient interest" in the determination of the application, the court must refuse to hear the application: s.1(5).

[After para.70–20: insert new section-headings, new paras 70–20A to 70–20D,   **70–20** *and new fnn.74a–74z as follows]*

Declaration of presumed death

Presumption of Death Act 2013

Applications The Presumption of Death Act 2013 came completely into force on   **70–20A** October 1, 2014.74a The Act applies where a person who is missing is thought to have died or has not been known to be alive for a period of at least seven years, and confers jurisdiction on the High Court to make a declaration on the application of any person that the missing person is presumed to be dead.74b The court's

---

74a Presumption of Death Act 2013 (Commencement and Transitional and Saving Provision) Order (SI 2014/1810). On the Presumption of Death Act 2013 and its effects, see also *Lewin on Trusts*, 19th edn (2015), para.26–058 onwards. Certain provisions had already come into effect on March 26, 2013.
74b Presumption of Death Act 2013 s.1(1), (2). No application may be made in respect of the Monarch: ss.1(5), 21(2).

jurisdiction is limited by the domicile or habitual residence of the missing person: the missing person must have been domiciled in England and Wales on the day when he or she was last known to be alive or must have been habitually resident in England and Wales throughout the period of one year ending with that day; but if these conditions are not satisfied it will be sufficient if the application is made by the missing person's spouse or civil partner and that person is domiciled in England and Wales on the day when the application is made or has been habitually resident in England and Wales throughout the period of one year ending with that day.[74c] In any case, the court must refuse to hear an application for a declaration if the application is made by someone other than the missing person's spouse, civil partner, parent, child or sibling, and the court considers that the applicant does not have a sufficient interest in the determination of the application.[74d] What constitutes sufficient interest is not defined by the Act and is therefore left to the appreciation of the court. Although it seems unlikely that a trustee or personal representative with a missing beneficiary would not have sufficient interest for the purposes of an application, there may be some merit in arranging for the application to be made by someone to whom the Act gives automatic standing, if such a person is willing to be the claimant. In such a case, the trustees or personal representatives should be joined as defendants.

The procedure for making applications under the Presumption of Death Act 2013 is contained in CPR Pt 57 and Practice Direction 57B. The claim may be made in either the Chancery Division or the Family Division and is brought using the Part 8 procedure as varied by Rule 57.19. Provision is made for particular persons (including the spouse or civil partner, parents, children and siblings of the missing person) to be given notice of the claim; and the claimant is also required within seven days of issuing the claim, to ensure that notice of the claim is published in a form which meets the requirements set out in Practice Direction 57B in at least one newspaper circulating in the vicinity of the last known address of the missing person.

70–20B **Declarations and consequential orders** On an application for a declaration, the court must make the declaration if it is satisfied that the missing person has died or has not been known to be alive for a period of at least seven years, and must include in the declaration a finding as to the date and time of the missing person's death.[74e] Subject to provisions relating to appeals, a declaration under the Act is conclusive of the missing person's presumed death and of the date and time of the death, and is effective against all persons and for all purposes, including for the purposes of (a) the acquisition of an interest in any property, and (b) the ending of a marriage or civil partnership to which the missing person is a party.[74f] When

---

[74c] Presumption of Death Act 2013 s.1(3), (4).
[74d] Presumption of Death Act 2013 s.1(5).
[74e] Presumption of Death Act 2013 s.2(1), (2). Where the court is satisfied that the missing person has died but is uncertain at which moment during a period the death occurred, it must find that the missing person is presumed to have died at the end of that period: s.2(3). Where the court is satisfied that the missing person has not been known to be alive for a period of at least seven years but is not satisfied that the missing person has died, the finding must be that the missing person is presumed to have died at the end of the period of seven years beginning with the day after the day on which he or she was last known to be alive: s.2(4).
[74f] Presumption of Death Act 2013 s.3(1), (2).

making a declaration the court has the power to determine any question which relates to an interest in property and arises as a result of the declaration and to determine the domicile of the missing person at the time of his or her presumed death; and may make such order as it considers reasonable in relation to any interest in property acquired as a result of the declaration.[74g]

Significantly, the court is also given the power, when making a declaration of presumed death, to direct that the value of any interest in property acquired as a result of the declaration is not to be recoverable by virtue of an order made under s.7(2), which deals with interests in property acquired as a result of the original declaration when an order varying or revoking the original declaration is made under s.5(1).[74h] In particular, the court may direct that the value of the interest is not to be recoverable in any circumstances or that it is not to be recoverable where the conditions specified in the order are met.[74i] The Act therefore enables the court to protect beneficiaries who receive distributions as the consequence of a declaration of presumed death against subsequent claims by the missing person if he or she subsequently reappears. Since such protection is not available to beneficiaries on the making of a *Benjamin* order,[74j] an application under the Act is likely to seem more attractive to them than an application for a *Benjamin* order.

The Act also provides for the court to direct trustees (which term includes executors, administrators and personal representatives)[74k] to take out insurance in respect of any claim which might arise under s.7(2) if their trust is affected by a declaration made under the Act; and the premium for such insurance may be paid out of the trust property.[74l] And before paying a capital sum to a person as a result of a declaration under the Act, an insurer is entitled to require that person to take out insurance in respect of any claim which the insurer may make in the event of the making of a variation order under s.5(1).[74m]

Variation orders A declaration made under the Act may be varied or revoked by an order, known as a "variation order", of the High Court on the application of any person, but the court must refuse to hear such an application if it considers that the applicant does not have sufficient interest in the determination of the application.[74n] A variation order does not revive a marriage or civil partnership that was brought to an end by virtue of a declaration under the Act, nor does it affect an interest in property acquired as a result of such a declaration unless the court makes an order under s.7 of the Act.[74o] **70–20C**

When making a variation order, the court may determine any question which relates to an interest in property and arises as a result of the variation order, and determine the domicile of the missing person at the time of his or her presumed

---

[74g] Presumption of Death Act 2013 s.4(1), (2).
[74h] Presumption of Death Act 2013 s.4(3).
[74i] Presumption of Death Act 2013 s.4(4).
[74j] See para.70–18, above.
[74k] Presumption of Death Act 2013 s.20(1).
[74l] Presumption of Death Act 2013 s.13(1), (3). A trust is affected by a declaration under the Act if it arises as a result of the declaration or property held by the trust is affected by the declaration: s.13(2).
[74m] Presumption of Death Act 2013 s.14(1). The policy must be taken out in the person's own name and for the benefit of the insurer: s.14(2).
[74n] Presumption of Death Act s.5.
[74o] Presumption of Death Act 2013 s.6(1) (interests in property), (2) (marriage and civil partnership).

death, and must also, under s.7(2), make such further order (if any) as it considers reasonable in relation to any interest in property acquired as a result of the original declaration.[74p] An order made under s.7(2) does not affect income which has accrued between the making of the original declaration and the making of the variation order, nor does it affect or provide grounds to challenge a related good faith transaction or an interest in property acquired under such a transaction.[74q]

When considering what order to make under s.7(2), the court must also, as far as practicable, observe the principles set out in s.8.[74r] The first principle, which is relevant where property is being or has been administered under a trust, is that the person who, but for s.6(1) (which provides for a variation order not to affect an interest in property acquired as a result of the original declaration), would have an interest in the relevant property by virtue of the variation order, and a person who, but for s.6(1), would have acquired an interest in the relevant property from that person should be entitled to have made over to him or her by the trustee in full satisfaction of that interest the following: (a) the interest in the relevant property or an equivalent interest in property representing the relevant property, to the extent that such property is still in the hands of the trustee when the variation order is made, and (b) the value of the interest in the relevant property, to the extent that such property has been distributed.[74s] The intention of this principle is clear: the formerly missing person, and any person claiming through him or her, should so far as possible be put into the position he or she would have been in but for the original declaration. It is unclear what is meant by a trustee's "making over" an interest in relevant property where the interest would not give an immediate right to the entirety of the corpus itself (as under a bare trust); but it seems probable that acts recognising and giving effect to the person's interest would satisfy the requirement, for example, ceasing to pay income to the person entitled as the result of the original declaration and paying it to the formerly missing person.[74t]

The second principle is that where an insurer has paid a capital sum as the result of the original declaration it, or any part of it, should be repaid to the insurer if the facts on which the variation order was made justify it.[74u]

The Act also provides, in s.7(8), for trustees (which includes executors, administrators and personal representatives) to be liable to a person who has entitlement under a trust in virtue of an order under s.7(2), where that person suffers a loss on account of any breach of trust by the trustee in the administration or distribution of all or part of the property subject to the order. This appears to be a statement of the obvious, but the intention of the section may be to establish the entitled person's right to sue the trustees for breaches of trust which occurred

---

[74p] Presumption of Death Act 2013 s.7(1) (determination of questions and of domicile), (2) (further orders). Unless the court considers that there are exceptional circumstances making it appropriate to make an order under s.7(2), such an order cannot be made if the application for a variation order was made more than five years after the making of the original declaration: s.7(3).

[74q] Presumption of Death Act 2013 s.7(5) (income), (6) (good faith transactions). A definition of "good faith transaction" which protects those who acquire interests in good faith and for value is provided in s.7(7).

[74r] Presumption of Death Act 2013 s.7(4).

[74s] Presumption of Death Act 2013 s.8(2), (3), (4).

[74t] See *Lewin on Trusts*, 19th edn (2015), para.26–071.

[74u] Presumption of Death Act 2013 s.8(5), (6).

before the making of the order under s.7(2). The trustee nonetheless retains the benefit of any restriction of liability under any primary or subordinate legislation of the United Kingdom parliament or the Welsh National Assembly or any provision in a deed regulating the administration of the trust.[74v] Curiously, restrictions of liability provided under the terms of a will do not appear to fall within the strict terms of this provision.

Cases determined under the common law

Where an application for a declaration is not required to be made under the Presumption of Death Act 2013, because the conditions as to the domicile or habitual residence of the missing person or the applicant cannot be met, the common law principles for determining whether a person is presumed to be dead will continue to apply. In cases of seven years' absence, where no statute applies, on proof (1) that there were persons who would be likely to have heard of the missing person over that period; (2) that those persons had not heard of him; (3) that all due inquiries appropriate to the circumstances had been made, in the absence of affirmative evidence of life during the relevant period, a presumption of law arises that the missing person died at some time within the seven-year period.[74w]   **70–20D**

The common law does not presume that death occurred at any particular point during the seven-year period. The time at which the missing person died is not a matter of presumption, but of evidence, and the onus of proving that the death took place at any particular time within the seven years lies upon the person who claims a right to the establishment of which that fact is essential.[74x] It is to be noted, however, that where a court or tribunal makes a declaration that a missing person is presumed to be dead other than on an application under the Act, s.2(2) to 2(4) of the Act will apply to the court or tribunal making the declaration.[74y] The court must therefore include in its declaration a finding as to the date and time of the missing person's death, applying inter alia the provisions of s.2(3) and 2(4) where relevant.[74z]

[74v] Presumption of Death Act 2013 s.8(9), (10).
[74w] *Chard v Chard* [1956] P. 259; and see *Lewin on Trusts*, 19th edn (2015), para.26–076 et seq.
[74x] *In re Phené's Trusts* (1869–70) L.R. 5 Ch. App. 139.
[74y] Presumption of Death Act 2013 s.16(2).
[74z] See fn.74e, above.

CHAPTER 71

ADEMPTION AND SATISFACTION

C.—ADEMPTION

Ademption by change effected by statute or act of third parties

Transactions during the incapacity of the testator

71–18 *[Replace fn.109 text with the following]*

Johnson v Maclarn [2002] N.S.W.S.C. 97 (New South Wales); *Mulhall v Kelly* [2006] V.S.C. 407, (2006) 1 A.S.T.L.R. 394 (Victoria); *Ensor v Frisby* [2010] 1 Qd. R. 146 (Queensland); *Moylan v Rickard* [2010] Q.S.C. 327 (Queensland); even where the attorney knew the content of the will: *Re Hartigan* Unreported 1997 (SC of Western Australia); *Simpson v Cunning* [2011] V.S.C. 466, (2011) 4 A.S.T.L.R. 584 (Victoria); *Public Trustee of Qld v Lee* [2011] Q.S.C. 409, [2012] 2 Qd R. 473 (Queensland). Acceptance has not been universal, however: *Re Viertel* was not followed in *Public Trustee of Qld v Stibbe* [2012] Q.S.C. 357 (Queensland) or in *The Trust Company Ltd v Gibson* [2012] Q.S.C. 183, [2014] 1 Qd R. 553 (Queensland), and was subject to trenchant obiter criticism by Campbell J.A. in *RL v NSW Trustee and Guardian* [2012] N.S.W.C.A. 39, (2012) 84 N.S.W.L.R. 263 (New South Wales). Other decisions have merely noted the conflict in the authorities concerning the correctness of *Re Viertel*: *Re Blake (Deceased)* [2009] V.S.C. 184; (2009) 25 V.R. 27 (Victoria); *Power v Power* [2011] N.S.W.S.C. 288 (New South Wales); *Public Guardian v JM* [2014] W.T.L.R. 979. Scottish jurisprudence has arrived at the same result as *Re Viertel* but by a different route: *Turner v Turner* [2012] CSOH 41; 2012 S.L.T. 877 (Scotland). Appendix B of Campbell J.A.'s judgment in *RL v NSW Trustee and Guardian* [2012] N.S.W.C.A. 39; (2012) 84 N.S.W.L.R. 263 (New South Wales) at [125]–[187] contains a comprehensive and scholarly analysis of this "minefield" (*Public Guardian v JM* [2014] W.T.L.R. 979 at [53]).

D.—SATISFACTION

Presumption against double portions

Portions

71–21 *[Add at end of fn.121]*

; *Re Frost (Deceased)* [2013] EWHC 435 (Ch); [2013] W.T.L.R. 673; [2014] W.T.L.R. 77.

Satisfaction (or ademption) of legacies by portions

The donor's intention

[Add at end of fn.181]

71–35

; *Re Frost (Deceased)* [2013] EWHC 435 (Ch) at [28].

CHAPTER 73

INCAPACITY TO TAKE

B.—HOMICIDE

The forfeiture rule

Manslaughter

73–04 *[Add at end of fn.20]*

; *Chadwick v Collinson* [2014] EWHC 3055 (Ch.); M. Pawlowski [2014] T.E.L&T.J. (December) 8.

The Forfeiture Act 1982

73–12 *[Insert new para.73–12A and fnn.55a–55c after para.73–12]*

73–12A In *Dunbar v Plant*, Phillips L.J. identified the "first and paramount consideration" for the court in applying the Act as whether the culpability attending the beneficiary's criminal conduct was such as to justify the application of the forfeiture rule at all.[55a] Mummery L.J. considered that the court was required "to look at the case in the round, pay regard to all the material circumstances, including the conduct of the offender and the deceased, and then ask whether 'the justice of the case requires' a modification of the effect of the forfeiture rule." He identified among the factors which the court is entitled to take into account, the relationship between the offender and the deceased; the degree of moral culpability for what happened; the nature and gravity of the offence; the intentions of the deceased; the size of the estate and the value of the property in dispute; the financial position of the offender; and the moral claims and wishes of those who would be entitled to take the property on the application of the rule.[55b] Subsequent cases have adopted the approach that while the first and paramount consideration is that identified by Phillips L.J., it is not the only factor to be considered, and other factors for consideration include those identified by Mummery L.J.[55c]

[55a] *Dunbar v Plant* [1998] Ch. 412 at 438.
[55b] *Dunbar v Plant* [1998] Ch. 412 at 427H–428A.
[55c] *Re Murphy* [2003] W.T.L.R. 687; *Chadwick v Collinson* [2014] EWHC 3055 (Ch.).

Joint tenancy

[Replace para.73–15 with the following text and fnn.69–72]   **73–15**

Although the effect of the forfeiture rule upon a joint tenancy has not been expressly decided by an English court, it is accepted that it operates to sever the deceased's interest from that of the killer. There is a strong dictum in *Re K* at first instance,[69] and strong Commonwealth authority,[70] that the joint tenancy is severed in equity, and the concession made in *Dunbar v Plant* to the same effect was approved by Mummery L.J as having been correctly made.[70a] Mummery L.J.'s approval was in turn relied on in *Chadwick v Collinson* as a statement of the law.[70b] Only in this way can the criminal survivor be prevented from benefiting from his crime without depriving him, or his estate, of property which by severance he could have made his own at any time. This seems to have been the approach of the court below in *Dunbar v Plant*,[71] but it was held by a majority of the Court of Appeal that the survivor of a genuine suicide pact might benefit by survivorship because in most cases public interest required no penal sanction against such a survivor.[72]

E.—UNINCORPORATED GROUP

[In fn.77, replace "Lewin on Trusts, 18th edn (2011), para.4–49 et seq." with the   **73–18**
following]

Lewin on Trusts, 19th edn (2015), para.4–054 onwards

Uncertainty

[Add at end of fn.78]

; *Re St Andrew's (Cheam) Lawn Tennis Club Trust* [2012] EWHC 1040 (Ch); [2012] 1 W.L.R. 3487.

[Add at end of fn.79]

; *Re St Andrew's (Cheam) Lawn Tennis Club Trust* [2012] EWHC 1040 (Ch); [2012] 1 W.L.R. 3487.

---

[69] *Re K* [1985] Ch. 85 at 100F.
[70] *Schobelt v Barber* [1967] 10 R. 349; *Rasmanis v Jurewitsch* (1969) 70 S.R. (N.S.W.) 407; *Re Pechar* [1969] N.Z.L.R. 574; *Re Gore* [1972] I.O.R. 550. As to severance, see further para.41–31, above.
[70a] *Dunbar v Plant* [1998] Ch. 412 at 418B.
[70b] *Chadwick v Collinson* [2014] EWHC 3055 (Ch.) at [5].
[71] *Dunbar v Plant* [1998] Ch. 412 at 420, 426.
[72] *Dunbar v Plant* [1998] Ch. 412 at 435. The dissenting judgment of Mummery L.J. does not seem to rely on "severance" but rather on the exercise of the statutory discretion under s.2 of the Forfeiture Act 1982.

73–19 *[Replace last sentence of fn.83 with the following]*

See *Snell's Equity*, 33rd edn (2015), para.22-021 onwards; *Lewin on Trusts*, 19th edn (2015), para.4–035 onwards.

F.—GIFTS FOR A PURPOSE

73–20 *[In fn.84, replace "Lewin on Trusts, 18th edn (2011), paras 4–42-4–48" with the following]*

Lewin on Trusts, 19th edn (2015), paras 4–042—4–053.

[In fn.85, replace "Lewin on Trusts, 18th edn (2011), Ch.29; Snell's Equity, 32nd edn (2010), Ch.10" with the following]

Lewin on Trusts, 19th edn (2015), Ch.29; *Snell's Equity*, 33rd edn (2015), Ch.10.

G.—ATTESTING WITNESS AND SPOUSE OR CIVIL PARTNER

Effect of nullity of gift

No right to grant

73–33 *[Insert after the first sentence of fn.119]*

Rule 16 of the Draft Probate Rules is to the same effect.

H.—FORMER SPOUSE OR CIVIL PARTNER

Deaths on or after January 1, 1996

73–37 *[Replace text in para.73–37 with the following text and fnn.126–128]*

There followed a revision of s.18A, by s.3 of the Law Reform (Succession) Act 1995. The new s.18A applies in respect of deaths occurring on or after January 1, 1996, and provides that where, after a testator has made a will, a decree of a court of civil jurisdiction in England and Wales dissolves or annuls his marriage, or his marriage is dissolved or annulled and the divorce or annulment is entitled to recognition[126]: (a) provisions of the will appointing executors or trustees or conferring a power of appointment, if they appoint or confer the power on the former spouse, shall take effect as if the former spouse had died on the date on which the marriage is dissolved or annulled; and (b) any property which, or an interest in which, is devised or bequeathed to the former spouse shall pass as if the former spouse had died on that date.[127]

---

[126] By virtue of Pt II of the Family Law Act 1986.

[127] Section 18A(1)(a), (b). The right in the surviving former spouse to apply for financial provision under the Inheritance (Provision for Family and Dependants) Act 1975 is preserved: s.18A(2).

It is to be noticed that the section continues to provide for its provisions to be subject to a contrary intention expressed in the will.[128]

[Insert new section-heading, new para.73–39 and new fnn.130–133 as follows]   **73–38**

I.—POLITICAL PARTIES

Section 54(1)(a) of the Political Parties, Elections and Referendums Act 2000 provides that a donation received by a registered political party must not be accepted by the party if the person by whom the donation would be made is not, at the time of its receipt by the party, a permissible donor. An individual is a permissible donor if he is an individual registered in an electoral register,[130] or, if the political party is one whose entry in the register of political parties includes a statement that it intends to contest one or more elections to the European Parliament in the combined region, if he is a Gibraltar elector.[131] In relation to a donation in the form of a bequest, permissible donor means, when referring to an individual, an individual who was, at any time within the period of five years ending with the date of his death, registered in an electoral register or who was a Gibraltar elector.[132] Section 56 requires a donation received from a person who is not a permissible donor to be returned within 30 days; and s.58 gives the Court power to order forfeiture of an amount equal to the donation where it has not been returned to the donor in accordance with the Act.   **73–39**

In *Re Robson (Deceased)*,[133] the executor sought directions from the court as to the distribution of the estate. The deceased, who was a British citizen, had moved to Spain on his retirement and had died there. He had owned no property in the United Kingdom after moving to Spain. In his will he left the residue of his estate to a registered political party in the United Kingdom, the British National Party; but at the time of his death he had not been registered in an electoral register in the United Kingdom at any time during the previous five years. The deceased's two sons claimed that the deceased's gift of his residuary estate failed by reason of the Act and that the residue passed to them on intestacy. In response to this claim,

---

[128] See also *Theobald on Wills*, 17th edn (2010), para.12–028, but note that this paragraph of *Theobald* requires correction to recognise that s.18A continues to provide for the supremacy of a contrary intention expressed in the will.

[130] Political Parties, Elections and Referendums Act 2000 s.54(2)(a). Under s.54(8), "electoral register" means a register of parliamentary or local government electors maintained under s.9 of the Representation of the People Act 1983; a register of relevant citizens of the European Union prepared under the European Parliamentary Elections (Franchise of Relevant Citizens of the Union) Regulations 2001; or a register of peers prepared under regulations under s.3 of the Representation of the People Act 1985.

[131] Political Parties, Elections and Referendums Act 2000 s.54(2A)(a). Under s.160(1), "Gibraltar elector" means an individual who is registered in the Gibraltar register (as defined by s.14 of the European Parliament (Representation) Act 2003), or, if the first version of that register has not been published, who is registered in the register of electors used for House of Assembly elections, or who is resident in Gibraltar, aged 16 or over and is a Commonwealth citizen or a citizen of the European Union (other than a Commonwealth citizen).

[132] Political Parties, Elections and Referendums Act 2000 ss.54(3), (3A). "Bequest" includes any form of testamentary disposition: s.160(1).

[133] *Re Robson (Deceased)* [2014] Ch. 470.

three bequest trustees of the British National Party executed a deed of variation to give the residuary estate to the trustees of a settlement formed for the purpose of receiving the gift under the deed of variation.

Having found that the deceased was not a permissible donor, the court found that, for the purposes of s.54(1)(a) of the Act, the British National Party had received and accepted the gift by executing the deed of variation. It declined, however, to direct the executor to distribute the residuary estate to the trustees of the settlement created by the deed, on the ground that the trustees of the settlement had no better right than the British National Party to take the gift, and the British National Party could not have enforced the right to receive a donation in breach of the prohibition contained in s.54 of the Act. The executor was instead directed to distribute the residuary estate to the fourth and fifth defendants as the beneficiaries of the Deceased's estate on intestacy.

CHAPTER 74

ELECTION

A.—MEANING OF THE DOCTRINE

Equity

[In fn.1 replace "Snell's Equity, 32ⁿᵈ edn (2010), para.6–12 et seq." with the following]   **74–02**

Snell's Equity, 33rd edn (2015), para.6-012 onwards;

Basis of the doctrine

[Add at end of fn.9]   **74–03**

; and see the careful analysis and criticism of the doctrine by Strauss QC (sitting as a Deputy Judge) in *Scarfe v Matthews* [2012] EWHC 371; [2012] W.T.L.R. 1579 at [28] onwards. See also Wilson [2012] T.E.L.&T.J. (November) 2, and Bird and Saunders [2013] P.C.B. 34.

[Replace last sentence of fn.11 with the following]

In *Scarfe v Matthews* [2012] EWHC 371; [2012] W.T.L.R. 1579 at [34] the proposition that the basis of the rule lies in the "highest principles of equity" was stated not to carry much conviction.

[Add at end of fn.12]

; *Lissenden v C.A.V. Bosch Ltd* [1940] A.C. 412 at 419.

B.—OPERATION OF THE DOCTRINE

The property must not be inalienable

[Insert the following new text and fn.48a at the end of the second paragraph of para.74–10]   **74–10**

It has been held *obiter* that where beneficiaries assert their right to property contrary to the terms of the will, and the inevitable effect of enforcing that claim is to give them a benefit under the will which otherwise they would not have (where, for example, children assert their forced heirship rights over foreign property which the testator had left to another person, and are therefore entitled to the benefit of a legacy of the tax payable in respect of that foreign property), equity will intervene to require that they compensate the beneficiary disappointed as the result of their claim, notwithstanding that if they had not asserted their right they would not have received any gift under the will.[48a]

[48a] *Scarfe v Matthews* [2012] W.T.L.R. 1579 at [52]–[58].

CHAPTER 76

ABATEMENT

A.—INTRODUCTION

[Add the following before the first sentence]

As stated above in para.75–01, abatement arises where the estate is insufficient to meet the interests of all beneficiaries and the question is how the deficiency is to be borne.

76–01

CHAPTER 77

FUTURE LEGACIES

B.—TIME FOR PAYMENT

Legacy postponed beyond eighteen

77–03   *[In fn.9, replace "Lewin on Trusts, 18th edn (2011), para.5–99 onwards; Megarry & Wade: Law of Real Property, 7th edn (2008), para.9–152 onwards" with the following]*

Lewin on Trusts, 19th edn (2015), para.5–152 onwards; *Megarry & Wade: Law of Real Property*, 8th edn (2012), para.9–163 onwards.

Executor as trustee

77–05   *[In the second sentence, replace "entitled and of full age" with the following]*

entitled are of full age

[In fn.14 replace "Lewin on Trusts, 18th edn (2011), para.13–16 onwards" with the following]

Lewin on Trusts, 19th edn (2015), para.13–020 onwards.

[In fn.15 replace "Lewin on Trusts, 18th edn (2011), para.24–19 onwards" with the following]

Lewin on Trusts, 19th edn (2015), para.24–024 onwards.

CHAPTER 78

PAYMENT AND RECEIPT

A.—INFANT LEGATEES

Courses open to executor

[Replace last sentence of fn.24 with the following]

See *Lewin on Trusts*, 19th edn (2015), para.36–133 and Chs 31 and 32.

78–05

C.—PERSONS LACKING MENTAL CAPACITY

Protective trusts

[Replace fn.45 text with the following]

The topic of protective trusts is considered in *Lewin on Trusts*, 19th edn (2015), para.5–180 onwards; *Snell's Equity*, 33rd edn (2015), para.22–006 onwards.

78–10

E.—ASSIGNEE OF LEGACY

[In fn.51 replace "Lewin on Trusts, 18th edn (2011), para.33–26 et seq" with the following]

Lewin on Trusts, 19th edn (2015), para.33–028 onwards.

78–12

[In fn.57 replace "Lewin on Trusts, 18th edn (2011), para.33–13 onwards" with the following]

Lewin on Trusts, 19th edn (2015), para.33–016.

CHAPTER 79

INCOME, INTEREST AND ANNUITIES

B.—INTEREST

79–03   *[Replace fn.27 text with the following]*

The current rate may be found at *https://www.gov.uk/pay-court-funds-office* [Accessed January 2, 2015].

[Remove second last paragraph in section (beginning "Interest on the surviving . . .")]

[Add new paragraph at end of section]

In cases where a fixed net sum is payable to the surviving spouse or civil partner on an intestacy, however, interest runs from the date of death. For deaths after October 1, 2014, interest on the surviving spouse's fixed net sum on intestacy is fixed at the Bank of England base rate: Administration of Estates Act s.46(1A). For deaths before that date, the rate was fixed at 6 per cent by art.2 of the Intestate Succession (Interest and Capitalisation) Order 1977 as amended.

Compound interest

79–04   *[Add at end of fn.38]*

One example where compound interest appears to be payable is following the over-payment of VAT: *Littlewoods Retail Ltd v R.C.C.* [2014] EWHC 868 (Ch).

CHAPTER 80

EQUITABLE APPORTIONMENT

A.—INTRODUCTION

[Replace the first three paragraphs of the section with the following text and fnn.1 to 4–5 and 6]   **80–01**

In relation to any death on or after October 1, 2013, the old rules of equitable apportionment have been abolished by s.1 of the Trusts (Capital and Income) Act 2013. Those rules, together with the rule in *Allhusen v Whittell* considered above,[1] were developed by equity[2] to ensure fairness between the tenant for life and the remainderman, and were known collectively as the rule in *Howe v Lord Dartmouth*,[3] although they consisted of at least three different rules.

Even before their abolition, the old rules of equitable apportionment were frequently excluded by well-drawn wills because of their complexity,[4-5] though conversely testators may still wish to incorporate them expressly into new will trusts, as without them there may in some cases be a potential for unfairness, as noted by the Law Commission when recommending their abolition.[6] Moreover, the old rules will continue to concern personal representatives for some time to come, as the 2013 Act does not apply to trusts created before October 1, 2013.

C.—THE RULE IN *RE CHESTERFIELD'S TRUSTS*

[Add at end of fn.58]   **80–11**

For a case where the rule was excluded, see *Pagliaro v Thomas* [2008] W.T.L.R. 1417.

---

[1] *Allhusen v Whittell* (1867) L.R. 4 Eq. 295. See para.69–09, above, and as to the difficulty of applying the rule see *Caldecott v Caldecott* (1842) 1 Y. & C.C.C. 312 and Gover, *Capital and Income*, 3rd edn (1933), p.132.

[2] As to legal apportionment under the Apportionment Act 1870, see para.45–76 onwards.

[3] *Howe v Lord Dartmouth* (1802) 7 Ves. 137. The rule is discussed in 7 Conv.(N.S.) 128. See also *Snell's Equity*, 33rd edn (2015), para.29–008 onwards.

[4-5] Kessler, *Drafting Trusts and Will Trusts*, 12th edn (2015) at para.21.60; Brighouse, *Precedents of Wills, Williams on Wills*, 9th edn, especially para.38.17 onwards; Mitchell "Trusts for Sale in Wills— excess baggage" (1999) 63 Conv. 84, 98–103; *Re Chance* [1962] Ch. 593 at 608.

[6] Law Com. No.315, para.6.59.

CHAPTER 81

ASSENTS

E.—WHO MAY ASSENT?

Assent by one executor

81–18   *[Add before the first sentence of fn.130]*

The same applies to administrators: *Fountain Forestry Ltd v Edwards* [1975] Ch. 1.

I.—THE TRUSTS OF LAND AND APPOINTMENT OF TRUSTEES ACT 1996

81–26   *[In fn.181 replace "Lewin on Trusts, 18th edn (2011), Ch.37" with the following]*
Lewin on Trusts, 19th edn (2015), Ch.37.

CHAPTER 82

DISTRIBUTION ON INTESTACY

[Replace "para.70–22" with the following]

para.70–02

82–01

A.—STATUTORY DISTRIBUTION

[Add the following text after the second sentence]

For deaths after October 1, 2014, the Inheritance and Trustees' Powers Act 2014 makes further changes to the interest of the surviving spouse.

82–02

D.—THE SURVIVING SPOUSE OR CIVIL PARTNER

[Add the following text after the first paragraph]

For deaths after October 1, 2014, the surviving spouse of civil partner's rights under s.46(1)(i) of the Administration of Estates Act 1925, as amended by the Inheritance and Trustees' Powers Act 2014, are much increased. If the deceased had no issue, then he or she will take the deceased's entire estate absolutely. But if the deceased died leaving issue, the surviving spouse or civil partner is entitled to the deceased's personal chattels, a fixed net sum, and one half of the residuary estate absolutely.

82–05

The statutory legacy

[Add at end of paragraph]

For deaths after October 1, 2014, only the first sum is relevant. The new provisions inserted by the Inheritance and Trustees' Powers Act 2014 ensure that the fixed net sum will be increased by statutory instrument in line with inflation. Interest on the fixed net sum is payable from the date of death until payment at the Bank of England rate in effect on the date of death: s.46(1A).

82–06

J.—ESTATES PUR AUTRE VIE

[Add at end of paragraph]

For deaths after October 1, 2014, the spouse or civil partner would receive half the capital and income.

82–19

[225]

CHAPTER 83

REFUNDING, FOLLOWING, TRACING AND SUBROGATION

C.—THE PROPRIETARY REMEDY—FOLLOWING, TRACING AND CLAIMING

83–12   *[In fnn.61 and 64, replace "Snell's Equity, 32nd edn (2010)" with the following]*
Snell's Equity, 33rd edn (2015), para.30–054 onwards.

[Add at end of fn.61]

Tracing is possible even into an asset passed on before the trust monies were paid to the person transferring them, provided the inference that they were intended to be substitutions: *Reflo Ltd (in liquidation)* [2014] EWCA Civ 360.

Appendix One

STATUTES

[Insert the following three Acts at the end of Appendix 1]

[Other amendments to legislation include the following:

Section 51 of the Administration of Justice Act 1985 has been repealed by the Crime and Courts Act 2013.

Section 1 of the Family Law Reform Act 1987 has been amended by the Marriage (Same Sex Couples) Act 2013.

Section 17 of the Law of Property (Miscellaneous Provisions) Act 1994 has been amended by the Public Bodies (Abolition of Administrative Justice and Tribunals Council) Order 2013.

Sections 15ZA,15A, 15B and 25 the Inheritance (Provision for Family and Dependants) Act 1975 are affected by the Crime and Courts Act 2013, which replaces references to the County Court with references to the family court.]

Trusts (Capital and Income) Act 2013

CHAPTER 1

1 Disapplication of apportionment etc. rules   A–253

(1) Any entitlement to income under a new trust is to income as it arises (and accordingly section 2 of the Apportionment Act 1870, which provides for income to accrue from day to day, does not apply in relation to the trust).

(2) The following do not apply in relation to a new trust—

    (a) the first part of the rule known as the rule in *Howe v. Earl of Dartmouth* (which requires certain residuary personal estate to be sold);

    (b) the second part of that rule (which withholds from a life tenant income arising from certain investments and compensates the life tenant with payments of interest);

    (c) the rule known as the rule in *Re Earl of Chesterfield's Trusts* (which requires the proceeds of the conversion of certain investments to be apportioned between capital and income);

    (d) the rule known as the rule in *Allhusen v. Whittell* (which requires a contribution to be made from income for the purpose of paying a deceased person's debts, legacies and annuities).

(3) Trustees have power to sell any property which (but for subsection (2)(a)) they would have been under a duty to sell.

(4) Subsections (1) to (3) have effect subject to any contrary intention that appears—

(a) in any trust instrument of the trust, and
(b) in any power under which the trust is created or arises.

(5) In this section "new trust" means a trust created or arising on or after the day on which this section comes into force (and includes a trust created or arising on or after that day under a power conferred before that day).

A–254   **2   Classification of certain corporate distributions as capital**

(1) A receipt consisting of a tax-exempt corporate distribution is to be treated for the purposes of any trust to which this section applies as a receipt of capital (even if it would otherwise be treated for those purposes as a receipt of income).

(2) Subsection (1) has effect subject to any contrary intention that appears—

(a) in any trust instrument of the trust, and
(b) in any power under which the trust is created or arises.

(3) The following are tax-exempt corporate distributions for the purposes of this section and section 3—

(a) a distribution that is an exempt distribution by virtue of section 1076, 1077 or 1078 of the Corporation Tax Act 2010, and
(b) any other distribution of assets (in any form) by a body corporate, where the distribution is of a description specified by an order made by the Secretary of State by statutory instrument.

(4) An order under subsection (3)(b) may specify a description of distribution only if neither income tax nor capital gains tax is chargeable in respect of a distribution of that description.

(5) A statutory instrument containing an order under subsection (3)(b) is subject to annulment in pursuance of a resolution of either House of Parliament.

(6) This section applies to any trust, whether created or arising before or after this section comes into force.

3   Power to compensate income beneficiary

A–255   (1) This section applies in any case where—

(a) by virtue of section 2 a tax-exempt corporate distribution made by a body corporate is treated for the purposes of a trust to which that section applies as a receipt of capital, and
(b) the trustees are satisfied that it is likely that, but for the distribution, there would have been a receipt from the body corporate that would have been a receipt of income for the purposes of the trust.

(2) The trustees may make a payment out of the capital funds of the trust, or transfer any property of the trust, to an income beneficiary for the purpose set out in subsection (3) (and any such payment or transfer is to be treated as a payment or transfer of capital).

(3) The purpose is placing the income beneficiary (so far as practicable) in the position in which the trustees consider that the beneficiary would have been had there been the receipt of income mentioned in subsection (1)(b).

(4) In this section "income beneficiary", in relation to a trust, means a person entitled to income arising under the trust, or for whose benefit such income may be applied.

Presumption of Death Act 2013

CHAPTER 13

Declaration of presumed death   A–256

1 Applying for declaration   A–257

(1) This section applies where a person who is missing—

(a) is thought to have died, or
(b) has not been known to be alive for a period of at least 7 years.

(2) Any person may apply to the High Court for a declaration that the missing person is presumed to be dead.

(3) The court has jurisdiction to hear and determine an application under this section only if—

(a) the missing person was domiciled in England and Wales on the day on which he or she was last known to be alive,
(b) the missing person had been habitually resident in England and Wales throughout the period of 1 year ending with that day, or
(c) subsection (4) is satisfied.

(4) This subsection is satisfied if the application is made by the spouse or civil partner of the missing person and—

(a) the applicant is domiciled in England and Wales on the day on which the application is made, or
(b) the applicant has been habitually resident in England and Wales throughout the period of 1 year ending with that day.

(5) The court must refuse to hear an application under this section if—

(a) the application is made by someone other than the missing person's spouse, civil partner, parent, child or sibling, and

(b) the court considers that the applicant does not have a sufficient interest in the determination of the application.

(6) This section has effect subject to section 21(2).

A–258 2 Making declaration

(1) On an application under section 1, the court must make the declaration if it is satisfied that the missing person—

(a) has died, or

(b) has not been known to be alive for a period of at least 7 years.

(2) It must include in the declaration a finding as to the date and time of the missing person's death.

(3) Where the court—

(a) is satisfied that the missing person has died, but

(b) is uncertain at which moment during a period the missing person died, the finding must be that the missing person is presumed to have died at the end of that period.

(4) Where the court—

(a) is satisfied that the missing person has not been known to be alive for a period of at least 7 years, but

(b) is not satisfied that the missing person has died,

the finding must be that the missing person is presumed to have died at the end of the period of 7 years beginning with the day after the day on which he or she was last known to be alive.

A–259 3 Effect of declaration

(1) A declaration under this Act is conclusive of—

(a) the missing person's presumed death, and

(b) the date and time of the death.

(2) A declaration under this Act is effective against all persons and for all purposes, including for the purposes of—

(a) the acquisition of an interest in any property, and

(b) the ending of a marriage or civil partnership to which the missing person is a party.

(3) But subsections (1) and (2) apply to a declaration only if—

    (a) it has not been appealed against and the period for bringing an appeal has ended, or

    (b) it has been appealed against and the appeal (and any further appeal)

has been unsuccessful.

(4) For the purposes of subsection (3), an appeal has been unsuccessful if—

    (a) it has been dismissed or withdrawn, and

    (b) any period for bringing a further appeal has ended.

4 Other powers of court making declaration

A–260

(1) When making a declaration under this Act, the court may—

    (a) determine any question which relates to an interest in property and arises as a result of the declaration, and

    (b) determine the domicile of the missing person at the time of his or her presumed death.

(2) When making a declaration under this Act, the court may make such order as it considers reasonable in relation to any interest in property acquired as a result of the declaration.

(3) An order under subsection (2) may direct that the value of any interest in property acquired as a result of the declaration is not to be recoverable by virtue of an order made under section 7(2).

(4) It may, in particular, direct that the value of the interest—

    (a) is not to be recoverable in any circumstances, or

    (b) is not to be recoverable where conditions specified in the order are met.

Variation order

5 Varying and revoking declaration

A–261

(1) On an application by any person, a declaration under this Act may be varied or revoked by an order of the High Court (a "variation order").

(2) The court must refuse to hear an application for a variation order if it considers that the applicant does not have a sufficient interest in the determination of the application.

6 Effect of variation order

A–262

(1) A variation order does not affect an interest in property acquired as a result of a declaration under this Act (but see section 7).

(2) A variation order does not revive a marriage or civil partnership that was brought to an end by virtue of a declaration under this Act.

(3) Except as otherwise required by subsection (1) or (2)—

(a) where a variation order varies a declaration, subsections (1) and (2) of section 3 have effect in relation to the declaration as varied by the order, and

(b) where a variation order revokes a declaration, those subsections cease to have effect in relation to the declaration.

(4) But subsection (3) applies only if—

(a) the variation order has not been appealed against and the period for bringing an appeal has ended, or

(b) the variation order has been appealed against and the appeal (and any further appeal) has been unsuccessful.

(5) For the purposes of subsection (4), an appeal has been unsuccessful if—

(a) it has been dismissed or withdrawn, and

(b) any period for bringing a further appeal has ended.

A–263   7   Other functions of court making variation order

(1) When making a variation order, the court may—

(a) determine any question which relates to an interest in property and arises as a result of the variation order, and

(b) determine the domicile of the missing person at the time of his or her presumed death.

(2) When making a variation order, the court must make such further order (if any) as it considers reasonable in relation to any interest in property acquired as a result of the declaration varied or revoked by the order ("the original declaration") (but see subsections (3), (5) and (6)).

(3) The court must not make an order under subsection (2) if the application for the variation order was made after the end of the period of 5 years beginning with the day on which the original declaration was made, unless it considers that there are exceptional circumstances which make it appropriate to do so.

(4) In considering what order to make under subsection (2), the court must, as far as practicable, have regard to the principles in section 8.

(5) An order under subsection (2) does not affect income that accrued in the period—

(a) beginning with the day on which the original declaration was made, and

(b) ending with the day on which the variation order was made.

(6) An order under subsection (2) does not affect or provide grounds to challenge—

(a) a related good faith transaction, or

(b) an interest in property acquired under such a transaction.

(7) A "related good faith transaction" is a transaction under which a person acquires an interest in the property that is the subject of the order (or any part of it) in good faith and for value from—

    (a) a person who acquired an interest in the property (or any part of it) as a result of the original declaration, or

    (b) a person who acquired an interest in the property (or any part of it) from a person described in paragraph (a), whether directly or indirectly.

(8) Where a person has entitlement under a trust by virtue of an order under subsection (2), the trustee is liable to that person for any loss suffered by that person on account of any breach of trust by the trustee in the administration or distribution of all or part of the property that is the subject of the order.

(9) Subsection (8) does not apply to the extent that the trustee's liability is restricted under any enactment or by any provision in a deed regulating the administration of the trust.

(10) In subsection (9) "enactment" includes an enactment contained in—

    (a) an instrument made under an Act, or

    (b) an Act or Measure of the National Assembly for Wales or an instrument made under such an Act or Measure.

8 Principles

A–264

(1) These are the principles referred to in section 7(4).

(2) The first principle is relevant where property ("the relevant property") is being or has been administered under a trust.

(3) The first principle is that—

    (a) a person who, but for section 6(1), would have an interest in the relevant property by virtue of a variation order, and

    (b) a person who, but for section 6(1), would have acquired an interest in the relevant property from a person described in paragraph (a),

should be entitled to have made over to him or her by the trustee in full satisfaction of that interest the things listed in subsection (4).

(4) Those things are—

    (a) the interest in the relevant property or an equivalent interest in property representing the relevant property, to the extent that such property is still in the hands of the trustee when the variation order is made, and

    (b) the value of the interest in the relevant property, to the extent that such property has been distributed.

(5) The second principle is relevant where an insurer has paid a capital sum as a result of a declaration varied or revoked by a variation order.

(6) The second principle is that the capital sum, or any part of the capital sum,

should be repaid to the insurer if the facts in respect of which the variation order was made justify such repayment.

(7) The references in subsections (5) and (6) to a capital sum do not include a capital sum distributed by way of an annuity or other periodical payment.

Further provision about declarations and orders

A–265   **9   Giving notice of application**

(1) A person who makes an application under this Act for a declaration or a variation order must send to the persons specified by rules of court—

    (a) notice of the application, and
    (b) any other information specified by rules of court.

(2) An application under this Act for a declaration or a variation order must be advertised in accordance with rules of court.

(3) The court must refuse to hear an application under this Act for a declaration or a variation order if the requirements in this section have not been met.

A–266   **10   Attorney General**

(1) In proceedings on an application under this Act for a declaration or a variation order, the court may at any stage direct that papers relating to the matter be sent to the Attorney General.

(2) It may do so on the application of a party to the proceedings or without such an application being made.

(3) Where the Attorney General incurs costs in connection with an application under this Act for a declaration or a variation order, the court may make such order as it considers appropriate as to the payment of the costs by parties to the proceedings.

(4) Subsection (3) applies whether the costs are incurred by virtue of a direction under subsection (1), an intervention under section 11(2) or otherwise.

A–267   **11   Right to intervene**

(1) The missing person's spouse, civil partner, parent, child or sibling may intervene in proceedings on an application under this Act for a declaration or a variation order.

(2) The Attorney General may intervene in such proceedings, whether or not the court directs papers relating to the application to be sent to the Attorney General.

(3) Any other person may intervene in such proceedings only with the permission of the court.

(4) References in this section to intervening in proceedings include—

    (a) arguing before the court any question in relation to the application which the court considers it necessary to have fully argued,
    (b) in proceedings on an application for a declaration under this Act, seeking a determination or order under section 4, and

(c) in proceedings on an application for a variation order, seeking a determination or order under section 7.

12 Information

(1) In proceedings on an application under this Act for a declaration or a variation order, the court may by order at any stage require a person who is not a party to the proceedings to provide it with specified information that it considers relevant to the question of whether the missing person is alive or dead.

(2) It may do so only where it considers it necessary for the purpose of disposing of the proceedings.

(3) It may do so on the application of a party to the proceedings or without such an application being made.

(4) The order may not require the provision of information—

(a) which is permitted or required by any rule of law to be withheld on grounds of public interest immunity,

(b) which any person would be entitled to refuse to provide on grounds of legal professional privilege, or

(c) whose provision might incriminate the person providing it, or that person's spouse or civil partner, of an offence.

(5) Before making an order under this section, the court must send notice of its intention to make the order to any person who, in its opinion, is likely to be affected by the order.

(6) The court may discharge or vary an order made under this section on an application made by any person who, in the opinion of the court, is affected by it.

(7) In this section "specified" means specified in an order under this section.

13 Insurance against claims: trustees

(1) If the court so directs, the trustee of a trust affected by a declaration under this Act must as soon as reasonably practicable take out an insurance policy in respect of any claim which may arise by virtue of an order under section 7(2).

(2) For the purposes of this section, a trust is affected by a declaration under this Act if—

(a) it arises as a result of the declaration, or

(b) property held under the trust is affected by the declaration.

(3) A premium payable by the trustee in accordance with a direction under this section may be paid out of money or other property held under the trust.

14 Insurance against claims: insurers paying capital sums

(1) Before paying a capital sum to a person as a result of a declaration under this Act, an insurer may require the person to take out an insurance policy in respect of any claim which the insurer may make in the event of a variation order being made.

[235]

(2) The policy must be taken out—

    (a) in the person's own name, and

    (b) for the benefit of the insurer.

(3) Subsection (1) does not apply where the sum is paid in respect of an annuity or other periodical payment.

(4) In this section "insurer" means any person who provides for the payment of a benefit on a person's death.

Register of Presumed Deaths

A–271   **15 Register of Presumed Deaths**

(1) The Registrar General must maintain a register which is to be called the Register of Presumed Deaths.

(2) The register must be maintained in the General Register Office.

(3) The register may be maintained in any form the Registrar General considers appropriate.

(4) Schedule 1 (further provision about Register of Presumed Deaths) has effect.

Other determinations

A–272   **16 Other determinations about death of missing person**

(1) No declaration which may be applied for under section 1 may be made otherwise than under this Act.

(2) Where a court or tribunal makes a declaration that a missing person is presumed to be dead (other than on an application under this Act), subsections (2) to (4) of section 2 apply to the court or tribunal as they apply to the High Court when it makes a declaration under this Act.

(3) Schedule 2 (amendment of provisions about presumption of death) has effect.

(4) Apart from subsections (1) to (3) and Schedule 2, nothing in the preceding provisions of this Act affects any power or duty that a court or tribunal has other than under this Act to determine a question relating to the death of a missing person.

Supplementary

A–273   **17 Power to amend periods of time**

The Secretary of State may by regulations amend this Act by increasing or reducing a period of time referred to in—

    (a) section 1(1)(b),

    (b) section 2(1) or (4), or

    (c) section 7(3).

18   Consequential and supplementary etc provision

A–274

(1) The Secretary of State may by regulations make consequential, supplementary, incidental, transitional, transitory or saving provision in relation to any provision of this Act.

(2) Regulations under this section may amend, repeal or revoke an enactment passed or made before, or in the same Session as, this Act is passed.

(3) In this section "enactment" includes an enactment contained in—

(a)   an instrument made under an Act, or

(b)   an Act or Measure of the National Assembly for Wales or an instrument made under such an Act or Measure.

19   Regulations

A–275

(1) Regulations under this Act are to be made by statutory instrument.

(2) A statutory instrument containing the following regulations (whether alone or with other provision) may not be made unless a draft of the instrument has been laid before, and approved by a resolution of, each House of Parliament—

(a)   regulations under section 17;

(b)   regulations under section 18 which amend or repeal an Act (including an Act or Measure of the National Assembly for Wales).

(3) Any other statutory instrument containing regulations made by the Secretary of State under this Act is subject to annulment in pursuance of a resolution of either House of Parliament.

20   Interpretation

A–276

(1) In this Act—

"the court" means the High Court (except in section 16(2));

"interest in property" means an interest in property of any description, including an estate in land and a right over property;

"the missing person", in relation to a declaration under this Act or an application, determination or order made in connection with such a declaration, means the person who is or would be the subject of the declaration;

"the Registrar General" means the Registrar General for England and Wales;

"sibling" means a sibling of the full blood or the half blood;

"trustee" includes an executor, administrator or personal representative;

"variation order" has the meaning given in section 5.

(2) References in this Act to a party to proceedings include a person intervening in the proceedings in accordance with section 11.

21   Application to Crown

A–277

(1) This Act binds the Crown.

(2) But an application may not be made under this Act for a declaration in respect of Her Majesty.

A–278 **22 Commencement**

(1) The following come into force on the day on which this Act is passed—

(a) section 9 so far as it confers a power to make rules,
(b) section 15(4) and Schedule 1 so far as they confer a power to make regulations,
(c) sections 17 to 21,
(d) this section, and
(e) sections 23 and 24.

(2) Subject to subsection (1), the provisions of this Act come into force on such day as the Secretary of State may by order appoint.

(3) An order under this section must be made by statutory instrument. (4) An order under this section may—

(a) appoint different days for different purposes, and
(b) include transitional, transitory or saving provision.

A–279 **23 Extent**

This Act extends to England and Wales.

A–280 **24 Short title**

This Act may be cited as the Presumption of Death Act 2013.

SCHEDULES

SCHEDULE 1   Section 15

REGISTER OF PRESUMED DEATHS

A–281 *Entries in Register of Presumed Deaths*

1 (1) When a declaration under this Act satisfies section 3(3)(a) or (b), the court must send to the Registrar General—

(a) a copy of the declaration, and
(b) any prescribed information.

(2) On receipt of a copy of a declaration in accordance with sub-paragraph (1), the Registrar General must—

(a) make an entry in the Register of Presumed Deaths containing the name of the missing person and such other information as may be prescribed in relation to that person's presumed death,

(b) secure that the entry made in the Register of Presumed Deaths is included in the index of the registers of deaths, and

(c) make traceable the connection between the entry in the Register of Presumed Deaths and the index of the registers of deaths.

(3) In this paragraph "prescribed" means prescribed by regulations made by the Registrar General with the approval of the Secretary of State.

Amendment and cancellation of entries in Register

A–282

2 (1) When a variation order satisfies section 6(4)(a) or (b), the court must send to the Registrar General—

(a) a copy of the order, and
(b) any prescribed information.

(2) Where the variation order varies a declaration, on receipt of a copy of the order in accordance with sub-paragraph (1), the Registrar General must—

(a) amend the entry in the Register of Presumed Deaths in relation to the missing person, and
(b) amend any entry relating to that person made in the index of the registers of deaths in accordance with paragraph 1(2)(b).

(3) Where the variation order revokes a declaration, on receipt of a copy of the order in accordance with sub-paragraph (1), the Registrar General must—

(a) cancel the entry in the Register of Presumed Deaths relating to the missing person, and
(b) cancel any entry relating to that person made in the index of the registers of deaths in accordance with paragraph 1(2)(b).

(4) In this paragraph "prescribed" means prescribed by regulations made by the Registrar General with the approval of the Secretary of State.

Searches and certified copies

A–283

3 (1) Any right to search the index of the registers of deaths includes the right to search entries included in it in accordance with paragraph 1(2)(b).

(2) Any person is entitled to have a certified copy of an entry in the Register of Presumed Deaths (but see paragraph 6).

(3) The Registrar General must cause a certified copy of an entry in the Register of Presumed Deaths to be sealed or stamped with the seal of the General Register Office.

(4) No certified copy of an entry in the Register of Presumed Deaths is to be of any force or effect unless it is sealed or stamped in accordance with sub-paragraph (3).

(5) Section 34(5) of the Births and Deaths Registration Act 1953 (certified copy on form different from original entry deemed to be true copy) applies in relation to a copy of an entry in the Register of Presumed Deaths as it applies in relation to a copy of an entry in a register made under that Act.

Proof of death

A–284

4 A certified copy of an entry in the Register of Presumed Deaths in relation to a person is to be received as evidence of the person's death, without further or other proof, if it purports to be sealed or stamped in accordance with paragraph 3(3).

Correction and annotation of Register

A–285

5 (1) Where it appears to the Registrar General that there is a clerical error in the Register of Presumed Deaths, the Registrar General may authorise a person to correct the error.

(2) Where it appears to the court that there is an error in the Register of Presumed Deaths, the court may direct the Registrar General to secure that the error is corrected.

(3) The Registrar General may annotate, or cancel the annotation of, any entry in the Register of Presumed Deaths.

(4) Sub-paragraph (5) applies where it appears to the Registrar General that the death of a missing person to whom an entry in the Register of Presumed Deaths relates—

    (a)   has been registered in a register of deaths made under the Births and Deaths Registration Act 1953, or

    (b)   has been recorded in a register kept or maintained under the law of a country or territory outside England and Wales corresponding in nature to a register described in paragraph (a).

(5) The Registrar General must annotate the relevant entry in the Register of Presumed Deaths accordingly.

A–286   *Fees*

6 (1) A fee of a prescribed amount is payable to the Registrar General for a certified copy of an entry in the Register of Presumed Deaths.

(2) The Registrar General may refuse to provide such a copy until the prescribed fee is paid, except as otherwise prescribed.

(3) In this paragraph "prescribed" means prescribed by regulations made by the Secretary of State.

A–287   *Interpretation*

7 In this Schedule "the index of registers of deaths" means the index kept in the General Register Office of certified copies of entries in the registers of deaths made under the Births and Deaths Registration Act 1953.

SCHEDULE 2   Section 16

AMENDMENT OF PROVISIONS ABOUT PRESUMPTION OF DEATH

A–288   *Matrimonial Causes Act 1973 (c. 18)*

1 Omit section 19 of the Matrimonial Causes Act 1973 (presumption of death and dissolution of marriage).

A–289   *Domicile and Matrimonial Proceedings Act 1973 (c. 45)*

2 In section 5 of the Domicile and Matrimonial Proceedings Act 1973 (jurisdiction of High Court and county courts), omit—

    (a)   subsection (1)(b) (and the "and" before it);

    (b)   subsection (4).

A–290   *Civil Partnership Act 2004 (c. 33)*

3 (1) Section 222 of the Civil Partnership Act 2004 (proceedings for presumption of death order) is amended as follows.

(2) After "presumption of death order" insert "on an application made by a civil partner".

(3) Omit paragraphs (a) and (b).

(4) After those paragraphs insert—

    "(ba)   at the time the application is made, the High Court does not have jurisdiction to entertain an application by that civil partner under section 1 of the Presumption of Death Act 2013 for a declaration that the other civil partner is presumed to be dead, and".

A–291   *Consequential repeal*

4 In consequence of the repeal in paragraph 1, omit paragraph 7 of Schedule 8 to the Family Law Act 1996.

Inheritance and Trustees' Powers Act 2014

CHAPTER 16

1 Intestacy: surviving spouse or civil partner

A–292

(1) Section 46 of the Administration of Estates Act 1925 (succession to real and personal estate on intestacy) is amended as follows.

(2) For the Table in paragraph (i) of subsection (1) substitute—

"TABLE

(1) If the intestate leaves no issue:	the residuary estate shall be held in trust for the surviving spouse or civil partner absolutely.
(2) If the intestate leaves issue:	(A) the surviving spouse or civil partner shall take the personal chattels absolutely;
	(B) the residuary estate of the intestate (other than the personal chattels) shall stand charged with the payment of a fixed net sum, free of death duties and costs, to the surviving spouse or civil partner, together with simple interest on it from the date of the death at the rate provided for by subsection (1A) until paid or appropriated; and
	(C) subject to providing for the sum and interest referred to in paragraph (B), the residuary estate (other than the personal chattels) shall be held—
	(a) as to one half, in trust for the surviving spouse or civil partner absolutely, and
	(b) as to the other half, on the statutory trusts for the issue of the intestate.

The amount of the fixed net sum referred to in paragraph (B) of case (2) of this Table is to be determined in accordance with Schedule 1A."

(3) For subsection (1A) substitute—

[241]

"(1A) The interest rate referred to in paragraph (B) of case (2) of the Table in subsection (1)(i) is the Bank of England rate that had effect at the end of the day on which the intestate died."

(4) After subsection (4) insert—

"(5) In subsection (1A) "Bank of England rate" means—

(a) the rate announced by the Monetary Policy Committee of the Bank of England as the official bank rate, or
(b) where an order under section 19 of the Bank of England Act 1998 (reserve powers) is in force, any equivalent rate determined by the Treasury under that section.

(6) The Lord Chancellor may by order made by statutory instrument amend the definition of "Bank of England rate" in subsection (5) (but this subsection does not affect the generality of subsection (7)(b)).

(7) The Lord Chancellor may by order made by statutory instrument—

(a) amend subsection (1A) so as to substitute a different interest rate (however specified or identified) for the interest rate for the time being provided for by that subsection;
(b) make any amendments of, or repeals in, this section that may be consequential on or incidental to any amendment made by virtue of paragraph (a).

(8) A statutory instrument containing an order under subsection (6) is subject to annulment pursuant to a resolution of either House of Parliament.

(9) A statutory instrument containing an order under subsection (7) may not be made unless a draft of the instrument has been laid before and approved by a resolution of each House of Parliament."

A–293   **2   The fixed net sum**

(1) In the Administration of Estates Act 1925, after the First Schedule insert the Schedule set out in Schedule 1 to this Act (which provides for the determination of the fixed net sum).

(2) The Family Provision Act 1966 is repealed.

A–294   **3   Definition of "personal chattels"**

(1) For paragraph (x) of section 55(1) of the Administration of Estates Act 1925 (definitions) substitute—

"(x) "Personal chattels" means tangible movable property, other than any such property which—
consists of money or securities for money, or
was used at the death of the intestate solely or mainly for business purposes, or
was held at the death of the intestate solely as an investment:".

(2) If a will or codicil containing a reference to personal chattels defined (in whatever form of words) by reference to section 55(1)(x) of the Administration of Estates Act 1925 was executed before the coming into force of subsection (1), then unless the contrary intention appears subsection (1) is to be disregarded in interpreting the reference to personal chattels.

4 Adoption and contingent interests

A–295

(1) In section 69 of the Adoption and Children Act 2002 (rules of interpretation for instruments concerning property), in subsection (4)—

(a) omit "or" after paragraph (a), and
(b) after paragraph (b) insert ", or
(c) any contingent interest (other than a contingent interest in remainder) which the adopted person has immediately before the adoption in the estate of a deceased parent, whether testate or intestate."

(2) The amendments made by subsection (1) have effect only in relation to adoptions whose date is the day this section comes into force or later.

5 Presumption of prior death

A–296

In section 18 of the Family Law Reform Act 1987 (succession on intestacy), after subsection (2) insert—

"(2ZA) Subsection (2) does not apply if a person is recorded as the intestate's father, or as a parent (other than the mother) of the intestate—

(a) in a register of births kept (or having effect as if kept) under the Births and Deaths Registration Act 1953, or
(b) in a record of a birth included in an index kept under section 30(1) of that Act (indexes relating to certain other registers etc)."

6 Amendments of Inheritance (Provision for Family and Dependants) Act 1975

A–297

Schedule 2 amends the Inheritance (Provision for Family and Dependants) Act 1975.

7 Date when representation is first taken out

A–298

Schedule 3 amends enactments relating to the determination, for various purposes, of the date on which representation with respect to the estate of a deceased person is first taken out.

8 Power to apply income for maintenance

A–299

In section 31 of the Trustee Act 1925 (power to apply income for maintenance and to accumulate surplus income during a minority), in subsection (1)—

    (a) in paragraph (i) for "as may, in all the circumstances, be reasonable," substitute "as the trustees may think fit," and

    (b) omit the words from "Provided that" to the end.

A–300   **9 Power of advancement**

(1) Section 32 of the Trustee Act 1925 (power of advancement) is amended as follows.

(2) In subsection (1), in the words before the proviso—

    (a) after "subject to a trust," insert "or transfer or apply any other property forming part of the capital of the trust property," and

    (b) after "payment" insert ", transfer".

(3) In subsection (1), in paragraph (a) of the proviso—

    (a) for the words from the beginning to "amount" substitute "property (including any money) so paid, transferred or applied for the advancement or benefit of any person must not, altogether, represent more than", and

    (b) omit "one-half of".

(4) In paragraph (b) of that proviso for "the money so paid or applied" substitute "the money or other property so paid, transferred or applied".

(5) In paragraph (c) of that proviso—

    (a) after "payment" (in both places) insert ", transfer", and

    (b) for "paid" substitute "or other property paid, transferred".

(6) After subsection (1), insert—

"(1A) In exercise of the foregoing power trustees may pay, transfer or apply money or other property on the basis (express or implied) that it shall be treated as a proportionate part of the capital out of which it was paid, transferred or applied, for the purpose of bringing it into account in accordance with proviso (b) to subsection (1) of this section."

A–301   **10 Application of sections 8 and 9**

(1) Section 8 applies in accordance with subsections (4) and (5).

(2) Section 9, apart from subsection (3)(b), applies in relation to trusts whenever created or arising.

(3) Section 9(3)(b) applies in accordance with subsections (4) and (5).

(4) Subject to subsection (5), the provisions mentioned in subsections (1) and (3) apply only in relation to trusts created or arising after the coming into force of those provisions.

(5) Those provisions also apply in relation to an interest under a trust (not falling within subsection (4)) if the interest is created or arises as a result of the exercise, after the coming into force of those provisions, of any power.

11 Minor and consequential amendments

A–302

Schedule 4 makes minor and consequential amendments.

12 Short title, commencement, application and extent

A–303

(1) This Act may be cited as the Inheritance and Trustees' Powers Act 2014.

(2) This section comes into force on the day on which this Act is passed, but otherwise this Act comes into force on such day as the Lord Chancellor may by order made by statutory instrument appoint.

(3) An order under subsection (2) may appoint different days for different purposes.

(4) The provisions of this Act, except sections 4 and 8 to 10, apply only in relation to deaths occurring after the coming into force of the provision concerned.

(5) Subject to subsection (6), this Act extends to England and Wales only.

(6) The repeals made by paragraph 4 of Schedule 4 extend to the United Kingdom.

SCHEDULES

SCHEDULE 1

Section 2   A–304

DETERMINATION OF THE FIXED NET SUM

The following is the Schedule inserted after the First Schedule to the Administration of Estates Act 1925—

"SCHEDULE 1A

DETERMINATION OF THE FIXED NET SUM

1 This Schedule has effect for determining the fixed net sum referred to in paragraph (B) of case (2) of the Table in section 46(1)(i).

2 On the coming into force of this Schedule, the amount of the fixed net sum is the amount fixed by order under section 1(1)(a) of the Family Provision Act 1966 immediately before the coming into force of this Schedule.

3 (1) The Lord Chancellor may from time to time by order made by statutory instrument specify the amount of the fixed net sum.

(2) An order under sub-paragraph (1) relates only to deaths occurring after the coming into force of the order.

(3) The first order under sub-paragraph (1) supersedes paragraph 2 of this Schedule.

(4) A statutory instrument containing an order under sub-paragraph (1) is subject to annulment pursuant to a resolution of either House of Parliament.

(5) Sub-paragraph (4) does not apply in the case mentioned in paragraph 6(3), or in the case of an instrument which also contains provision made by virtue of paragraph 8.

4 (1) This paragraph applies where—

(a)   a figure for the consumer prices index for a month has become available, and

(b)   the consumer prices index for that month is more than 15% higher than the consumer prices index for the base month.

(2) The Lord Chancellor must, before the end of the period of 21 days beginning with the day on which the figure mentioned in sub- paragraph (1)(a) becomes available ("the publication date"), make an order under paragraph 3(1).

(3) But if the Lord Chancellor determines under paragraph 6 that the order should specify an amount other than that mentioned in paragraph 6(1), the Lord Chancellor is to be taken to have complied with sub-paragraph (2) if, within the period of 21 days beginning with the publication date—

(a)   a draft of a statutory instrument containing the order is laid before each House of Parliament, and
(b)   paragraph 6(4) is complied with.

(4) In this paragraph—

"the base month" means—
(a)   the month in which this Schedule came into force, or
(b)   if one or more orders under paragraph 3(1) have been made before the publication date, the most recent month for which a figure for the consumer prices index was available when the Lord Chancellor made the most recent of those orders;
"consumer prices index" means—
(a)   the all items consumer prices index published by the Statistics Board, or
(b)   if that index is not published for a relevant month, any substituted index or index figures published by the Statistics Board.

5 The Lord Chancellor must ensure that the power under paragraph 3(1) is exercised in such a way that an order is made—

(a)   before the end of the period of 5 years beginning with the date this Schedule comes into force, and then
(b)   before the end of the period of 5 years since the date on which the last order under paragraph 3(1) was made, and so on.

6 (1) Unless the Lord Chancellor otherwise determines, an order under paragraph 3(1) must specify the amount given by paragraph 7(2) or (as the case requires) 7(3).

(2) If the Lord Chancellor does otherwise determine—

(a)   an order under paragraph 3(1) may provide for the fixed net sum to be of any amount (including an amount equal to or lower than the previous amount), and
(b)   the Lord Chancellor must prepare a report stating the reason for the determination.

(3) A statutory instrument containing an order under paragraph 3(1) that specifies an amount other than that mentioned in sub- paragraph (1) of this paragraph may not be made unless a draft of the instrument has been laid before and approved by a resolution of each House of Parliament.

(4) The Lord Chancellor must lay the report before Parliament no later than the date on which the draft of the instrument containing the order is laid before Parliament.

7 (1) The amount mentioned in paragraph 6(1) is found as follows.

(2) If the consumer prices index for the current month is higher than that for the base month, the amount to be specified in the order is found by—

(a)   increasing the amount of the previous fixed net sum by the same percentage as the percentage increase in the consumer prices index between the base month and the current month, and
(b)   if the resulting figure is not a multiple of £1,000, rounding it up to the nearest multiple of £1,000.

(3) If the consumer prices index for the current month is the same as, or lower than, that for the base month, the amount specified in the order is to be the same as the amount of the previous fixed net sum.

(4) In this paragraph—

"the base month" means—

    (a)   in the case of the first order under paragraph 3(1), the month in which this Schedule came into force, and

    (b)   in the case of each subsequent order, the month which was the current month in relation to the previous order;

"the current month" means the most recent month for which a figure for the consumer prices index is available when the Lord Chancellor makes the order;

"consumer prices index" has the same meaning as in paragraph 4.

8 (1) The Lord Chancellor may by order made by statutory instrument amend paragraphs 4 and 7 so as to—

    (a)   substitute for references to the consumer prices index (as defined) references to another index, and

    (b)   make amendments in those paragraphs consequential on that substitution.

(2) A statutory instrument containing an order under sub-paragraph (1) may not be made unless a draft of the instrument has been laid before and approved by a resolution of each House of Parliament."

SCHEDULE 2

Section 6   **A–305**

AMENDMENTS OF INHERITANCE (PROVISION FOR FAMILY AND DEPENDANTS) ACT 1975

1 The Inheritance (Provision for Family and Dependants) Act 1975 is amended as follows.

Children of the family

A–306

2 (1) Section 1 (application for financial provision from deceased's estate) is amended as follows.

(2) In subsection (1)(d), for the words from "who" to the end substitute "who in relation to any marriage or civil partnership to which the deceased was at any time a party, or otherwise in relation to any family in which the deceased at any time stood in the role of a parent, was treated by the deceased as a child of the family;".

(3) After subsection (2) insert—

"(2A) The reference in subsection (1)(d) above to a family in which the deceased stood in the role of a parent includes a family of which the deceased was the only member (apart from the applicant)."

Maintenance

A–307

3 In section 1 (application for financial provision from deceased's estate), for subsection (3) substitute—

"(3) For the purposes of subsection (1)(e) above, a person is to be treated as being maintained by the deceased (either wholly or partly, as the case may be) only if the deceased was making a substantial contribution in money or money's worth towards the reasonable needs of that person, other than a contribution made for full valuable consideration pursuant to an arrangement of a commercial nature."

Powers of court

A–308

4 (1) Section 2 (powers of court to make orders) is amended as follows.

(2) In subsection (1), at the end insert—

"(h) an order varying for the applicant's benefit the trusts on which the deceased's estate is held (whether arising under the will, or the law relating to intestacy, or both)."

(3) After subsection (3) insert—

"(3A) In assessing for the purposes of an order under this section the extent (if any) to which the net estate is reduced by any debts or liabilities (including any inheritance tax paid or payable out of the estate), the court may assume that the order has already been made."

A–309   *Matters to which court is to have regard*

5 (1) Section 3 (matters to which court is to have regard when exercising powers under section 2) is amended as follows.
(2) In subsection (2), at the end of each of the final two sentences insert "; but nothing requires the court to treat such provision as setting an upper or lower limit on the provision which may be made by an order under section 2."
(3) In subsection (3)—

(a)   for paragraph (a) substitute—
   "(a) to whether the deceased maintained the applicant and, if so, to the length of time for which and basis on which the deceased did so, and to the extent of the contribution made by way of maintenance;
   (aa) to whether and, if so, to what extent the deceased assumed responsibility for the maintenance of the applicant;";
(b)   in paragraph (b) for "assuming and discharging that responsibility" substitute "maintaining or assuming responsibility for maintaining the applicant".

(4) In subsection (4), for the words from "regard" to the end substitute

"regard—
(a)   to the length of time for which and basis on which the deceased maintained the applicant, and to the extent of the contribution made by way of maintenance;
(b)   to whether and, if so, to what extent the deceased assumed responsibility for the maintenance of the applicant."

A–310   *Time limit for applications*

6 In section 4 (time-limit for applications), at the end insert "(but nothing prevents the making of an application before such representation is first taken out)".

A–311   *Joint tenancies*

7 (1) Section 9 (property held on joint tenancy) is amended as follows.
(2) In subsection (1)—

(a)   omit the words from ", before the end" to "first taken out," and
(b)   omit ", at the value thereof immediately before his death,".

(3) After subsection (1) insert—

"(1A) Where an order is made under subsection (1) the value of the deceased's severable share of the property concerned is taken for the purposes of this Act to be the value that the share would have had at the date of the hearing of the application for an order under section 2 had the share been severed immediately before the deceased's death, unless the court orders that the share is to be valued at a different date."

DETERMINATION OF DATE WHEN REPRESENTATION IS FIRST TAKEN OUT

1 In section 31 of the Matrimonial Causes Act 1973 (variation, discharge, etc, of certain orders for financial relief), for subsection (9) substitute—

"(9) The following are to be left out of account when considering for the purposes of subsection (6) above when representation was first taken out—

    (a) a grant limited to settled land or to trust property,

    (b) any other grant that does not permit any of the estate to be distributed,

    (c) a grant limited to real estate or to personal estate, unless a grant limited to the remainder of the estate has previously been made or is made at the same time,

    (d) a grant, or its equivalent, made outside the United Kingdom (but see subsection (9A) below).

(9A) A grant sealed under section 2 of the Colonial Probates Act 1892 counts as a grant made in the United Kingdom for the purposes of subsection (9) above, but is to be taken as dated on the date of sealing."

2 For section 23 of the Inheritance (Provision for Family and Dependants) Act 1975 (determination of date on which representation was first taken out) substitute—

"23 Determination of date on which representation was first taken out

(1) The following are to be left out of account when considering for the purposes of this Act when representation with respect to the estate of a deceased person was first taken out—

    (a) a grant limited to settled land or to trust property,

    (b) any other grant that does not permit any of the estate to be distributed,

    (c) a grant limited to real estate or to personal estate, unless a grant limited to the remainder of the estate has previously been made or is made at the same time,

    (d) a grant, or its equivalent, made outside the United Kingdom (but see subsection (2) below).

(2) A grant sealed under section 2 of the Colonial Probates Act 1892 counts as a grant made in the United Kingdom for the purposes of this section, but is to be taken as dated on the date of sealing."

3 In section 20 of the Administration of Justice Act 1982 (rectification of wills), for subsection (4) substitute—

"(4) The following are to be left out of account when considering for the purposes of this section when representation with respect to the estate of a deceased person was first taken out—

    (a) a grant limited to settled land or to trust property,

    (b) any other grant that does not permit any of the estate to be distributed,

    (c) a grant limited to real estate or to personal estate, unless a grant limited to the remainder of the estate has previously been made or is made at the same time,

    (d) a grant, or its equivalent, made outside the United Kingdom (but see subsection (5)).

(5) A grant sealed under section 2 of the Colonial Probates Act 1892 counts as a grant made in the United Kingdom for the purposes of subsection (4), but is to be taken as dated on the date of sealing."

4 (1) Schedule 1 to the Children Act 1989 (financial provision for children) is amended as follows.

(2) In paragraph 7 (variation of orders for secured periodical payments after death of parent), for sub-paragraph (6) substitute—

"(6) The following are to be left out of account when considering for the purposes of sub-paragraph (2) when representation was first taken out—

(a) a grant limited to settled land or to trust property,
(b) any other grant that does not permit any of the estate to be distributed,
(c) a grant limited to real estate or to personal estate, unless a grant limited to the remainder of the estate has previously been made or is made at the same time,
(d) a grant, or its equivalent, made outside the United Kingdom (but see sub-paragraph (6A)).

(6A) A grant sealed under section 2 of the Colonial Probates Act 1892 counts as a grant made in the United Kingdom for the purposes of sub-paragraph (6), but is to be taken as dated on the date of sealing."

(3) In paragraph 11 (alteration of maintenance agreements after death of one of the parties), for sub-paragraph (4) substitute—

"(4) The following are to be left out of account when considering for the purposes of sub-paragraph (3) when representation was first taken out—

(a) a grant limited to settled land or to trust property,
(b) any other grant that does not permit any of the estate to be distributed,
(c) a grant limited to real estate or to personal estate, unless a grant limited to the remainder of the estate has previously been made or is made at the same time,
(d) a grant, or its equivalent, made outside the United Kingdom (but see sub-paragraph (4A)).

(4A) A grant sealed under section 2 of the Colonial Probates Act 1892 counts as a grant made in the United Kingdom for the purposes of sub-paragraph (4), but is to be taken as dated on the date of sealing."

5 In Schedule 5 to the Civil Partnership Act 2004, in paragraph 60 (variation of secured periodical payments order where person liable has died), for sub- paragraph (6) substitute—

"(6) The following are to be left out of account when considering for the purposes of sub-paragraph (3) when representation was first taken out—

(a) a grant limited to settled land or to trust property,
(b) any other grant that does not permit any of the estate to be distributed,
(c) a grant limited to real estate or to personal estate, unless a grant limited to the remainder of the estate has previously been made or is made at the same time,
(d) a grant, or its equivalent, made outside the United Kingdom (but see sub-paragraph (7)).

(7) A grant sealed under section 2 of the Colonial Probates Act 1892 counts as a grant made in the United Kingdom for the purposes of sub-paragraph (6), but is to be taken as dated on the date of sealing."

SCHEDULE 4   Section 11

MINOR AND CONSEQUENTIAL AMENDMENTS

A–313   *Administration of Estates Act 1925*

1 (1) The Administration of Estates Act 1925 is amended as follows.

(2) Omit section 46(3) (which relates to deaths in circumstances where it is uncertain which of two people survived the other).

(3) Omit section 47A (right of surviving spouse to have own life interest redeemed).

(4) In section 48 (powers of personal representative in respect of interests of surviving spouse), in subsection (2), omit the following—

    (a)   paragraph (b), and the word "and" after paragraph (a), and
    (b)   the words "in either case".

(5) In section 49 (application of Part 4 of Act to partial intestacies), omit subsection (4).

Intestates' Estates Act 1952

A–314

2 (1) Schedule 2 to the Intestates' Estates Act 1952 (rights of surviving spouse or civil partner as respects home) is amended as follows.

(2) Omit paragraph 1(4).

(3) In paragraph 3, for sub-paragraph (3) substitute—

"(3) The court may extend the period of 12 months referred to in sub- paragraph (1)(a) if the surviving spouse or civil partner applies for it to be extended and satisfies the court that a period limited to 12 months would operate unfairly—

    (a)   in consequence of the representation first taken out being probate of a will subsequently revoked on the ground that the will was invalid, or
    (b)   in consequence of a question whether a person had an interest in the estate, or as to the nature of an interest in the estate, not having been determined at the time when representation was first taken out, or
    (c)   in consequence of some other circumstances affecting the administration or distribution of the estate.

(4) For the purposes of the construction of the references in this paragraph to the first taking out of representation, there shall be left out of account—

    (a)   a grant limited to settled land or to trust property,
    (b)   any other grant that does not permit any of the estate to be distributed,
    (c)   a grant limited to real estate or to personal estate, unless a grant limited to the remainder of the estate has previously been made or is made at the same time,
    (d)   a grant, or its equivalent, made outside the United Kingdom (but see sub-paragraph (5)).

(5) A grant sealed under section 2 of the Colonial Probates Act 1892 counts as a grant made in the United Kingdom for the purposes of sub-paragraph (4), but is to be taken as dated on the date of sealing."

Administration of Justice Act 1977

A–315

3 In section 28 of the Administration of Justice Act 1977, omit subsection (1).

Inheritance Tax Act 1984

A–316

4 In the Inheritance Tax Act 1984—

    (a)   in section 17 (changes in distribution of deceased's estate, etc.), omit paragraph (c);
    (b)   omit section 145 (redemption of surviving spouse's or civil partner's life interest).

Appendix Two

RULES AND ORDERS

[Due to space constraints, it has not been possible to include new statutory instruments. For the current version of the Chancery Guide, the reader should consult the latest version (October 2013) online: http://www.justice.gov.uk/ downloads/courts/chancery-court/chancery-guide.doc.]

Part 57
Probate and Inheritance

[Add at end of paragraph]   A–409

V PROCEEDINGS UNDER THE PRESUMPTION OF DEATH ACT 2013

Scope and interpretation

57.17 (1) This Section contains rules about proceedings under the Presumption   **A–409A**
of Death Act 2013.

(2) In this Section, terms used in the Presumption of Death Act 2013 Act have the meaning given by that Act, and—

- (a) "the 2013 Act" means the Presumption of Death Act 2013;
- (b) "a claim for a declaration of presumed death" means a claim under section 1 of the 2013 Act for a declaration that a missing person is presumed to be dead;
- (c) "a claim for a variation order" means a claim for an order under section 5 of the 2013 Act varying or revoking a declaration of presumed death.

Proceedings to be in the High Court

57.18 (1) Proceedings under the 2013 Act must be issued in the High Court in   **A–409B**
either—

- (a) the Chancery Division; or
- (b) the Family Division.

(2) The Civil Procedure Rules apply to proceedings under the 2013 Act which are brought in the Family Division, except that the provisions of the Family Procedure Rules 2010(a) relating to the drawing up and service of orders apply instead of the provisions in Part 40 and Practice Direction 40B.

Procedure for claims for a declaration of presumed death or a variation order

A–409C   **57.19** (1) A claim for a declaration of presumed death or for a variation order must be made by issuing a claim form in accordance with Part 8.

(2) In addition to the matters set out in rule 8.2 (contents of the claim form), the claim form must also include or be accompanied by the information required by Practice Direction 57B.

(3) Rules 8.2A, 8.3, 8.4 and 8.5 apply as modified by paragraphs (4) to (7) of this rule (and references elsewhere in these Rules to a defendant and to an acknowledgment of service are, where relevant, to be read as references to the substitute terms in rules 8.2A, 8.3, 8.4 and 8.5 as so modified).

(4) Rule 8.2A (issue of claim form without naming defendants) applies as if for "without naming a defendant" in paragraph (1) there were substituted 'without serving notice on any person'.

(5) Rule 8.3 (acknowledgment of service) applies—

(a)   as if, instead of referring to a defendant, it referred to a person giving notice of intention to intervene or applying for permission to intervene, as the case may be;

(b)   as if, instead of referring to an acknowledgment of service, it referred to a notice of intention to intervene or an application for permission to intervene, as the case may be; and

(c)   subject to paragraph (7), with the substitution of 21 days for 14 days as the time within which the notice of intention to intervene or application for permission to intervene must be filed and served.

(6) Rules 8.4 (consequence of not filing an acknowledgment of service) and 8.5 (filing and serving written evidence) apply—

(a)   as if, instead of referring to a defendant, they referred to a person giving notice of intention to intervene or applying for permission to intervene, as the case may be; and

(b)   as if, instead of referring to an acknowledgment of service, they referred to a notice of intention to intervene or an application for permission to intervene, as the case may be.

(7) If the claim form is served out of the jurisdiction under rule 6.32 or 6.33, the period for filing notice of intention to intervene or an application for permission to intervene, as the case may be, and any written evidence, is 7 days longer than the relevant period for serving an acknowledgement of service specified in rule 6.35 or Practice Direction 6B.

Giving notice of claim

57.20 (1) Where the claim is for a declaration of presumed death, the claimant **A–409D** must give notice of the claim by serving a copy of it on the following persons (where not the claimant)—

(a) the spouse or civil partner of the missing person;

(b) any parent of the missing person;

(c) any child of the missing person;

(d) any sibling of the missing person;

(e) if there are no persons within sub-paragraphs (a) to (d), the nearest relative of the missing person known to the claimant; and

(f) any other person (including in particular any insurance company) appearing to the claimant to have an interest in the claim.

(2) Where the claim is for a variation order, the claimant must give notice of the claim by serving a copy of it on the following persons (where not the claimant)—

(a) the person who was the claimant for the declaration of presumed death or (as the case may be) previous variation order which it is sought to have varied or revoked;

(b) the spouse or civil partner of the missing person;

(c) any parent of the missing person;

(d) any child of the missing person;

(e) any sibling of the missing person;

(f) if there are no persons within sub-paragraphs (b) to (e), the nearest relative of the missing person known to the claimant; and

(g) any other person (including in particular any insurance company) appearing to the claimant to have an interest in the claim.

(3) Notice under paragraph (1)(a) to (f) or paragraph (2)(a) to (g) must be given within 7 days after the claim is issued.

Advertisement of claim

57.21 (1) The claimant (whether the claim is for a declaration of presumed **A–409E** death or for a variation order) must, within 7 days of issue of the claim, ensure that notice of the claim is published—

(a) in a form which meets the requirements set out in Practice Direction 57B; and

(b) in at least one newspaper circulating in the vicinity of the last known address of the missing person.

(2) The claimant must, at least 5 days before the hearing, file a copy of the page of the newspaper bearing the advertisement of notice of the claim required by paragraph (1) and the date on which it was published.

Interveners

A–409F   **57.22** (1) The Attorney General, or a person who is entitled to intervene in proceedings under section 11(1), must first notify the court of the intention to intervene in accordance with the requirements of Practice Direction 57B.

(2) Any other person who wishes to intervene in such proceedings must submit an application for permission to intervene in accordance with the requirements of Practice Direction 57B.

(3) Where the court grants permission to intervene, it may do so on conditions and may give case management directions.

(4) The court may direct that a person who intervenes in proceedings, other than the Attorney General, be joined as a claimant or defendant.

Requirement to provide information

A–409G   **57.23** (1) An application for an order under section 12(1) of the 2013 Act must be supported by evidence and must in particular—

   (a) specify or describe the information in respect of which the order is sought;
   (b) set out the reasons why the person making the application believes that the person against whom the order is sought is likely to have such information; and
   (c) include any further details, where known, of the missing person which are likely to assist in providing the information sought.

(2) The person making the application must serve a copy of the application notice on the person against whom the order is sought, and on every other party to the proceedings (within the meaning of section 20(2) of the 2013 Act), at least 14 days before the date fixed for the hearing of the application.

(3) An application for discharge or variation under section 12(6) of an order made under section 12(1) may be made without notice unless the court directs otherwise.

A–429   *[Add the following new Practice Direction after para.A–429]*

Practice Direction 57B—Proceedings under the Presumption of Death Act 2013

A–429A   *This Practice Direction supplements CPR Part 57*

CONTENTS OF THIS PRACTICE DIRECTION

Procedure for claims – Rule 57.19

Claim for declaration of presumed death – claim form

1.1 The claim form for a claim for a declaration of presumed death must include   **A–429B**
or be accompanied by the following (where known)—
   (1) Information about the claimant

     (a) the claimant's name and address;
     (b) the relationship of the claimant to the missing person; and
     (c) if the claimant is not the missing person's spouse, civil partner, parent, child or sibling, details of the claimant's interest in the determination of the application;

   (2) Information about the missing person

     (a) the missing person's name and surname, and any other names by which the missing person is or has formerly been known;
     (b) the missing person's gender;
     (c) the missing person's maiden surname (if any);
     (d) the missing person's date and place of birth;
     (e) the occupation of the missing person;
     (f) the occupation, name and surname of —

       (i) the missing person's spouse or civil partner (or late spouse or civil partner if the marriage or civil partnership ended on death);
       (ii) where the missing person was under 16 years of age, the missing person's parents;

     (g) the missing person's National Insurance number;
     (h) the date on which missing person is thought to have died, or on which the missing person was last known have been alive;
     (i) on which of the grounds in section 1(4) of the 2013 Act the court is considered to have jurisdiction to entertain the claim;
     (j) the usual or last known address of the missing person; and
     (k) the name and address of the spouse or civil partner, parents, children or siblings of the missing person (if any, and if not the claimant);

   (3) Information about steps taken to trace the missing person

     (a) details of any enquiries made or other steps taken to trace the missing person or confirm when the missing person was last known to be alive; and
     (b) details of the results of such enquiries or other steps;

   (4) Information about the missing person's property

     (a) an estimate of the total value of the assets of the missing person;
     (b) details of property owned by the missing person; and

(c) details of the interest of any other person in the missing person's property which it is sought to have determined by the court; and

(5) Information about advertisement and recipients of notice of the claim

(a) details of the newspaper in which the claimant proposes to advertise the claim; and
(b) details of the persons to whom the claimant is giving notice of the claim and, where notice is being given to a person under rule 57.20(1)(f), the nature of that person's interest in the claim.

Claim for variation order

1.2 The claim form for a variation order must include or be accompanied by the following (where known)—
(1) Information about the claimant

(a) the claimant's name and address;
(b) the relationship of the claimant to the missing person; and
(c) details of the claimant's interest in the determination of the application;

(2) Information about previous claim and missing person's property

(a) details of the declaration of presumed death or (as the case may be) previous variation order which it is sought to have varied or revoked;
(b) details of the circumstances which are claimed to justify a variation order, and evidence of the enquiries made and other steps taken to verify them and their outcomes; and
(c) details of any interest in property acquired as a result of the declaration of presumed death or (as the case may be) previous variation order which it is sought to have varied or revoked; and

(3) Information about advertisement and recipients of notice of the claim

(a) details of the newspaper in which the claimant proposes to advertise the claim; and
(b) details of the persons to whom the claimant is giving notice of the claim and, where notice is being given to a person under rule 57.20(2)(g), the nature of that person's interest in the claim.

Issue of claim form without serving notice on any person

1.3 For the purposes of rule 8.2A as modified by rule 57.19, an application for permission to issue a claim form, whether the claim is for a declaration or presumed death or for a variation order, may be made only where the claimant believes there to be no person within paragraph (1)(a) to (f) or paragraph (2)(a) to (g) of rule 57.20. The application must explain why the claimant believes that there is no such person.

Case management – first directions hearing

1.4 A claim (whether for a declaration of presumed death or for a variation order) must be listed for case management directions either—

(a) more than 28 days (but where practicable no more than 56 days) after issue; or

(b) where the claim form has been served outside the jurisdiction, more than 7 days (but where practicable no more than 35 days) after the period for filing provided for by rule 57.19(7), to allow for time for those served with notice of the claim or who respond to the advertisement of the claim to file notice of intention to intervene or an application for permission to intervene as the case may be.

1.5 The court must notify all those who have filed notice of intention to intervene or an application for permission to intervene of the date of the directions hearing.

Advertisement of claim – Rule 57.21

2.1 The advertisement of the claim required by section 9(2) of the 2013 Act and   **A–429C**
rule 57.21(1)(a) must be in the form set out below, or contain the equivalent information about the claim and the possibility of applying, and where and by when to apply, to the Court—

IN THE HIGH COURT OF JUSTICE
[CHANCERY] [FAMILY] DIVISION
Case Number ......
IN THE MATTER OF AN APPLICATION FOR A DECLARATION OF THE PRESUMED DEATH OF (INSERT NAME)
A claim has been issued in the High Court of Justice, for a [declaration] [variation of a declaration] that (insert name), whose last known address was (insert address) is presumed to be dead. Any person having an interest may apply to the Court to intervene in the matter.
If you wish to apply to the Court, you should do so at [Court address] as soon as possible, and if possible within 21 days of the date of this notice. Delay may harm your prospects of being able to intervene.
[If the claimant is legally represented]
(Name)
Claimant's Legal Representative
(Address)
[If the claimant is not legally represented]
(Claimant's address for service)

Interveners – Rule 57.22

A–429D   **3.1** The Attorney General, or a person who is entitled to intervene in the proceedings by virtue of section 11(1) (the missing person's spouse, civil partner, parent, child or sibling) should notify the intention to intervene as early as possible by filing, and serving on the claimant, notice in writing, specifying—

    (a) the intervener's name and address;
    (b) the intervener's relationship to the missing person (where the intervener is not the Attorney General);
    (c) the reasons for intervening; and
    (d) particulars of any determination or order sought under section 11(4)(b) or (c) of the 2013 Act.

3.2 An application under rule 57.22(2) for permission to intervene must be served on the claimant and must specify—

    (a) the applicant's relationship to the missing person or other interest in the proceedings;
    (b) the reasons for seeking to intervene; and
    (c) particulars of any determination or order sought under section 11(4)(b) or (c) of the 2013 Act.

TABLE OF DISTRIBUTION ON INTESTACY

A-475 *[Please replace existing Table with the following]*

This table applies to the estates of those dying intestate on or after.

Table of Distribution of Intestacy where Death Occurred after October 1, 2014[1] For those dying before this date, please refer to Appendix Three in the main work.

Surviving relatives in order of precedence	Distribution of estate	Notes
1. Spouse or civil partner	If living issue then: (a) Personal chattels,[2] and (b) Fixed net sum[3] absolutely, and (c) One half of the residue absolutely; If no living issue, then the whole estate absolutely (even if other relatives are alive)	The spouse or civil partner must survive for 28 days. The surviving spouse or civil partner may acquire by appropriation any matrimonial home owned by the deceased.
2. Issue[4]	If the deceased was survived by a spouse or civil partner by more than 28 days, then half the residue on the statutory trusts; Otherwise: the whole estate on the statutory trusts	Statutory trusts are set out in s.47 of the Administration of Estates Act 1925. In summary, they are for the children (or other relative as the case may be) living at the death who attain 18 or marry under that age, and any living issue of children who predecease the intestate per stirpes, so that no issue shall take whose parent is living.
3. Parent(s)	The whole estate absolutely, in equal shares if more than one	The parents do not take on statutory trusts.

4. Brother(s) and/or sister(s) of the whole blood	The whole estate on the statutory trusts	Deceased brothers and sisters are represented by their issue (i.e. nephews and nieces of the intestate).
5. Brother(s) and/or sister(s) of the half blood	The whole estate on the statutory trusts	See note to No. 4.
6. Grandparent(s)	The whole estate absolutely, in equal shares if more than one	The grandparents do not take on statutory trusts.
7. Uncle(s) and/or aunt(s) of the whole blood	The whole estate on the statutory trusts	Deceased uncles and aunts are represented by their issue (i.e. cousins of the intestate).
8. Uncle(s) and/or aunt(s) of the half blood	The whole estate on the statutory trusts	See note to No. 7.
9. The Crown/Duchy of Lancaster/Duchy of Cornwall	The whole estate	No relation more remote than a grandparent or the descendant of a grandparent can claim on intestacy. The Crown will usually modify its strict rights by providing for dependants of the intestate, related or not, and certain others. This is a discretionary power.[7]

[1] The Inheritance and Trustees' Powers Act 2014 came into force on this date. For details see Chs 19 and 82.
[2] The meaning of this phrase has changed with effect for deaths intestate occurring after October 1, 2014.
[3] This is currently £250,000. This figure will be increased in line with inflation at least every five years.
[4] From this class downwards, the existence of relatives in one class means that there is no need to consider any further class.

[262]

Appendix Four

MEANS-TESTED BENEFITS AND TAX CREDITS

[In the row entitled "Income-Based Jobseekers Allowance" add to the column "Main Conditions of Entitlement"]   A–476

Normally aged 18 or over.

[Add the following new row describing the new benefit "Universal Credit (UC)" to the table after "Income Support (IS)"]

Universal Credit (UC)	Aged between 18 and state pension credit age (some exceptions); be in Great Britain; not subject to immigration control; not be in education and have accepted a claimant commitment.	Basic financial needs are compared with financial resources. UC is paid monthly in arrears.	Upper: £16,000 Lower: £6,000 There is assumed monthly income £4.35 for each £250 or less of capital between £6,000 and £16,000.	Claims cannot normally be backdated. In certain circumstances, when it would not have been reasonable to claim earlier, claims may be backdated one month.

[On the row entitled "State Pension Credit" change the age requirement to the following]

Age: must be over the qualifying age.

[On the row entitled "Housing Benefit" add to Method of Calculation the following]

– The Benefit Cap may be applied.
– The Spare Room Subsidy deduction may be applied.

[On the row entitled "Council Tax Benefit" replace all the material in the table with the following]

Council Tax Benefit has been replaced with local authority Council Tax Reduction Schemes. The Schemes, which were introduced on April 1, 2013, have qualifying conditions, backdating rules, etc. determined locally.

[On the row entitled "Discretionary Social Fund" delete all reference to Community Care Grants (CCG) and Crisis Loans (CL) and replace with the following]

Since April 2013 local authorities have taken over the administration of grants and loans for situations formerly covered by CCG and CL. The qualifying conditions, backdating rules, etc. are determined locally. The Discretionary Social Fund has been abolished and Budgeting Loans are administered by the Department of Work and Pensions now. Applications for Budgeting Loans should be made to the local Jobcentre Plus office.

[On the row entitled "Discretionary Social Fund" under Main Conditions of Entitlement add the following to the section "Budgeting Loans" after "qualifying benefit"]

IS, IBJSA, income-related ESA and SPC.

[On the row entitled "Regulated Social Fund" change the title to the following]

Social Fund

[On the row now entitled "Social Fund" under Main Conditions of Entitlement add the following to the section Sure Start Maternity Grant after "SPC"]

Universal Credit (UC)

[On the row now entitled "Social Fund" under Main Conditions of Entitlement replace "over 60" in the section Winter Fuel Payments with the following]

over the qualifying age for pension credit

[On the row now entitled "Social Fund" add the following to Method of Calculation]

Sure Start Maternity Grant £500

NON-MEANS-TESTED BENEFITS

DISABILITY BENEFITS

A–477   *[On the row entitled "Disability Living Allowance" add the following paragraph under "Main Conditions of Entitlement"]*

Disability Living Allowance (DLA) is now a benefit only for disabled children up to the age of 16. Disabled adults under 65 may still be in receipt of DLA but will gradually transfer to Personal Independence Payment (PIP) after being reassessed. All new claims from disabled adults between the ages of 16 and 64 will be for PIP.

[On the row entitled "Disability Living Allowance" in "Main Conditions of Entitlement for Mobility Component Higher Rate" replace "getting CC highest rate" with the following]

getting CC higher rate

[On the row entitled "Disability Living Allowance" add the following paragraph under "Care Component"]

The age should be changed from "under 65" to "under 16" and the words "or 16 or over and cannot prepare cooked main meal" should be deleted.

[On the row entitled "Disability Living Allowance" replace all of "Method of Calculation of Care Component" with the following]

– Higher rate as per AA higher rate.
– Lower rate as per AA lower rate.

[After "Disability Living Allowance" add the following paragraph describing the new benefit Personal Independence Payment (PIP)]

Personal Independence Payment (PIP)	Age: 16 - under 65 when the claim is made; must pass PIP assessment for the three months before the claim and show that the assessment criteria would be met for the subsequent nine months unless terminally ill. Residence conditions; not subject to immigration control. There are separate assessments for the 'daily living component' and the 'mobility component'.	The daily living component and the mobility component each have a standard rate and an enhanced rate depending on the assessment	No	No	None

[On the row entitled "Severe Disablement Allowance" add the following to Main Conditions of Entitlement]

Apart from recipients of SDA who reached pension age before April 6, 2014 all recipients of SDA should have been reassessed and transferred to Employment and Support Allowance.

BENEFITS FOR PARENTS AND CARERS

[On the row entitled "Carer's Allowance" add the following to Main Conditions of Entitlement]

Caring for a person receiving Personal Independence Payment (PIP) daily living component (at either rate).

[On the row entitled "Child Benefit" add the following to Method of Calculation]

Child Benefit is taxed if one partner receives between £50,000 and £60,000 "adjusted net income". For net incomes above £60,000 the tax equals the child benefit so it is possible to elect not to receive child benefit.

INDEX

This index has been prepared using Sweet and Maxwell's Legal Taxonomy. Main index entries conform to keywords provided by the Legal Taxonomy except where references to specific documents or non-standard terms (denoted by quotation marks) have been included. These keywords provide a means of identifying similar concepts in other Sweet and Maxwell publications and on-line services to which keywords from the Legal Taxonomy have been applied. Readers may find some differences between terms used in the text and those which appear in the index. Suggestions to *sweetandmaxwell.taxonomy@thomson.com*. **(All references are to paragraph number)**.